Artificial Intelligence, Game Theory and Mechanism Design in Politics

Tshilidzi Marwala

Artificial Intelligence, Game Theory and Mechanism Design in Politics

palgrave
macmillan

Tshilidzi Marwala
United Nations University
Tokyo, Japan

ISBN 978-981-99-5102-4 ISBN 978-981-99-5103-1 (eBook)
https://doi.org/10.1007/978-981-99-5103-1

Cover illustration: Maram_shutterstock.com

This Palgrave Macmillan imprint is published by the registered company Springer Nature
Singapore Pte Ltd.
The registered company address is: 152 Beach Road, #21-01/04 Gateway East, Singapore
189721, Singapore

PREFACE

In this book, we study the convergence of artificial intelligence (AI), game theory, and mechanism design in providing ideas and novel tools to the intricate world of politics in the constantly changing world. This work, located at the crossroads of these fields, attempts to understand their enormous consequences for political science.

AI now impacts almost every facet of our lives, including politics. It is transforming political processes from policy formulation to public opinion analyses. However, AI is a tool with enormous power that may be used for good or evil; hence, it necessitates our comprehension, investigation, and ethical evaluation.

Game theory, the mathematical study of strategic interaction, provides a solid foundation for studying political behavior. It enables us to decipher the intricate network of acts and reactions among political actors, whether people, groups, or nations. Furthermore, by outlining probable strategies and outcomes, game theory equips us with a toolbox for navigating the volatile waters of politics.

Mechanism design, a branch of game theory, enables us to create systems that incentivize rational people to achieve socially desirable outcomes. As a result, mechanism design can offer a more equal and efficient political landscape, from developing fair voting systems to formulating public goods-providing programs.

This book investigates how these technologies are used in political contexts, highlighting their possible benefits and drawbacks. The book draws on my substantial research in artificial intelligence and related technologies, as well as real-world examples, to offer a picture of a political environment that is both inspiring and frightening.

This book is intended for students, academics, policymakers, and everyone else interested in the future of politics. It does not necessitate a technical background because it has been designed with accessibility in mind, transforming complicated concepts into exciting and understandable text. Above all, it is intended to elicit thought, create conversation, and motivate action.

As you read this book, I hope you will share my excitement and curiosity about the potential of combining AI, game theory, and mechanism design. These are enormously powerful weapons; how we use them in politics will influence our shared future. This is more than a book; it is an invitation to embark on a journey to comprehend and shape that future.

Welcome to the fascinating world of politics, artificial intelligence, game theory, and mechanism design.

Tokyo, Japan   Tshilidzi Marwala
July 2023

Acknowledgments

First and foremost, I am grateful to my family for their constant support and patience while writing this book. Thank you to my wife, Jabulile, for her unique viewpoint and to our children, Khathu, Thendo, and Denga, whose laughter and curiosity inspire me daily.

I want to thank my editor, Uma Vinesh, for her thorough review and insightful comments. She improved this book in ways I could not have predicted.

Thank you to the Palgrave Macmillan team for believing in my initiative and assisting in its completion. Your effort and professionalism are much appreciated.

I would also want to thank the authors and researchers whose works were the foundation and inspiration for this book. I am grateful for your insight and contributions to the field.

Finally, I want to express my heartfelt gratitude to you, dear reader. This book is for you, and I hope it inspires and enlightens you as much as it had me when I was writing it.

Thank you very much. Ndi a livhuwa nga maanda!

CONTENTS

ABOUT THE AUTHOR

Tshilidzi Marwala is the Rector of the United Nations (UN) University and UN Under-Secretary-General. He was previously the Vice-Chancellor and Principal of the University of Johannesburg. He was born at Duthuni Village in the Limpopo Province of South Africa. He obtained a Ph.D. in Artificial Intelligence from the University of Cambridge in 2000 and a Bachelor of Science in Mechanical Engineering from Case Western Reserve University, graduating with a Magna Cum Laude in 1995. He is an artificial intelligence engineer, computer scientist, mechanical engineer, and university administrator. He has also served as a trustee of the Nelson Mandela Foundation and on the board of Nedbank. He has published 27 books and over 300 papers, supervised 37 doctoral graduates, and holds five patents. He is a fellow of the American Academy of Arts and Sciences, the World Academy of Science, the African Academy of Science, and the Academy of Science of South Africa.

ABBREVIATIONS

ACO	Ant Colony Optimization
AI	Artificial Intelligence
AIS	Artificial Immune System
ANNs	Artificial Neural Networks
AU	African Union
BC	Business Continuity
CNNs	Convolutional Neural Networks
DQN	Deep Q-Network
DR	Disaster Recovery
EP	Evolutionary Programming
EU	European Union
FNNs	Feedforward Neural Networks
GANs	Generative Adversarial Networks
GRU	Gated Recurrent Unit
IDS	Intrusion Detection Systems
IPS	Intrusion Prevention Systems
LSTM	Long Short-Term Memory
MAD	Mutually Assured Destruction
MLPs	Multi-layer Perceptrons
NLP	Natural Language Processing
PPO	Proximal Policy Optimization
PSO	Particle Swarm Optimization
RL	Reinforcement Learning
RNNs	Recurrent Neural Networks
SA	Simulated Annealing

UN   United Nations
VPNs   Virtual Private Networks
WTO   World Trade Organization

LIST OF FIGURES

LIST OF TABLES

Introduction to Artificial Intelligence, Game Theory, and Mechanism Design in Politics

1.1 Introduction to International Politics

Politics has always been a complicated, ever-changing field marked by shifting power, conflict, and cooperative dynamics. However, in today's fast-changing globe, various issues, such as globalization, technical breakthroughs, and altering geopolitical landscapes, influence the international political arena, presenting states with both difficulties and opportunities (Alexander, 1998). Here, we look at the fundamental concerns affecting politics, the causes of change, and the techniques governments can use to adapt and survive in this volatile climate.

Globalization has significantly altered the international political scene, resulting in greater interdependence among nations and the distribution of power among state and non-state actors (Ampuja, 2012; Conner & Torimoto, 2004; Horvath & Szakolczai, 2018; Mimiko, 2012). While growing connectivity has aided trade, investment, and cooperation, it has also created new problems, such as the spread of transnational threats such as terrorism, cybercrime, and climate change. As a result, old ideas of power and sovereignty are changing, necessitating the development of new tactics and frameworks for controlling and responding to these new problems.

Technological advancements in areas such as artificial intelligence (AI), blockchain, and cybersecurity have had a profound impact on international politics (Crossingham et al., 2008; Habtemariam et al.,

© The Author(s), under exclusive license to Springer Nature
Singapore Pte Ltd. 2023
T. Marwala, *Artificial Intelligence, Game Theory and Mechanism Design
in Politics*, https://doi.org/10.1007/978-981-99-5103-1_1

2005; Lagazio & Marwala, 2006; Marwala & Lagazio, 2004, 2011; Ndzendze & Marwala, 2021, 2022). These technologies provide new prospects for improving efficiency, security, and international cooperation but also introduce risks and vulnerabilities that must be handled. Therefore, nations must establish comprehensive policies to manage the associated problems and dangers as they continue to invest in and adopt cutting-edge technology, ensuring that these breakthroughs are used responsibly and ethically.

The geopolitical environment is continually altering, with growing countries like Russia and China confronting the United States (US) and European powers (Carmody, 2013; Chun, 2016). As governments compete for influence and resources, the shifting balance of power is causing growing competition and tensions in diverse regions. In this situation, governments must engage in proactive diplomacy and create international collaboration to address common concerns and maintain global stability.

Multilateralism and international institutions play an essential role in global politics by offering frameworks and methods for nations to collaborate on common challenges and goals (Newman et al., 2006; Yahuda, 2011). However, multilateralism has come under strain in recent years, with some countries pursuing more nationalist and protectionist policies that jeopardize the efficacy and credibility of international organizations. Nations must reaffirm their commitment to international cooperation, collaborating to reform and improve these institutions in the face of growing challenges to ensure multilateralism's future relevance and effectiveness.

Climate change and environmental issues have gained prominence in international politics, with governments acknowledging the critical need to address these serious issues (Dessler & Parson, 2019). As the effects of climate change worsen, nations must adopt and execute aggressive climate policies, collaborate on innovative solutions, and invest in the transition to a more sustainable and resilient global economy. As a result, nations can safeguard the environment while creating new economic growth and development prospects.

This book investigates AI, game theory, and mechanism design in politics.

1.2   AI

AI has quickly progressed from a fascinating branch of computer science to a revolutionary worldwide phenomenon, impacting many industries and redefining modern discourse (Marwala, 2021; Marwala & Hunt, 1999; Moloi & Marwala, 2021; Muller et al., 2022). Its dynamic interactions with international politics are beginning to take shape, impacting diplomatic relations, power dynamics, security, and economic development. AI introduces new difficulties and uncertainties that require careful handling by presenting significant possibilities for improving governance.

AI technologies such as machine learning and natural language processing have far-reaching ramifications in international politics. These technologies can analyze massive amounts of data faster and more precisely than human analysts, giving governments and institutions crucial decision-making insights. However, AI's dual-use character—its ability to be used for both positive and destructive purposes—has enormous consequences for international security and political relations.

AI is altering fighting and defense strategies in worldwide security. Drones, cyber warfare tools, and surveillance technology are increasingly becoming part of national security systems. Moreover, the race for artificial intelligence mastery among significant powers such as the United States and China is creating a new battleground in which technological prowess dictates geopolitical influence and security strength.

AI tools can help in diplomacy by forecasting political trends, assessing foreign policy, and even engaging in digital diplomacy. However, diplomacy automation might dehumanize diplomatic operations, raising questions regarding accountability, transparency, and ethical implications.

AI provides a lot of promise for economic development. It can potentially increase efficiency, stimulate innovation, and generate income. However, AI's financial gains are now unequally distributed, with technologically advanced countries enjoying the lion's share. This condition exacerbates global inequality and can potentially create an "AI digital divide" across nations, causing difficulties in international relations.

Furthermore, AI's impact on labor markets can cause socio-economic upheavals, potentially leading to political instability. As certain jobs are replaced by technology, countries must handle the risk of greater unemployment and social discontent, which can echo through international politics.

As AI pervades international politics, the necessity for effective governance and ethical principles becomes more pressing. Privacy, data ownership, AI bias, and the threat of autonomous weapons are all controversial issues that necessitate international collaboration.

However, due to various cultural norms, political systems, and economic interests, attaining worldwide consensus on AI ethics and legislation is a big task. Furthermore, the tension between AI as a weapon for social control in authoritarian regimes and a tool for boosting democratic processes in liberal democracies confuses the situation even further. This polarization raises the possibility of a "splinternet," in which the internet fragments along national or regional lines, diminishing global connectedness and cooperation.

1.3   Game Theory

The study of strategic interaction through game theory has proven beneficial in comprehending the complex dynamics of political science (Aumann & Shapley, 1974; Dutta, 1999; Luce & Raiffa, 1957). Game theory provides a framework for analyzing and forecasting the outcomes of international disputes, cooperation, and negotiation by modelling states as rational players attempting to maximize their interests. This book examines how game theory is used in politics, focusing on diplomacy, conflict resolution, and international law. Figure 1.1 depicts the method of game theory.

As depicted in Fig. 1.1, in game theory, we have players and rules, and the players interact until they achieve an equilibrium which is undetermined at the start. As a result, the game's conclusion is unknowable in game theory.

In diplomacy, game theory models can depict the dynamics of state negotiation, cooperation, and competition. The "Prisoner's Dilemma,"

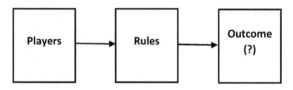

Fig. 1.1   Illustration of game theory

a classic game theory model described in Table 1.1, is an effective tool for comprehending the difficulties of international collaboration. When two persons commit a crime, they are separated and given the following options: If one player confesses and the other player does not, the person who confesses receives three years in prison. In contrast, the person who does not confess is sentenced to 20 years in prison. They are both set free if they do not confess. Both are sentenced to five years in prison if they confess. Nash equilibrium is a concept in game theory that describes a stable state of strategic interaction among multiple players in which no individual player has the incentive to alter their strategy unilaterally. In the case above, the Nash equilibrium inevitably leads to confession. It demonstrates how two rational actors may refuse to cooperate even though it is in their best interests because they fear being used by the other (Nash, 1950). In diplomacy, such scenarios frequently play out, where mutual distrust can lead to squandered opportunities for cooperation.

Climate change is one example of this, as countries may hesitate to invest in costly environmental protection measures unless they are satisfied that others would do the same. Policymakers can use game theory models to understand these dynamics better and devise methods to increase collaboration.

Game theory is also essential in conflict resolution. The "Chicken Game," in which two parties rush at each other, and the first to yield is the "chicken," is a model that is frequently used in conflicts where the consequence of not backing down is disastrous. For example, the Cold War's nuclear arms race can be viewed as a "Chicken Game," in which the United States and the Soviet Union faced the decision of escalation or retreat to avoid mutual devastation.

Game theory assists policymakers in understanding alternative outcomes and designing ways to minimize conflict by offering a mathematical description of such circumstances. In international law, game theory helps to explain why states comply with unenforceable rules and accords. The concept of the "Iterated Prisoner's Dilemma," in which the

Table 1.1 Prisoner's Dilemma			Player 2	
			Confess	Don't Confess
	Player 1	Confess	(5,5)	(3,20)
		Don't Confess	(20,3)	(0,0)

game is played repeatedly, demonstrates how states might adopt cooperative methods over time. Even without an enforcement mechanism, states may follow international law to establish a reputation for cooperation and prevent reprisal.

The World Trade Organization's dispute resolution system is one example. Despite the lack of a binding enforcement mechanism, most countries follow the rules because failure to do so could result in retaliation and damage to their reputation, influencing future encounters.

Despite its usefulness, game theory has limitations when applied to international politics. It frequently assumes governments are unitary and rational actors, an oversimplification that may fail to account for domestic politics, irrational conduct, or the complexities of international interactions. Furthermore, because game theory is strategic, it can overlook the relevance of norms, values, and culture in molding state behavior.

1.4   Mechanism Development

Mechanism design theory, a subset of game theory, is becoming more widely recognized as a useful instrument in international politics (Diamantaras et al., 2009; Marwala & Hurwitz, 2017; Milgrom, 2004). In contrast to classical game theory, which investigates how rational players operate under a given set of rules, mechanism design is concerned with developing the rules to accomplish desired results, as shown in Fig. 1.2. We have players and a desired outcome here. The goal is to identify the rules to achieve the desired outcome.

This section investigates the use of mechanism design in international politics, namely in international collaboration, conflict resolution, and global governance.

Due to asymmetric knowledge, competing interests, and the free-rider dilemma, international collaboration frequently confronts difficulties.

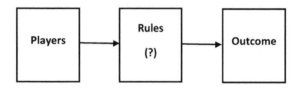

Fig. 1.2   Illustration of mechanism design

Mechanism design can assist in addressing these difficulties by establishing processes that align the interests of various parties toward cooperation. This is accomplished by carefully arranging incentives and disincentives so that, given the tactics of others, the best plan for each player leads to the desired collective outcome.

For example, in the case of climate change, countries may be hesitant to reduce emissions for fear that others may benefit from their efforts. Mechanism design can contribute to developing international agreements that incentivize emission reductions while penalizing non-compliance and fostering global cooperation.

Mechanism design can also be helpful in dispute resolution. Mechanism design can aid in resolving international conflicts by developing norms and protocols that encourage peaceful resolution and discourage escalation. Furthermore, utilizing mechanism design, the negotiation process, which frequently involves strategic considerations, asymmetric information, and bargaining, may be modelled and optimized.

Consider discussions on resource allocation or territorial disputes. Mechanisms can be created to guarantee that distribution is equitable and agreeable to all stakeholders, lowering the probability of conflict. In addition, protocols that reward compromise and penalize aggressive posture could be used to incentivize peaceful dialogue.

The design of mechanisms has significant consequences for global governance because various players with disparate interests must be coordinated toward common aims. Furthermore, mechanism design can help with the construction of international organizations, the execution of international law, and the creation of global economic systems.

For example, voting procedures in international organizations might be devised to improve fairness, efficiency, and representation. Similarly, international trade laws can be developed to balance different countries' interests while promoting global economic progress. Given the strategic behavior of governments, mechanism design allows these systems to be carefully built to accomplish desired outcomes.

While mechanism design provides intriguing tools for international politics, it also poses some difficulties. The complexity of global interactions, the diversity of participants, and a lack of enforcement skills might make it challenging to put designed procedures in place and execute them. Furthermore, the theory implies rational behavior, which may not always be true in practice. Moreover, the question of "who" designs the mechanisms is an important issue to consider.

1.5   CONCLUSION AND OUTLINE OF THE BOOK

AI, game theory, and mechanism design are increasingly influential factors in international politics. Together, the computing capacity of AI, the strategic concepts of game theory, and the ability of mechanism design can engineer desired outcomes to form a potent mix that can potentially transform the landscape of world politics. This section looks at how the junction of these three ideas might influence international diplomacy, conflict resolution, and global government.

AI can improve the use of game theory in international diplomacy by enabling real-time analysis of massive volumes of data, predicting outcomes, and strategizing effective responses. For example, machine learning algorithms can forecast states' behavior in negotiations or conflicts by modelling complex game theory situations such as the Prisoner's Dilemma or the Chicken Game. This capability can give politicians and diplomats crucial insights, allowing them to foresee the maneuvers of other actors and make strategic judgments.

Mechanism design can improve these processes by introducing mechanisms that encourage cooperation while discouraging adversarial behavior. For example, diplomats can build agreements and treaties that are more likely to be approved and adhered to by all sides by combining AI's predictive capability with the strategic structure of mechanism design.

AI and game theory can give a framework for understanding and managing disputes in conflict resolution. AI can model and anticipate conflict scenarios, while game theory can provide insights into these conflicts' strategic dynamics. AI can also help create dispute resolution mechanisms by modelling and forecasting the impact of various strategies.

In territorial disputes or arms control discussions, for example, AI can model various allocation tactics or disarmament stages, and game theory can provide insights into how governments would respond to these strategies. The design of a mechanism can then be used to shape the negotiating process to incentivize a peaceful conclusion.

AI, game theory, and mechanism design can revolutionize the design of international institutions, the execution of international law, and the administration of global economic systems in global governance. For example, AI can evaluate global patterns and forecast the impact of policies; game theory can provide insights into state strategy; and mechanism design can develop rules and incentives that promote collaboration and mutual gain.

Integrating AI, game theory, and mechanism design in international politics, on the other hand, is complicated. Effective modelling and prediction of outcomes can be challenging because of global affairs' complexity, the actors' diversity, and the unpredictable nature of human behavior. Furthermore, ethical concerns about the employment of AI, such as privacy, bias, and the risk of autonomous decision-making, present substantial obstacles that must be addressed.

The second chapter discusses game theory and politics, while the third chapter discusses mechanism design and politics. The fourth chapter discusses artificial intelligence and politics, while the fifth chapter discusses data and politics. Deep learning and politics are discussed in Chapter 6, while natural language processing and politics are discussed in Chapter 7. Chapter 8 concerns evolutionary programming and politics, whereas Chapter 9 concerns cybersecurity and international politics. Chapter 10 concerns social media and politics, while Chapter 11 concerns robotics and politics. Chapter 12 is on AI-powered blockchain and politics. Finally, the conclusion and lessons from mechanism design, game theory, and AI in politics are covered in Chapter 13.

REFERENCES

Alexander, F. (1998). *Encyclopedia of world history*. Oxford University Press.

Ampuja, M. (2012). *Theorizing globalization: A critique of the mediatization of social theory* (Vol. 47). Brill.

Aumann, R. J., & Shapley, L. S. (2015 [1974]). *Values of non-atomic games*. Princeton University Press.

Carmody, P. (2013). *The rise of the BRICS in Africa: The geopolitics of South-South relations*. Bloomsbury Publishing.

Chun, K. H. (2016). *The BRICs superpower challenge: Foreign and security policy analysis*. Routledge.

Conner, T., & Torimoto, I. (Eds.). (2004). *Globalization redux: New name*. University Press of America.

Crossingham, B., Marwala, T., & Lagazio, M. (2008). Optimized rough sets for modelling interstate conflict. In *2008 IEEE International Conference on Systems, Man and Cybernetics* (pp. 1198–1204). IEEE.

Dessler, A. E., & Parson, E. A. (2019). *The science and politics of global climate change: A guide to the debate*. Cambridge University Press.

Diamantaras, D., Cardamone, E. I., Campbell, K., Deacle, S., & Delgado, L. (2009). *A toolbox for economic design*. Palgrave Macmillan.

Dutta, P. K. (1999). *Strategies and games: Theory and practice*. MIT Press.

Habtemariam, E., Marwala, T., & Lagazio, M. (2005). Artificial intelligence for conflict management. In *Proceedings. 2005 IEEE International Joint Conference on Neural Networks, 2005* (Vol. 4, pp. 2583–2588). IEEE.

Horvath, A., & Szakolczai, A. (2018). Political anthropology. In W. Outhwaite & S. Turner (Eds.), *Sage handbook of political sociology* (pp. 189–204). Sage.

Lagazio, M., & Marwala, T. (2006). Assessing different Bayesian neural network models for militarized interstate dispute: Outcomes and variable influences. *Social Science Computer Review, 24*(1), 119–131.

Luce, R. D., & Raiffa, H. (1957). *Games and decisions: Introduction and critical survey.* Wiley.

Marwala, T. (2021). *Rational machines and artificial intelligence.* Academic Press.

Marwala, T., & Hunt, H. E. M. (1999). Fault identification using finite element models and neural networks. *Mechanical Systems and Signal Processing, 13*(3), 475–490.

Marwala, T., & Hurwitz, E. (2017). Mechanism design. In *Artificial intelligence and economic theory: Skynet in the market* (pp. 111–124). Springer.

Marwala, T., & Lagazio, M. (2004). Modeling and controlling interstate conflict. In *2004 IEEE International Joint Conference on Neural Networks (IEEE Cat. No. 04CH37541)* (Vol. 2, pp. 1233–1238). IEEE.

Marwala, T., & Lagazio, M. (2011). *Militarized conflict modeling using computational intelligence.* Springer Science & Business Media.

Milgrom, P. R. (2004). *Putting auction theory to work.* Cambridge University Press.

Mimiko, N. O. (2012). *Globalization: The politics of global economic relations and international business.* Carolina Academic Press.

Moloi, T., & Marwala, T. (2021). *Artificial intelligence and the changing nature of a firm.* Springer International Publishing.

Muller, D., Buarque, F., & Marwala, T. (2022). *On rationality, artificial intelligence and economics.* World Scientific Press.

Nash, J. F., Jr. (1950). Equilibrium points in n-person games. *Proceedings of the National Academy of Sciences, 36*(1), 48–49.

Ndzendze, B., & Marwala, T. (2021). *AI and emerging technologies in international relations.* World Scientific.

Ndzendze, B., & Marwala, T. (2022). *Artificial intelligence and international relations theories.* Palgrave Macmillan.

Newman, E., Rhakur, R., & Tirman, J. (2006). *Multilateralism under challenge.* United Nations Press.

Yahuda, M. (2011). *The international politics of the Asia-Pacific.* Routledge.

CHAPTER 2

Game Theory in Politics

2.1 Introduction to Game Theory

Game theory, a branch of mathematics, is an analytical tool used to model and predict strategic interactions among rational individuals (Aumann, 1987; Bierman & Fernandez, 1998; Camerer, 2011; Dutta, 1999; Fisher, 1930; Marwala, 2013; Marwala & Hurwitz, 2017). These interactions often involve situations where the outcome for an individual depends not only on their own decisions but also on the decisions made by others. Since its inception, game theory has found applications in various fields, such as economics, political science, psychology, computer science, biology, and philosophy.

The foundation of game theory lies in the idea of a "game," a theoretical construct representing a situation where multiple players interact. Each player, or "agent," has a set of possible actions or "strategies," and the game's outcomes depend on the strategies chosen by all players. Furthermore, these outcomes are typically associated with "payoffs," which can be considered the numerical representation of the players' preferences.

Game theory is divided into two main branches: cooperative and non-cooperative game theory. Cooperative game theory deals with games where binding agreements are possible, while non-cooperative game theory deals with games where players cannot commit.

© The Author(s), under exclusive license to Springer Nature
Singapore Pte Ltd. 2023
T. Marwala, *Artificial Intelligence, Game Theory and Mechanism Design
in Politics*, https://doi.org/10.1007/978-981-99-5103-1_2

Several important concepts are fundamental to understanding game theory. One such concept is the "Nash Equilibrium," named after the mathematician John Nash, which represents a state of the game where no player can unilaterally improve their payoff by changing their strategy, given the other players' strategies (Bernheim et al., 1987; Carmona & Podczeck, 2009; Harsanyi, 1973; Kreps, 1987; Nash, 1950; Wilson, 1971). Another important concept is "dominant strategy," which is a strategy that is best for a player regardless of what strategies the other players choose.

Through these and other concepts, game theory provides a mathematical way to analyze strategic situations. It helps us understand how rational decision-makers interact and how these interactions influence the overall outcome. Whether it is understanding international trade agreements, predicting election strategies, or designing auctions for internet advertising, game theory provides a robust framework for analyzing and predicting the complex world of strategic interactions.

2.2   TYPES OF GAMES

In game theory, games can be classified into different types based on various factors, such as the number of players, the timing of players' moves, the nature of payoffs, and the ability to cooperate. Below we discuss the main types of games.

In cooperative games, players can form binding agreements and collaborate to achieve a common goal. In addition, these agreements often involve the sharing of payoffs. In contrast, in non-cooperative games, players cannot make binding agreements; each player acts independently to maximize their own payoff.

In simultaneous games, all players make their decisions simultaneously without knowing the other players' decisions. A payoff matrix often represents these games. Sequential games, conversely, involve players making their decisions in turns, with each player aware of the previous players' decisions. These games are typically represented using a game tree.

In a zero-sum game, the sum of the payoffs to all players is zero for every combination of strategies. In other words, one player's gain is the other player's loss. Poker is an example of a zero-sum game. On the other hand, non-zero-sum games are games in which the total gain or loss is not fixed. As a result, the players' interests are not always directly opposed, and both players can gain or lose simultaneously.

In symmetric games, all players are identical in strategy and payoff. The classic example is the Prisoner's Dilemma, where players face the same choices and payoffs (Amadae, 2016). On the other hand, asymmetric games have players that differ in some way, such as having different strategies, payoffs, or different amounts of information.

Perfect information games are games in which all players know the moves made by all other players. Chess is a classic example. On the other hand, imperfect information games are games in which players do not know all the previous actions. An example is card games like poker, where players do not know the cards held by the other players.

In static games, players make their decisions once and simultaneously, while in dynamic games, players make decisions more than once and possibly in reaction to other players' actions.

The rules, strategies, and payoffs are known to all players in complete information games. In contrast, in incomplete information games, players have private information that other players do not know.

Game theory utilizes these various types of games to model real-world scenarios and predict outcomes based on players' strategic interactions. The type of game used depends on the specific details and requirements of the scenario being modelled. In the next sections, we discuss these games within the context of international politics.

2.3   Cooperative vs Non-Cooperative Games in International Politics

Game theory has found profound application in international politics. The two primary types of games in this model, cooperative and non-cooperative, serve as insightful lenses through which the complexities of global political dynamics can be better understood. The cooperative game model explores scenarios where nations can form binding agreements, while non-cooperative games depict situations where nations act independently to maximize their interests. This section delves into applying these two types of games in international politics and how they shape global interactions.

Cooperative game theory is employed when nations enter treaties, alliances, or any form of binding agreement for mutual benefits. Side payments, binding agreements, and enforceable contracts characterize this theoretical model. International organizations like the United Nations (UN), the African Union (AU), the European Union (EU), and the

World Trade Organization (WTO) exemplify cooperative game structures. These institutions are platforms where nations negotiate, form coalitions, and establish binding rules on their members.

The Paris Agreement on Climate Change is a quintessential example of a cooperative game in international politics. Signatory nations have agreed to binding targets for reducing greenhouse gas emissions, with the common goal of mitigating the impacts of climate change. Although sovereign nations have disparate economic and political interests, they cooperate for the greater global good, acknowledging the interconnectedness of our planet's climate system.

Conversely, non-cooperative game theory comes into play when nations act independently, pursuing their interests with little or no regard for collective objectives. Nations cannot make enforceable commitments here, and their strategic interaction determines the outcome.

A prime example of a non-cooperative game in international politics is the arms race during the Cold War. The United States and the Soviet Union, each seeking to ensure its security and supremacy, amassed large quantities of nuclear weapons.[1] Yet, despite this global threat, each country made decisions independently, prioritizing its interests over global safety—a classic non-cooperative game scenario.

The prisoner's dilemma, one of the most famous non-cooperative games, also finds relevance in international politics. Nations often face situations where cooperation would lead to a better collective outcome, but the temptation to defect and pursue individual interests leads to suboptimal results for all. An example of this is in Table 2.1. Here is an example of an interaction between countries A and B with respective payoffs.

Table 2.1 Payoff Matrix for countries cooperating

		Country B Cooperate	Don't Cooperate
Country A	Cooperate	(10,10)	(5,20)
	Don't Cooperate	(20,5)	(0,0)

[1] https://www.jfklibrary.org/learn/about-jfk/jfk-in-history/the-cold-war.

To analyze Table 2.1, we use the minimax procedure. Cooperating gives the best outcome, while if one does not know what the other country is doing, the best strategy is not to cooperate (Nash equilibrium).

The dynamics of international politics often straddle both cooperative and non-cooperative games. Nations cooperate in certain aspects while competing in others. For instance, while countries might cooperate on environmental issues, they might compete intensely in the economic sphere, making independent decisions that maximize their welfare. Table 2.1 shows the net payoff if the two countries cooperate and share information. But it should be noted that it is recognized if and only they cooperate and share information.

Therefore, the key to effective international politics lies in striking a delicate balance between cooperation and competition. Game theory helps policymakers understand this balance by providing a framework to analyze strategic interactions between nations. Moreover, it underscores the importance of enforceable agreements for effective cooperation and highlights the consequences of defection and non-cooperation.

2.4   Simultaneous vs Sequential Games and International Politics

The distinction between simultaneous and sequential games provides a unique perspective on global political dynamics among its various classifications. Simultaneous games occur when all players make their decisions at the same time without knowing the decisions of others. In contrast, sequential games involve players making decisions one after another, with each player privy to the decisions made by those before them. This section explores the implications and applications of these two game types in international politics (Munoz-Garcia & Toro-Gonzalez, 2019; Sun, 2020).

Simultaneous games in international politics often arise when nations make decisions concurrently without knowledge of what the other nations will decide. These situations are prevalent in diplomacy, trade negotiations, and international crises.

The global geopolitical landscape is fraught with situations that can be modelled as simultaneous games. For instance, consider the negotiations surrounding trade agreements. Here, each country must decide its trade policy without knowing what policies the others will adopt. For instance, a country might choose to impose tariffs without knowing whether other countries will retaliate with their own tariffs or choose to maintain free trade.

Similarly, decisions on international environmental policy often represent simultaneous games. Countries make decisions about emission reductions without knowing what other countries will do. The success of collective action against climate change depends on the independent decisions of numerous countries, each acting without certain knowledge of the others' actions.

Sequential games, however, are pervasive in situations with a clear order of moves, with each player fully aware of the actions taken by those who moved before them. Moreover, these games often involve long-term strategic interactions and can model various scenarios in international relations.

An example of a sequential game in international politics is the process of disarmament negotiations. One country may decide to disarm because its adversary, that moves next, also disarms. The second country, aware of the first's decision, decides accordingly. In this case, the order of moves and the full knowledge of previous actions are crucial to the outcome.

The domino theory proposed during the Cold War, suggesting that if one country in a region came under the influence of communism, then the surrounding countries would follow sequentially, is another example of a sequential game.

The distinction between simultaneous and sequential games has significant implications for strategy in international politics. In simultaneous games, the uncertainty about other players' actions often leads to defensive and conservative strategies. In sequential games, however, the ability to react to others' actions allows for more calculated and adaptive strategies.

Choosing between a simultaneous and sequential game model can greatly affect analyzing a given political situation. The models can lead to different predictions and suggest different optimal strategies. Therefore, accurately identifying whether a case is best represented as a simultaneous or sequential game is a crucial step in the strategic analysis of international politics.

2.5 ZERO-SUM VS NON-ZERO-SUM GAMES

In the various classifications of games within this field, the distinction between zero-sum and non-zero-sum games provides a unique perspective on the nature of global interactions. A zero-sum game is a situation in which a corresponding loss to another party matches an advantage one party gains. Conversely, in a non-zero-sum game, the players' gains and losses do not necessarily cancel each other out, allowing for the possibility of mutual benefit or mutual loss. This section explores the applications and implications of these two types of games in international politics (Adler, 2013; Olson, 2010; Washburn, 2014).

Zero-sum games portray a picture of international relations characterized by pure competition, where one nation's gain is invariably another's loss. This perspective is often linked to realist theories in international relations, which view states as self-interested actors vying for power and security in an anarchic global system.

The Cold War era provides a classic example of a zero-sum game, where gains by the United States were viewed as losses by the Soviet Union, and vice versa. Their rivalry extended to various spheres, including military, technological, and ideological domains, with each advancement by one superpower perceived as a setback by the other.

Another instance of a zero-sum game in international politics is territorial disputes. When two countries claim the same piece of land, any gain for one is a direct loss for the other. The ongoing dispute over the South China Sea territories, claimed by multiple nations, is a contemporary example of a zero-sum game.[2]

Contrasting with the competitive view of zero-sum games, non-zero-sum games in international politics encapsulate scenarios where cooperation can lead to shared benefits or where conflict can result in shared losses. These games align more with liberal and constructivist international relations theories, emphasizing the potential for cooperative international structures and mutual benefits.

International trade is a prime example of a non-zero-sum game, where nations can mutually benefit from exchange. By specializing in their comparative advantage and trading, countries can both end up better off,

---

[2] https://www.cfr.org/global-conflict-tracker/conflict/territorial-disputes-south-chi na-sea.

demonstrating that international interactions need not always be a battle with winners and losers.

Similarly, global environmental issues like climate change represent non-zero-sum games. Here, the failure of nations to cooperate in reducing emissions could lead to shared losses for all. However, coordinated action could mitigate these damages, resulting in a better outcome for everyone.

The perception of international politics as a zero-sum or non-zero-sum game shapes a nation's foreign policy strategy. If international politics is seen as a zero-sum game, competitive strategies, power accumulation, and unilateral actions may be prioritized. Conversely, viewing international relations as a non-zero-sum game promotes cooperative strategies, mutual trust building, and multilateral actions.

However, it is crucial to note that these perceptions can be self-fulfilling. If states believe they are in a zero-sum game, they are likely to act competitively, thereby creating a reality of conflict and competition. On the other hand, recognizing the potential for non-zero-sum games can open the door for cooperation and shared benefits.

2.6   Symmetric vs Asymmetric Games

Politics, by nature, is a complex and multifaceted arena where nations interact and pursue their interests. These interactions often involve strategic choices and decisions that can be analyzed through game theory. Within game theory, games can be classified into two broad categories: symmetric and asymmetric. This section will delve into symmetric and asymmetric games' characteristics, implications, and applications in international politics (Beckenkamp et al., 2007; Hew & White, 2008).

Symmetric games are those in which the players possess identical strategies and payoffs. In international politics, symmetric games are often used to model situations where countries have similar capabilities, resources, or interests. These games can help scholars and policymakers understand the dynamics of power and cooperation in a more balanced international system.

One of the most well-known symmetric games in international politics is the Prisoner's Dilemma illustrated in Table 2.1 (Amadae, 2016; Chess, 1988; Collins, 2022; Schneider & Shields, 2022). This game represents a situation where two countries, each with the option to cooperate or defect, must decide how to act to pursue their interests. The key feature of this game is that both countries would be better off if they cooperated, but they may be tempted to defect, leading to suboptimal outcomes for both. The Prisoner's Dilemma can be applied to various scenarios in international politics, such as arms control negotiations, trade agreements, and climate change cooperation.

Asymmetric games, on the other hand, involve players with differing strategies, payoffs, or capabilities. These games are particularly relevant in international politics when analyzing the interactions between countries with unequal power, resources, or goals. Asymmetric games can help explain the strategies and behaviors of states in a hierarchical international system.

The Chicken Game is a prominent example of an asymmetric game in international politics (Rapoport & Chammah, 1966). This game captures the dynamics of brinkmanship, where two countries engage in a high-stakes standoff, hoping the other will back down first. The payoffs and strategies in the Chicken Game are not identical for both players, as one may have more at stake or possess greater capabilities to withstand the consequences of not backing down. This game can be applied to military confrontations, diplomatic crises, or trade disputes.

Understanding symmetric and asymmetric games in international politics can offer valuable insights into the strategic behavior of states and the dynamics of the international system. Moreover, these games can serve as a foundation for developing models that help predict the outcomes of political interactions and inform policy decisions.

For instance, symmetric games can help scholars and policymakers identify the conditions under which cooperation is more likely to emerge between states with similar capabilities or interests. On the other hand, asymmetric games can shed light on the power dynamics and strategic choices of states in an unequal international system, highlighting the role of bargaining, deterrence, and diplomacy in shaping state behavior.

2.7   STATIC VS DYNAMIC GAMES

International politics is a realm of strategic interactions where nations seek to maximize their interests while navigating the interests of others. Game theory provides a robust framework for understanding these interactions. However, one critical distinction within game theory is between static and dynamic games. This section explores the characteristics, implications, and applications of static and dynamic games in international politics.

Static games, also known as simultaneous games, are those in which players make their decisions simultaneously, or if they move sequentially, they do so without knowledge of the earlier players' actions. This feature captures situations where nations must make decisions without knowing what others have chosen, reflecting the uncertainty inherent in many international political scenarios.

The Prisoner's Dilemma is a classic example of a static game (Poundstone, 1993; Rapoport et al., 1965). Two nations must each decide whether to cooperate or defect without knowing the other's choice. While cooperation would result in the highest total benefit, the game structure tempts each player to defect, leading to a socially suboptimal outcome. This model can be applied to various issues in international politics, such as climate change negotiations, where countries must decide whether to reduce emissions without knowing whether others will do the same.

Dynamic games, also known as sequential games, are those in which players make their decisions in a particular order, and later players have information about earlier players' actions. These games model situations where nations can observe and respond to the actions of others, reflecting the strategic dynamics of many international political scenarios.

The Ultimatum Game is a common example of a dynamic game. For example, one nation (the proposer) proposes how to divide a resource (such as aid, trade benefits, or territory), and the other (the responder) can accept or reject the proposal. If the responder accepts, the resource is divided as proposed, but if the responder rejects, neither gets anything. This game can illustrate power dynamics in international negotiations, as the proposer has the power to set the terms, but the responder has the power to veto.

Understanding static and dynamic games in international politics offers valuable insights into the strategic behavior of states. For example, static games can help illustrate the challenges of cooperation under uncertainty, as countries may struggle to coordinate their actions without knowing what others will do. This can inform strategies to enhance transparency and build trust, such as through international institutions or diplomacy.

On the other hand, dynamic games can shed light on the strategic dynamics of sequential interactions, where states can observe and respond to others' actions. This can inform strategies for managing power dynamics and strategic responses, such as negotiation tactics, signaling, or deterrence.

Moreover, the distinction between static and dynamic games can also inform the analysis of institutional design in international politics. For example, international organizations might be designed to transform what would otherwise be a static game (with its challenges of uncertainty) into a dynamic game, where states can make more informed choices based on observing the actions of others.

2.8 GAME THEORY AND INTERNATIONAL POLITICS

Game theory has been widely used to analyze the dynamics of conflict and war. For instance, the famous Prisoner's Dilemma illustrates the challenges of cooperation in the face of mutual distrust. In addition, game-theoretic models, such as the concept of mutually assured destruction (MAD), were employed during the Cold War to study deterrence and arms races, positing that the threat of catastrophic retaliation would prevent rational actors from engaging in nuclear warfare.[3]

Game theory can help explain the strategic choices made by states in diplomatic interactions and negotiations. The bargaining model of war, for example, suggests that conflicts arise due to the inability of states to agree on the division of contested goods or resources. Understanding the strategic incentives enables policymakers to devise more effective negotiation strategies and conflict resolution mechanisms.

Game theory has been applied to understand the dynamics of international trade, where countries face the dilemma of pursuing protectionist policies to benefit domestic industries or embracing free trade to maximize global welfare. The concept of the Nash equilibrium, named after mathematician John Nash, has been particularly influential in understanding the strategic interactions in trade negotiations and the formation of trade agreements.

Game theory has been used to study the formation and effectiveness of international institutions and regimes. For example, the collective action problem, which arises when actors have incentives to free-ride on the contributions of others, has been employed to understand the challenges of maintaining cooperation in areas such as climate change mitigation and

---

[3] http://www.nuclearfiles.org/menu/key-issues/nuclear-weapons/history/cold-war/strategy/strategy-mutual-assured-destruction.htm.

global security. By identifying the factors that promote or hinder cooperation, game theory can inform the design of more effective international institutions and regimes.

Game theory has made several significant contributions to the study of international politics. First, it has helped formalize and systematize strategic interaction analysis, providing a more rigorous and consistent framework for understanding complex dynamics. Furthermore, game theory has generated valuable insights into the strategic incentives and constraints actors face in various international contexts, informing the development of more effective policies and strategies.

Despite its many contributions, game theory is not without limitations and challenges. One key concern is the reliance on rationality assumptions, which may not always hold true in the real world, as emotions, biases, or incomplete information may influence actors. Additionally, game-theoretic models can sometimes oversimplify complex international dynamics by reducing them to stylized interactions between a limited number of players. Finally, the predictive power of game theory can be limited by the difficulty of accurately modelling and the fact that it assumes rationality.

2.9   Conclusion

Game theory provides a useful framework for understanding and analyzing the strategic interactions that occur in international politics. By modelling decision-making processes and predicting outcomes based on the choices of rational actors, game theory offers insights into how states might behave in different scenarios and how conflicts might be resolved through negotiation and cooperation. However, game theory is not a perfect predictor of human behavior, and there are limitations to its applicability in complex real-world situations. It is important to recognize the assumptions and simplifications that underlie game-theoretic models, and to use them as tools for understanding rather than as definitive answers to complex questions. Overall, game theory can be a valuable tool for analyzing international politics, but it must be used in conjunction with other approaches and an understanding of the context-specific factors that shape decision-making processes.

References

Adler, I. (2013). The equivalence of linear programs and zero-sum games. *International Journal of Game Theory, 42*(1), 165.

Amadae, S. M. (2016). *Prisoners of reason: Game theory and neoliberal political economy.* Cambridge University Press.

Aumann, R. J. (1987). Game theory. In J. Eatwell, M. Milgate, & P. Newman (Eds.), *The new Palgrave: A dictionary of economics.* Macmillan.

Beckenkamp, M., Hennig-Schmidt, H., & Maier-Rigaud, F. P. (2007). Cooperation in symmetric and asymmetric prisoner's dilemma games. *MPI Collective Goods Preprint* (2006/25).

Bernheim, B. D., Peleg, B., & Whinston, M. D. (1987). Coalition-proof Nash equilibria I. concepts. *Journal of Economic Theory, 42*(1), 1–12.

Bierman, H. S., & Fernandez, L. F. (1998). *Game theory with economic applications.* Addison-Wesley.

Camerer, C. F. (2011). *Behavioral game theory: Experiments in strategic interaction.* Princeton University Press.

Carmona, G., & Podczeck, K. (2009). On the existence of pure-strategy equilibria in large games. *Journal of Economic Theory, 144*(3), 1300–1319.

Chess, D. M. (1988). Simulating the evolution of behavior: The iterated prisoners' dilemma problem. *Complex Systems, 2*(6), 663–670.

Collins, R. W. (2022). The Prisoner's Dilemma paradox: Rationality, morality, and reciprocity. *Think, 21*(61), 45–55.

Dutta, P. K. (1999). *Strategies and games: Theory and practice.* MIT Press.

Fisher, R. A. (1930). *The genetical theory of natural selection.* Clarendon Press.

Harsanyi, J. C. (1973). Oddness of the number of equilibrium points: A new proof. *International Journal of Game Theory, 2*(1), 235–250.

Hew, S. L., & White, L. B. (2008). Cooperative resource allocation games in shared networks: Symmetric and asymmetric fair bargaining models. *IEEE Transactions on Wireless Communications, 7*(11), 4166–4175.

Kreps, D. M. (1987). Nash equilibrium. In *The new Palgrave dictionary of economics.* Palgrave Macmillan.

Marwala, T. (2013). Multi-agent approaches to economic modeling: Game theory, ensembles, evolution and the stock market. In *Economic modeling using artificial intelligence methods* (pp. 195–213). Springer.

Marwala, T., & Hurwitz, E. (2017). Game theory. In *Artificial intelligence and economic theory: Skynet in the market* (pp. 75–88). Springer.

Munoz-Garcia, F., & Toro-Gonzalez, D. (2019). Pure strategy Nash equilibrium and simultaneous-move games with complete information. In *Strategy and game theory: Practice exercises with answers* (pp. 39–86). Springer.

Nash, J. F., Jr. (1950). Equilibrium points in n-person games. *Proceedings of the National Academy of Sciences, 36*(1), 48–49.

Olson, E. S. (2010). *Zero-sum game: The rise of the world's largest derivatives exchange*. Wiley.

Poundstone, W. (1993). *Prisoner's dilemma: John von Neumann, game theory, and the puzzle of the bomb*. Anchor.

Rapoport, A., & Chammah, A. M. (1966). The game of chicken. *American Behavioral Scientist, 10*(3), 10–28.

Rapoport, A., Chammah, A. M., & Orwant, C. J. (1965). *Prisoner's dilemma: A study in conflict and cooperation* (Vol. 165). University of Michigan Press.

Schneider, M., & Shields, T. (2022). Motives for cooperation in the one-shot Prisoner's Dilemma. *Journal of Behavioral Finance, 23*(4), 438–456.

Sun, C. H. (2020). Simultaneous and sequential choice in a symmetric two-player game with canyon-shaped payoffs. *The Japanese Economic Review, 71*(2), 191–219.

Washburn, A. (2014). Single person background. *Two-Person Zero-Sum Games,* 1–4.

Wilson, R. (1971). Computing equilibria of n-person games. *SIAM Journal on Applied Mathematics, 21*(1), 80–87.

CHAPTER 3

Mechanism Design in Politics

3.1 Introduction to Mechanism Design

The strategic design of rules and institutions in a system to achieve specified outcomes is called mechanism design (He et al., 2023; Hurwicz & Reiter, 2006; Kim, 2023; Marwala & Hurwitz, 2017; Myerson et al., 1989). This approach is called "reverse game theory" because, unlike traditional game theory, which begins with a game and attempts to predict results, mechanism design starts with the intended outcomes and works backwards to develop a game that would produce those outcomes. This provides a priceless tool for comprehending and constructing organizations or procedures that balance individual incentives with larger social goals, and this is shown in Table 3.1.

The essence of mechanism design is to create a situation, commonly called a "game," that drives participants to act in a way that results in the intended outcome. Understanding the preferences, strategies, and knowledge of the players is required. One of the most important features is the concept of incentive compatibility, which assures that players declare their real preferences rather than acting intentionally to influence the outcome.

Mechanism design integrates game theory, economics, and information theory ideas. It considers the activities of rational, self-interested agents with access to private information. The goal is to create methods that make these agents behave in a socially beneficial manner, even though they act in their self-interest.

© The Author(s), under exclusive license to Springer Nature Singapore Pte Ltd. 2023
T. Marwala, *Artificial Intelligence, Game Theory and Mechanism Design in Politics*, https://doi.org/10.1007/978-981-99-5103-1_3

Table 3.1 Mechanism design vs game theory

Method	Players	Rules	Outcome
Mechanism design	Known	Unknown	Known
Game theory	Known	Known	Unknown

Mechanism design has many applications in economics, politics, computer science, and operations research. For example, economics has been used to create auctions and markets, such as the spectrum auctions held by the US Federal Communications Commission.[1] These auctions are created to allocate spectrum while maximizing income efficiently.

Mechanism design can be used in political science to study and develop voting systems that encourage honest voting, discourage strategic voting, and successfully aggregate individual preferences into a collective choice.

Mechanism design is critical in computer science when building algorithms for distributed networks because individual nodes may have different goals. This is especially true when it comes to the internet and online platforms.

Mechanism design has also been used to maximize resource allocation in operations research, where individual units may have private information and objectives.

While mechanism design is a robust technique for developing organizations and procedures, it is fraught with difficulties. First, developing an incentive-compatible and individually rational mechanism in many real settings is difficult. Second, mechanism design frequently presupposes rational and self-interested players. However, other elements, such as cognitive biases, emotions, and social conventions, influence human behavior. Third, putting mechanisms in place can be difficult, particularly in complicated real-world settings with several interdependent variables and unforeseeable contingencies.

3.2   TYPES OF MECHANISM DESIGN

The types of mechanisms employed in mechanism design are determined by the game or system's specific aims, described below. The auction mechanism is used when an item or resource must be distributed among many parties (Fleck & Anatolitis, 2023; Liao et al., 2023; Mavungu

---

[1] https://www.fcc.gov/auctions.

et al., 2019). The auction mechanism ensures that the item or resource is assigned as effectively as possible.

Individual choices are aggregated into a collective judgment using voting methods (Großer, 2012; Kohli & Laskowski, 2018). As a result, even with identical individual preferences, different voting processes can produce different results.

When two sets of agents must be matched to each other, such as in the case of the National Resident Matching Program, which links medical students to residency programs (Gao et al., 2022; Hui et al., 2022; Thekinen & Panchal, 2017), matching techniques are utilized. The Gale-Shapley algorithm, utilized in the stable marriage problem, is an example of matching technique.

Market mechanisms enhance trade while maintaining market efficiency (Egan & Jakob, 2016; Thekinen & Panchal, 2017). They frequently include price and allocation regulations for commodities and services. The double auction technique, which is utilized in many financial markets, is one example.

Contract mechanisms are employed in principal-agent problems in which one party (the principal) wishes to have another party (the agent) act on their behalf (Du et al., 2017; Hensher & Wallis, 2005). For example, a contract describing the agent's conduct and the pay they will get is used as the mechanism. These strategies are intended to align the principal's and agent's incentives.

Mechanisms for public goods deliver non-exclusive and non-rival public products (Healy, 2010; Sinha & Anastasopoulos, 2019). As a result, they consider the level of public benefit provision and the allocation of the cost of providing the good.

Each of these systems has unique qualities and can result in different outcomes. The mechanism chosen is determined by the designer's individual objectives as well as the parameters of the environment, such as the number of agents, the knowledge they have, and their preferences.

3.3 AUCTION MECHANISM

Auction mechanisms, a market transaction in which products or services are sold to the highest bidder, may appear unrelated to international politics (Agastya et al., 2023; McClellan, 2023; Xing et al., 2011; Zhou & Serizawa, 2021). Closer investigation reveals, however, that auction processes are crucial in creating international political dynamics.

As a result, this section aims to untangle the complex relationship between auction mechanisms and international politics, concentrating on how auctions enhance resource allocation, influence strategic behavior, and influence global power relations.

Auctions are used internationally, from distributing telecommunication frequencies to allocating mineral rights. They contribute to resource allocation transparency, fairness, and efficiency. For example, global spectrum auctions establish the rights to utilize specific frequencies, which are critical for mobile communication. In addition, these auctions have far-reaching political consequences, influencing a country's scientific growth, economic competitiveness, and security dynamics.

Strategic conduct is inherent in auction procedures, which is essential to international politics. Bidders' strategy to maximize their interests in auctions is analogous to nations strategizing to promote their national interests internationally. For example, states strategically bid to balance their environmental commitments and economic interests in carbon credit auctions under the Kyoto Protocol.[2] These auctions impact global environmental politics and reflect state strategic interactions in the international system.

Auctions have the potential to reflect and affect global power relations. The entities with the highest bids in auctions frequently have considerable economic resources, implying a power advantage. For example, in the international art market, powerful countries and individuals often participate in auctions, and their bidding can affect cultural trends and global soft power. Similarly, natural resource auctions can reveal power discrepancies between wealthy and developing countries, adding to resource justice and international equity discussions.

On a negative note, auctions, particularly in the arms market, can be related to international crises. The best bidders frequently obtain modern weaponry, influencing power balances and increasing hostilities. This element of auctions poses significant ethical and political concerns, requiring international legislation and control.

---

[2] https://unfccc.int/process/the-kyoto-protocol/mechanisms/emissions-trading.

3.4   Voting Mechanism

The voting mechanism is critical to the functioning of democratic institutions because it represents varied views and facilitates collective decision-making (Filos-Ratsikas & Miltersen, 2014; Kim, 2017; Meir, 2018). While most people identify voting with national elections, it also plays a vital role in international politics. This section investigates the impact of voting mechanisms on international politics, focusing on their position in international organizations, their impact on global power relations, and the issues they pose.

International organizations rely on voting processes to function. Many organizations, like the United Nations (UN), World Trade Organization, African Union, European Union, International Monetary Fund, and others, rely on voting to make decisions. The design of these mechanisms, however, differs significantly. For example, each member state has one vote in the UN General Assembly, upholding the principle of sovereign equality. However, in the UN Security Council, a separate institution, the United States, Russia, China, the United Kingdom, and France have veto powers. This is a reason why there is a talk on the reform of the UN Security Council.

On the other hand, the IMF or World Bank employs a weighted voting system in which votes are awarded based on a country's quota, reflecting its economic power. These mechanisms influence global governance and diplomacy by shaping international collaboration and consensus-building.

Voting mechanisms in international politics, despite their importance, face significant obstacles. These include the danger of deadlock, which occurs when a lack of consensus prevents decision-making, and the risk of vote trading, in which countries exchange votes to advance their interests. There is also the issue of guaranteeing equal representation, which is especially difficult for underrepresented groups or smaller nations. Furthermore, when countries believe their opinions are not appropriately reflected in voting processes, the legitimacy of international judgments might be called into doubt.

3.5   Matching Mechanism

In mechanism design, pairing agents or assigning resources based on preferences and limitations to achieve certain goals or outcomes is called matching (Boudreau & Knoblauch, 2017; Johnson, 2013).

Matching mechanisms in international politics can facilitate collaboration between governments, international organizations, and non-state actors by aligning their incentives and objectives. For example, in[3] 2023, at the United Nations, Germany and Namibia were appointed co-facilitators of the Summit of the Future.[4] Another example at the UN is the appointment of Rwanda and Sweden to co-facilitate the intergovernmental process of the Global Digital Compact.

Mechanism design through matching can facilitate the allocation of peacekeeping forces, humanitarian aid, and other resources to foster stability and cooperation by evaluating the desires of opposing parties. This can lay the groundwork for long-term peace accords and conflict resolution. An example of this is the UN and AU partnership on peacekeeping mechanisms.[5]

Worldwide collaboration is required because of the global nature of climate change and environmental concerns. Matching systems can be used to distribute emission permits, adaptation and mitigation resources, or assign roles in environmental preservation activities. Mechanism design can foster global collaboration in addressing major ecological problems by aligning the incentives of different countries and considering their specific situations.

Matching mechanisms can also be used in international trade and economic ties, where governments must weigh domestic interests against the necessity for global collaboration. Mechanism design can encourage mutually beneficial outcomes and support global economic growth by establishing trade agreements and economic partnerships that adapt to the desires of different countries.

Matching mechanisms can help improve the effectiveness of foreign aid and development programs. Mechanism design can ensure that aid is delivered efficiently and targeted in locations with the most impact by matching donors with recipients based on their preferences and needs. This can help achieve global development goals while encouraging international cooperation in tackling global disparities.

---

[3] https://www.un.org/techenvoy/global-digital-compact/intergovernmental-process.

[4] https://www.idos-research.de/en/others-publications/article/germany-and-namibia-as-co-leads-for-the-united-nations-chances-and-challenges-on-the-road-to-the-2024-un-summit-of-the-future/.

[5] https://press.un.org/en/2022/sc15058.doc.htm.

Mechanism design matching mechanisms can contribute to international politics by providing a systematic strategy to align the incentives and interests of numerous parties. This can improve cooperation, minimize conflict, and increase global well-being. Furthermore, matching mechanisms can assist in overcoming collective action issues and mitigating the obstacles of asymmetric information, free-riding, and other problems that impede international collaboration.

Despite the apparent benefits, using matching mechanisms in international politics is fraught with difficulties and constraints. Some critical challenges include the difficulty of acquiring reliable information about diverse actors' preferences and limits, the possibility for manipulation and strategic behavior, and the need to adapt matching methods to the specific intricacies of international politics. Furthermore, adopting matching procedures may necessitate the establishment of new international institutions or modifying existing ones, which can present considerable logistical and political obstacles.

3.6 Market Mechanisms

The market mechanism, which concerns the design of markets to attain desirable features such as efficiency, fairness, and stability, is one of the essential topics in mechanism design (Xu et al., 2016; Wu et al., 2023; Ye et al., 2023; Zhou et al., 2023). This section covers market mechanisms and their consequences in international politics in mechanism design.

A market mechanism is a tool to coordinate economic activities. Its goal is to bring buyers and sellers together while modifying prices based on supply and demand to achieve equilibrium. The perfect market mechanism results in a Pareto-efficient allocation, in which no one may benefit without letting someone else suffer (Lecomber, 1979). Unfortunately, many markets are inefficient due to information asymmetry, externalities, and market power. These difficulties are addressed via mechanism design, which involves the development of rules and structures that drive market behavior toward desirable outcomes. For example, auction design, a subset of mechanism design, focuses on developing bidding rules to produce efficient results despite secret information and strategic behavior.

The market mechanism is more than just an economic notion; it is also important in international politics. International trade is one of the most visible examples of market mechanisms at work. Countries develop rules and conventions that govern the cross-border exchange of commodities and services through various trade agreements and treaties.

However, the design of these market systems can have significant political consequences. For example, WTO rules aim to encourage free commerce and avoid protectionism. These principles, however, have the potential to impact the balance of power among states. Moreover, they can cause contention, as evidenced by disagreements over agricultural subsidies and intellectual property rights.

The architecture of global market mechanisms can have far-reaching consequences for global politics. For starters, it can potentially change the allocation of economic power across states. For example, the structure of global financial markets can decide which countries have access to capital and on what terms.

Second, market systems can impact international relations and the likelihood of conflict or collaboration. Countries that are closely linked through trade, for example, may be less inclined to engage in military conflict, according to the "capitalist peace" theory (Gartzke, 2007; Gartzke & Hewitt, 2010).

Finally, the design of market systems can impact the international community's ability to address global concerns. For example, market-based methods such as carbon trading have been proposed to address climate change, but their effectiveness is highly dependent on their design.

3.7   Contract Mechanisms

Contract mechanisms are essential to the many tools used in mechanism design, especially to manage information asymmetry and incentivize desired behaviors (Zeng et al., 2018; Lumineau & Quélin, 2012; Page, 1991; Watson, 2007). This section delves into the concept of contract mechanisms in mechanism design and their ramifications in international politics.

Contracts are vital in mechanism design for coordinating interactions between parties, especially when information asymmetry exists. In principal-agent models, for example, if one party (the agent) has more information than the other (the principal), the principal might construct a contract that incentivizes the agent to operate in the principal's best interests.

Contract mechanisms can take many forms, such as performance-based contracts, in which the agent's income is based on measurable results. They may also involve screening or signaling systems, in which one party provides information about themselves through their actions or readiness to accept particular parameters. The goal is to design a system, frequently contained in the contract, that aligns all parties' interests and leads to an efficient and desired solution.

Contract mechanisms play an important role in international politics in various settings. Contracts between states include international treaties, trade agreements, and diplomatic agreements. These contracts specify the norms of interaction and include tools to encourage compliance and resolve possible issues.

International trade treaties, for example, frequently include provisions for dispute settlement, allowing parties to resolve issues without resorting to economic or military conflict. Similarly, climate agreements may contain methods to motivate countries to reduce greenhouse gas emissions, such as carbon trading or fines for non-compliance.

Contract mechanisms in international politics can have a considerable impact on world affairs. For starters, they can impact international relations by providing an organized, predictable framework for interaction that lowers uncertainty and promotes cooperation. Contract mechanisms that describe non-compliance penalties can deter infractions and encourage stability.

Second, contract mechanisms can impact the power balance in international relations. For example, nations with larger economies or military capabilities may be able to negotiate more advantageous contract conditions, reinforcing existing power arrangements.

Finally, contract arrangements can impact the international community's ability to address global concerns. The success of international efforts to prevent climate change, for example, relies heavily on the design of contract mechanisms in climate agreements.

3.8   PUBLIC GOODS MECHANISMS

Creating mechanisms to deliver and preserve public goods is an important component of mechanism design (Attiyeh et al., 2000; Chen & Hogg, 2008; Zhang et al., 2018). This section analyzes public goods mechanisms in the context of mechanism design.

Public goods are non-exclusive and non-rivalrous goods. This means that anyone can use them, and their usage by one individual does not limit their availability to others. Clean air, national defense, and public parks are a few examples. However, the supply of public goods is frequently fraught with difficulties due to the free-rider problem, in which individuals gain from the good without contributing to its provision.

Mechanism design is critical in addressing this issue. It entails creating procedures encouraging people to declare their genuine preferences for the public good and participate in its provision. These systems include taxation, voluntary donations, and conditional cooperation mechanisms, in which individuals give on the condition that others do the same.

It is vital in international politics to provide global public goods such as climatic stability, international security, and global health. These products benefit all countries, but their provision necessitates global cooperation and coordination.

Mechanism design gives techniques for addressing these issues. International accords, for example, frequently incorporate incentives to motivate countries to contribute to global public goods. For example, the Paris Agreement on Climate Change provides procedures to ensure transparency and accountability by requiring countries to report on their greenhouse gas emissions and efforts to reduce them.

The design of public goods systems can have far-reaching repercussions in international politics. It can influence how global public goods are provided and maintained. The efficacy of international accords' processes can determine whether countries collaborate to address global concerns or succumb to the free-rider problem.

Second, the design of these systems can influence the balance of power in international politics. Countries that give more to global public goods may gain influence and respect, while those that exploit them may face criticism or sanctions.

Finally, developing systems for public goods have the potential to influence the fairness and equity of global collaboration. As a result, it is critical to establish procedures that consider countries' varying resources and obligations to ensure that the cost of delivering global public goods is distributed fairly.

3.9   MECHANISM DESIGN IN POLITICS

Mechanism design creates institutions and norms that steer strategic behavior toward certain goals. This potent instrument can handle international political problems by examining the incentives and constraints faced by various global actors.

We learned about the significance of mechanism design in politics in this chapter. Mechanism design, for example, can make it easier to allocate peacekeeping soldiers, humanitarian supplies, and other resources to foster stability and cooperation. Furthermore, knowing the desires of opposing parties, this technique can assist in creating the framework for long-term peace agreements and conflict resolution.

Matching design can be used to distribute emission permits, adaptation and mitigation resources, or assign roles in environmental preservation activities. In addition, mechanism design can foster global collaboration in addressing major environmental problems by aligning the incentives of different countries and taking into account their specific situations.

Mechanism design can encourage mutually beneficial outcomes and support global economic growth by establishing trade agreements and economic partnerships that adapt to the desires of different countries.

Matching mechanisms, which connect donors with recipients based on their preferences and needs, can improve the effectiveness of international aid and development programs. This ensures that aid is allocated efficiently and directed toward locations with the greatest impact.

Mechanism design contributes to international politics by systematically matching various actors' incentives and interests. This encourages cooperation, reduces the risk of conflict, and improves global well-being. Furthermore, mechanism design can aid in resolving collective action problems and mitigating challenges given by asymmetric information, free-riding, and other issues impeding international collaboration.

However, there are obstacles and limitations to using mechanism design in international politics. First, the efficiency of mechanism design depends on having the correct knowledge of the parties involved, which can be difficult to obtain in international politics due to the complexity and diversity of actors. Second, mechanism design implies that individuals will rationally and truthfully declare their choices; yet, certain actors may manipulate or strategically undermine the desired consequences. Third, mechanism design frequently depends on simplistic models that may fail to convey the complexities and uncertainties inherent in international politics. As a result, it is critical to tailor mechanism design to the unique context of global interactions. Fourth, it is important to note who designs the mechanism, and often the parties benefiting from it are also responsible for designing the mechanism, which can create perverse incentives.

Implementing matching mechanisms may create new international institutions or modify existing ones, presenting considerable logistical and political obstacles. As a result, mechanism design can considerably impact international politics by providing new tools for understanding and tackling complicated global concerns. Moreover, mechanism design can help global peace, environmental protection, economic growth, and development by aligning the incentives and interests of multiple parties. However, to fully realize the potential for fostering global cooperation and welfare, scholars and policymakers must first overcome the problems and constraints of using mechanism design in international politics.

3.10   Conclusion

Mechanism design is critical in international politics because it is a potent tool for shaping outcomes in various circumstances. The influence of mechanism design is far-reaching, whether it is voting mechanisms that govern decision-making processes in international bodies, market mechanisms that govern global economic interactions, contract mechanisms that dictate the terms of international agreements, or mechanisms for public goods that underpin global cooperation for collective benefits.

The design of these processes can significantly influence the balance of power among nations, the effectiveness of international collaboration, and the global community's ability to handle essential concerns. Mechanism design in international politics demands a thoughtful and nuanced approach since it entails a delicate balance of economic theory, strategic considerations, and political realities.

The importance of mechanism design in international politics will rise as we move forward in a more interconnected world. Policymakers, scholars, and international leaders should thus continue to interact with these notions, refining and creating processes that can aid in achieving efficient, equitable, and sustainable global results. Finally, the intelligent application of mechanism design can contribute to a more cooperative and equitable international political scene, allowing us to better address our time's most important global problems.

References

Agastya, M., Feng, X., & Lu, J. (2023). Auction design with shortlisting when value discovery is covert. *Journal of Mathematical Economics, 107*(9), 102851.

Attiyeh, G., Franciosi, R., & Isaac, R. M. (2000). Experiments with the pivot process for providing public goods. *Public Choice, 102*(1–2), 93–112.

Boudreau, J. W., & Knoblauch, V. (2017). A marriage matching mechanism menagerie. *Operations Research Letters, 45*(1), 68–71.

Chen, K. Y., & Hogg, T. (2008). Experiments with probabilistic quantum auctions. *Quantum Information Processing, 7*, 139–152.

Du, J., Jiang, C., Han, Z., Zhang, H., Mumtaz, S., & Ren, Y. (2017). Contract mechanism and performance analysis for data transaction in mobile social networks. *IEEE Transactions on Network Science and Engineering, 6*(2), 103–115.

Egan, M., & Jakob, M. (2016). Market mechanism design for profitable on-demand transport services. *Transportation Research Part B: Methodological, 89*, 178–195.

Filos-Ratsikas, A., & Miltersen, P. B. (2014, December 14–17). Truthful approximations to range voting. In *Web and Internet Economics: 10th International Conference, WINE 2014. Proceedings 10* (pp. 175–188). Springer International Publishing.

Fleck, A. K., & Anatolitis, V. (2023). Achieving the objectives of renewable energy policy—Insights from renewable energy auction design in Europe. *Energy Policy, 173*, 113357.

Gao, J., Wong, T., Selim, B., & Wang, C. (2022). VOMA: A privacy-preserving matching mechanism design for community ride-sharing. *IEEE Transactions on Intelligent Transportation Systems, 23*(12), 23963–23975.

Gartzke, E. (2007). The capitalist peace. *American Journal of Political Science, 51*(1), 166–191.

Gartzke, E., & Hewitt, J. J. (2010). International crises and the capitalist peace. *International Interactions, 36*(2), 115–145.

Großer, J. (2012). Voting mechanism design: Modeling institutions in experiments. In B. Kittel, W. J. Luhan, & R. B. Morton (Eds.), *Experimental political science: Principles and practices* (pp. 72–91). Palgrave Macmillan.

He, B., Li, B., & Zhu, X. (2023). Carbon footprint prediction method for linkage mechanism design. *Environmental Science and Pollution Research, 30*(21), 1–18.

Healy, P. J. (2010). Equilibrium participation in public goods allocations. *Review of Economic Design, 14*, 27–50.

Hensher, D. A., & Wallis, I. P. (2005). Competitive tendering as a contracting mechanism for subsidizing transport: The bus experience. *Journal of Transport Economics and Policy (JTEP), 39*(3), 295–322.

Hui, D., Zhuo, L., & Xin, C. (2022). May. Quality-aware incentive mechanism design based on matching game for hierarchical federated learning. In *IEEE INFOCOM 2022-IEEE Conference on Computer Communications Workshops (INFOCOM WKSHPS)* (pp. 1–6). IEEE.

Hurwicz, L., & Reiter, S. (2006). *Designing economic mechanisms*. Cambridge University Press.

Johnson, T. R. (2013). Matching through position auctions. *Journal of Economic Theory, 148*(4), 1700–1713.

Kim, H. (2023). Bridging principal-agent and mechanism design theories: An integrated conceptual framework for policy evaluation. *Asia Pacific Education Review*, 1–14.

Kim, S. (2017). Ordinal versus cardinal voting rules: A mechanism design approach. *Games and Economic Behavior, 104*, 350–371.

Kohli, N., & Laskowski, P. (2018). Epsilon voting: Mechanism design for parameter selection in differential privacy. In *2018 IEEE Symposium on Privacy-Aware Computing (PAC)* (pp. 19–30). IEEE.

Lecomber, R. (1979). Resource depletion and the market mechanism. In *The economics of natural resources* (pp. 81–111). Palgrave.

Liao, Q., Tu, R., Zhang, W., Wang, B., Liang, Y., & Zhang, H. (2023). Auction design for capacity allocation in the petroleum pipeline under fair opening. *Energy, 264*, 126079.

Lumineau, F., & Quélin, B. V. (2012). An empirical investigation of interorganizational opportunism and contracting mechanisms. *Strategic Organization, 10*(1), 55–84.

Marwala, T., & Hurwitz, E. (2017). Mechanism design. In *Artificial intelligence and economic theory: Skynet in the market* (pp. 111–124). Springer.

Mavungu, M., Hurwitz, E., & Marwala, T. (2019). Modelling and computational simulation of optimal auction design and bidding strategies. *Journal of Economic and Financial Sciences, 12*(1), 6.

McClellan, A. (2023). Knowing your opponents: Information disclosure and auction design. *Games and Economic Behavior, 140*, 173–180.

Meir, R. (2018). Voting and mechanism design. In *Strategic voting* (pp. 47–66). Springer International Publishing.

Myerson, R. B., Eatwell, J., Milgate, M., & Peter, N. (1989). *Allocation, information and markets*. Palgrave Macmillan.

Page, F. H. (1991). Optimal contract mechanisms for principal-agent problems with moral hazard and adverse selection. *Economic Theory, 1*, 323–338.

Sinha, A., & Anastasopoulos, A. (2019). Distributed mechanism design with learning guarantees for private and public goods problems. *IEEE Transactions on Automatic Control, 65*(10), 4106–4121.

Thekinen, J., & Panchal, J. H. (2017). Resource allocation in cloud-based design and manufacturing: A mechanism design approach. *Journal of Manufacturing Systems, 43*, 327–338.

Vakilinia, I., Wang, W., & Xin, J. (2023). An incentive-compatible mechanism for decentralized storage network. *IEEE Transactions on Network Science and Engineering, 10*(4), 2294–2306.

Watson, J. (2007). Contract, mechanism design, and technological detail. *Econometrica, 75*(1), 55–81.

Wu, Q., Yan, C., & Qiu, Z. (2023). Deep reinforcement learning for strategic bidding in incomplete information market. In *Proceedings of the 7th PURPLE MOUNTAIN FORUM on Smart Grid Protection and Control (PMF2022)* (pp. 499–517). Springer Nature Singapore.

Xing, B., Gao, W. J., Battle, K., Nelwamondo, F. V., & Marwala, T. (2011). e-Reverse logistics for remanufacture-to-order: An online auction-based and multi-agent system supported solution. In *Proceedings of the Fifth International Conference on Advanced Engineering Computing and Applications in Sciences (ADVCOMP 2011)*. IARIA.

Xu, L., Jiang, C., Shen, Y., Quek, T. Q., Han, Z., & Ren, Y. (2016). Energy efficient D2D communications: A perspective of mechanism design. *IEEE Transactions on Wireless Communications, 15*(11), 7272–7285.

Ye, S., Long, C., Liu, X., Li, T., Wei, J., Yang, X., Li, D., Liu, L., & Yao, Y. (2023). Electricity market trading mechanism and business model under coordination of distribution and storage. In *The 37th Annual Conference on Power System and Automation in Chinese Universities (CUS-EPSA)* (pp. 781–794). Springer Nature Singapore.

Zeng, M., Li, Y., Zhang, K., Waqas, M., & Jin, D. (2018). Incentive mechanism design for computation offloading in heterogeneous fog computing: A contract-based approach. In *2018 IEEE International Conference on Communications (ICC)* (pp. 1–6). IEEE.

Zhang, M., Huang, J., & Zhang, R. (2018). Wireless power provision as a public good. In *2018 16th International Symposium on Modeling and Optimization in Mobile, Ad Hoc, and Wireless Networks (WiOpt)* (pp. 1–8). IEEE.

Zhou, Y., & Serizawa, S. (2021). *Multi-object auction design beyond quasi-linearity: Leading examples* (ISER Discussion Paper No. 1116).

Zhou, M., Wu, Z., & Li, G. (2023). Market mechanism design for enhancing the flexibility of power systems. In *Power system flexibility: Modeling, optimization and mechanism design* (pp. 241–271). Springer Nature Singapore.

CHAPTER 4

Artificial Intelligence in Politics

4.1 Introduction to Artificial Intelligence

Artificial intelligence (AI) is the creation of machines that mimic human intelligence using cognitive science, computer science, and data science, and it represents the pinnacle of human technological development (Leke & Marwala, 2019; Leke et al., 2017a; Marwala, 2001a, 2018; Marwala & Leke, 2019; Marwala et al., 2016, 2023). Machines may now perform tasks that previously required human intelligence while learning from experience and adapting to new inputs thanks to this cutting-edge technology. As we enter the twenty-first century, AI is changing many aspects of our lives, from the economy to culture, providing opportunities and challenges. This section studies the concept of AI, investigates its different applications, discusses potential challenges, and delves into ethical considerations.

A mathematician and cryptographer, Alan Turing, asked, "Can machines think?" in the middle of the twentieth century when AI first arose (Marwala, 2009). Some of the classes of AI include Narrow AI, which is designed to do a single task, such as speech recognition, and General AI, which has the potential to outperform humans in the majority of economically relevant tasks. In addition, algorithms, iterative learning, and massive volumes of data can help AI systems improve over time, demonstrating intelligence traditionally considered unique to humans.

T. Marwala, *Artificial Intelligence, Game Theory and Mechanism Design in Politics*, https://doi.org/10.1007/978-981-99-5103-1_4

AI technology has impacted several businesses, changing how we interact with the outside world (Marwala, 2015; Marwala et al., 2017; Xing & Marwala, 2018). AI in healthcare, for example, can forecast diseases, personalize medications, and improve patient care. Robo-advisors provide investment advice in the financial business, while AI algorithms detect questionable activities (Marwala, 2012). According to Marwala (2010), self-driving cars are becoming a reality in the automobile industry. Furthermore, AI has increased business productivity, enhanced supply chain management logistics, and allowed for more personalized school learning (Marwala, 2014). Moreover, the role of AI in the entertainment industry, notably in the development of video games and films, cannot be understated.

Despite its benefits, AI poses significant challenges. Job displacement is a serious problem as AI and automation continue performing the jobs humans previously handled. Furthermore, the "black box" problem is caused by the complexity of AI systems, which may result in unexpected results. Data privacy concerns frequently arise due to the massive volume of data that AI systems require to function properly. There is also the possibility that AI systems can be used for malevolent reasons, such as autonomous weapons or deepfake technology.

Our ability to manage AI has not kept pace with its rapid advancement, raising various ethical problems. People must be aware of all interactions with AI systems. Hence transparency is critical. Accountability is also crucial since it is necessary to understand who is to blame when an AI system causes harm. Another concern with AI is bias, as these systems frequently duplicate the biases in their training data, resulting in unfair outcomes. Finally, we must exert control over how artificial intelligence is used for monitoring and what this entails for people's privacy and civil liberties.

4.2   Types of Artificial Intelligence

AI can be classified in various ways, but one of the most frequently used is based on its capability or functioning. Currently, Narrow AI is the most commonly used type of AI. Narrow AI is focused on a single task, such as voice recognition, recommendation systems, or image recognition. These systems lack understanding and consciousness but can outperform in specific tasks. Siri, Alexa, and Google Assistant are a few examples.

General AI can perform any cognitive task that a human can. It can comprehend, learn, adapt, and apply knowledge in various tasks. Furthermore, General AI may use intellect to address different problems, displaying consciousness and self-awareness.

Superintelligent AI extends General AI while outperforming human intelligence in the most valuable tasks. Superintelligent AI is about more than just mimicking human intelligence; it is about transcending it. Superintelligent AI is frequently seen in science fiction and futuristic studies.

4.3   AI NARROW

Narrow AI meant to do a specific task, such as voice recognition or data processing, has become commonplace in our daily life. As a result, Narrow AI's influence in international politics is becoming more visible. This section delves into the impact of Narrow AI on politics, namely its role in global governance, diplomacy, and security.

Narrow AI offers tremendous potential to improve efficiency and decision-making in global governance (Marwala, 2001b). Narrow AI can process massive volumes of data, assisting in identifying patterns and trends in global phenomena like climate change and migration patterns. Narrow AI, for example, may analyze satellite data to track deforestation or the movement of displaced people, providing valuable insights to drive policy decisions (Abe et al., 2010; Gidudu et al., 2007, 2009). Furthermore, Narrow AI can help international institutions like the United Nations and the World Bank run more smoothly by automating mundane work and allowing for more effective resource allocation.

The impact of Narrow AI is also being felt in the diplomatic arena, leading to the emergence of "digital diplomacy" or "e-diplomacy." For example, Narrow AI-powered social media research can assist diplomats in framing statements or detecting future policy blowback (Fernandes et al., 2015). Furthermore, Narrow AI-powered real-time translation systems can break down language boundaries, improving international collaboration. However, the rise of digital diplomacy brings new obstacles, such as Narrow AI-powered disinformation efforts, which necessitate more rigorous cybersecurity safeguards and digital literacy.

Narrow AI has both beneficial and negative implications in the security sector. On the one hand, Narrow AI can improve threat detection, from detecting suspected terrorist activity online to monitoring border security using drones (Marwala, 2020). On the other hand, the use of Narrow AI in warfare, such as autonomous weapons systems, creates severe ethical and legal concerns. Furthermore, the drive to develop advanced AI capabilities may heighten geopolitical tensions, even leading to an "AI arms race."

4.4   GENERAL AI

General AI refers to systems that, like humans, can comprehend, learn, adapt, and apply knowledge across several tasks (Amin et al., 2023; Fjelland, 2020; Sewak, 2019; Szegedy, 2020). Although it is yet primarily theoretical, the emergence of General AI could have far-reaching consequences for international affairs. Therefore, this section investigates General AI's possible impact on worldwide politics, focusing on global power dynamics, international law, and global ethics implications.

The emergence of General AI has the potential to alter global power relations drastically. Countries that create General AI could gain a huge strategic advantage, potentially shifting the balance of power. This technological competition could intensify international tensions and lead to an AI weapons race, analogous to the Cold War nuclear arms race.[1] Ensuring equal distribution and use of general artificial intelligence will be a critical challenge for the global government.

General AI might likewise provide serious issues to international law. Existing legal systems are unprepared to deal with the intricacies of General AI, especially in areas such as liability, accountability, and rights. For example, who is liable if a General AI system causes harm? Who is to blame: the developer, the user, or AI? Furthermore, should General AI be awarded legal personality or rights if it acquires a level of consciousness? Major legal innovation and international cooperation would be required to address these difficulties.

General AI also raises grave ethical concerns. One of the biggest concerns is the possibility of abuse. General AI could be utilized for the wrong reasons, such as autonomous weapons or mass surveillance systems, endangering peace and human rights. There is also the potential of developing AI systems that reflect and perpetuate existing prejudices, resulting in inequitable outcomes. These ethical quandaries need

---

[1] https://www.cfr.org/timeline/us-russia-nuclear-arms-control#:~:text=The%20nuclear%20arms%20race%20was,the%20risk%20of%20nuclear%20war.

a global conversation on the values and principles that should govern the development and application of General AI.

4.5 SUPERINTELLIGENT AI

Superintelligent AI, a branch of General AI that outperforms human intellect in the most economically valuable tasks, represents a paradigm shift with far-reaching ramifications for international politics (Brundage, 2015; Davis, 2015; Russell, 2017; Shetty & Raj, 2022). While this form of AI is still theoretical and has yet to be realized, it is critical to address its possible implications for global power dynamics, ethical considerations, and international governance. This section delves into these ramifications and the significance of proactive policymaking.

Intelligent AI has the potential to alter global power dynamics radically. Nations or entities with such advanced AI could achieve unparalleled influence, potentially leading to imbalances. This might spark a new arms race as countries compete to develop or purchase Superintelligent AI. A race of this magnitude might exacerbate international tensions and threaten global peace. To avoid such a scenario, worldwide collaboration is required to control the development and usage of Superintelligent AI.

Intelligent AI brings serious ethical concerns. Theoretically, a Superintelligent AI may make decisions that affect billions of people, but humans may not completely comprehend its decision-making processes. This creates a lack of accountability and endangers human rights and democratic values. Furthermore, the potential for abusing Superintelligent AI, from mass surveillance to autonomous armament, poses serious challenges to peace and security.

Given the disruptive power of Superintelligent AI, existing international governance frameworks may be unprepared to deal with its consequences. Therefore, new global governance institutions must supervise its development and deployment to ensure that Superintelligent AI is used responsibly and benefits humanity. Furthermore, these mechanisms should promote openness, accountability, and inclusivity by bringing together various stakeholders such as governments, academics, the commercial sector, and civil society.

4.6   NEURAL NETWORKS

Neural networks have had a substantial impact on problem-solving and decision-making in a variety of disciplines. These computational models, inspired by the biological neural networks of the human brain, have provided the foundation for the development of intelligent systems (Marwala, 2000a, 2000b). This section presents an in-depth look into neural networks, including their history, structure, kinds, uses, and prospects.

Warren McCulloch and Walter Pitts created the first mathematical model of a neuron in 1943 (LeCun et al., 2015; McClelland et al., 1987; McCulloch & Pitts, 1943; Werbos, 1994). This marked the start of an era in which scientists and researchers began investigating the potential of artificial neural networks (ANNs) to mimic human cognition. Several advancements in the field over the years have resulted in the development of sophisticated neural network models, such as the perceptron, back-propagation, and deep learning, which have considerably increased the capabilities of ANNs (Marwala, 2003, 2004; Leke et al., 2017b).

The artificial neuron, a node or unit, is the essential building block at the center of a neural network. These neurons are grouped into input, hidden layer(s), and output layers. The input layer gets raw data from external sources, while the hidden layers execute complicated computations and modify the data to extract useful features. Conversely, the output layer offers the final results or predictions based on the hidden layers' analysis.

Weighted connections connect neurons in a neural network, regulating the strength of signals passed between neurons. These weights are iteratively modified during learning to reduce errors between the network's predictions and the output. Figure 4.1 depicts a multi-layer perceptron neural network (Marwala, 2001c; Msiza et al., 2007; Pires & Marwala, 2005). Different types of neural networks are developed to address specific problems and challenges. Some of the most common varieties are listed below. Feedforward neural networks, for example, comprise numerous layers with unidirectional connections in which information goes from the input layer to the output layer without looping back.

Recurrent neural networks (RNNs) have feedback connections that allow them to remember prior inputs. RNNs are thus particularly well suited to applications requiring sequences, such as time-series prediction

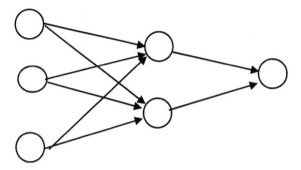

Fig. 4.1 A feedforward multi-layer perceptron with three input units, two hidden nodes, and one output unit

and natural language processing. Convolutional neural networks (CNNs) are neural networks that are specifically intended for image processing and computer vision tasks. CNNs detect local features inside pictures using convolutional layers, which are pooled and processed by fully connected layers for ultimate classification. Finally, because deep learning networks include numerous hidden layers, they can learn more abstract and complicated data representations. They are widely used in various applications, including image recognition, speech recognition, and natural language processing (Leke & Marwala, 2016; Leke et al., 2017b).

Neural networks have been used in various industries and areas with impressive results. In medical diagnostics, neural networks aid in disease detection and correct diagnosis, hence improving patient outcomes (Mistry et al., 2009; Ogunleye et al., 2019; Russell et al., 2008; Spiller & Marwala, 2007; Tim & Marwala, 2007). Credit scoring, fraud detection, and algorithmic trading are all made possible by neural networks, which provide more efficient and reliable decision-making in the financial sector (Khoza & Marwala, 2012; Lunga & Marwala, 2006; Marwala, 2013; Marwala & Hurwitz, 2017; Moloi & Marwala, 2020; Patel & Marwala, 2006; Pires & Marwala, 2004). Neural networks have contributed significantly to natural language processing improvements, powering applications such as language translation, sentiment analysis, and chatbots (Roy et al., 2020). Neural networks have been used to improve robot performance and monitor construction's structural stability (Vilakazi & Marwala, 2009). Neural networks have played an essential role in collecting meaningful information from visual data, from facial recognition systems to video surveillance (Abe et al., 2014; Machowski & Marwala, 2005).

Engineering, healthcare, and finance have all been transformed by neural networks (Tettey & Marwala, 2007). These computational models have also begun to considerably impact international politics (Marwala & Lagazio, 2011). Using neural networks in politics can improve decision-making processes, advance diplomatic negotiations, and transform global security. This section examines applications of neural networks in international politics and the obstacles and ethical considerations surrounding their use.

Large volumes of data can be analyzed by neural networks to find patterns and trends, allowing policymakers to make informed decisions based on correct forecasts. This could lead to more effective international policy formation that considers economic trends, social movements, and geopolitical dynamics.

Neural networks can help negotiators prepare for complex debates and design ideal strategies, to model diplomatic scenarios. Furthermore, by evaluating historical data and cultural nuances, these AI-driven simulations might provide valuable insights and allow more effective dialogue across nations.

By recognizing risks and vulnerabilities in cybersecurity, terrorism, and weapons proliferation, neural networks can improve global security (Marais & Marwala, 2004). Furthermore, by evaluating massive amounts of data from diverse sources, these AI systems may find trends and abnormalities, resulting in more effective prevention and reaction methods.

Despite the potential benefits, using neural networks in international politics poses several problems and ethical concerns. Because neural networks rely on massive volumes of data, data privacy and security become critical. Protecting sensitive information, such as diplomatic communications and national security data, is essential to preventing misuse and preserving international confidence. Furthermore, neural networks are vulnerable to biases in training data. This could lead to biased or unfair foreign policy decisions, increasing tensions and wars.

Understanding and explaining the decision-making processes of neural networks can be difficult because they are based on complicated algorithms and computations. Furthermore, the lack of transparency raises issues about accountability, particularly when AI-driven judgments substantially impact international relations.

The growing dependence on neural networks in international politics may limit human involvement, prompting concerns about the autonomy that these AI systems should be afforded. To ensure responsible and ethical use, balancing exploiting AI capabilities and keeping human control is critical.

4.7 Reinforcement Learning

Reinforcement learning (RL) is a branch of AI that allows agents to learn optimal behaviors by interacting with their environment through trial and error (Annaswamy, 2023; Auer et al., 2008; François-Lavet et al., 2018; Ng & Russell, 2000; Sutton & Barto, 2018). Its robust approach has helped solve complicated, dynamic issues in various disciplines, including robotics, gaming, finance, and healthcare. This section delves into the principles of RL and its essential components, algorithms, applications, challenges, and possibilities in the quickly changing AI world.

RL is based on interaction-based learning, in which an agent strives to maximize the cumulative rewards it obtains over time by executing activities within an environment. The agent explores and exploits its background knowledge to make educated judgments that result in optimal behavior.

The initial component of RL is an agent, a learning entity that interacts with its surroundings, makes decisions, and learns from the outcomes of those decisions. The environment is where the agent functions, offering the agent varied states, actions, and rewards. A state is a precise environment configuration that is the foundation for the agent's decision-making process. An action is an agent's conceivable motion or choice inside a particular state. Finally, a reward is a numerical value that represents the immediate feedback received by the agent after acting in a specific condition. Figure 4.2 shows an example of RL.

Reinforcement learning algorithms are classified as model-based or model-free. Model-based algorithms learn an explicit model of the dynamics of their environment, whereas model-free algorithms learn rules or value functions immediately from their experiences.

Value Iteration and Policy Iteration are model-based algorithms that compute the best policy by updating the value function and/or policy iteratively until they converge. Q-Learning is a common model-free, off-policy approach for determining the optimal policy by learning the action-value function (Q-function). The agent's Q-function is updated

Fig. 4.2
Reinforcement learning

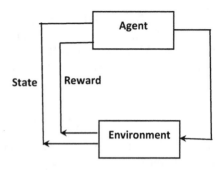

based on the experiences it gains through interacting with the environment. Deep Q-Network (DQN) is a Q-learning variation that uses deep neural networks as function approximators to handle high-dimensional state spaces, reaching human-level performance in various games. Finally, Proximal Policy Optimization is a model-free, on-policy technique that simplifies and improves the stability of policy gradient approaches, allowing for more efficient learning and performance in complicated contexts.

Reinforcement learning offers a wide range of applications in a variety of fields. RL has been used to teach robots a variety of activities, including locomotion, manipulation, and navigation, by allowing them to learn from their interactions with their surroundings. RL has shown remarkable success in understanding complicated games such as Go, chess, and poker, often outperforming humans (Hurwitz & Marwala, 2007; Marivate & Marwala, 2008; Marwala & Hurwitz, 2009). RL has been used in algorithmic trading and portfolio optimization, allowing for more efficient financial market decision-making. Finally, RL algorithms have been utilized in personalized medicine to optimize treatment options for patients with chronic diseases, resulting in improved patient outcomes.

The capacity of RL to solve complicated, dynamic problems has made it a formidable tool in various disciplines, ranging from robotics to finance. Reinforcement learning has also begun to impact international politics in recent years, providing solutions to diplomatic issues, improving decision-making processes, and forecasting global trends. This section discusses applications, problems, and consequences of reinforcement learning in international politics.

Reinforcement learning can analyze massive volumes of data, identify patterns, and make intelligent decisions based on accurate predictions. This could lead to more effective policy formation in international politics by considering economic trends, social movements, and geopolitical dynamics.

RL algorithms can simulate diplomatic scenarios, assisting negotiators in preparing for difficult discussions and devising ideal strategies. Furthermore, by evaluating historical data and cultural nuances, these simulations can provide significant insights and encourage more effective dialogue between nations.

By recognizing dangers and vulnerabilities in areas such as cybersecurity, terrorism, and weapons proliferation, reinforcement learning has the potential to improve global security. RL systems can find trends and anomalies by evaluating vast amounts of data from diverse sources, resulting in more effective prevention and reaction methods.

By monitoring social media data, news stories, and other sources, reinforcement learning can predict public attitudes on various international topics. This data can help governments better understand their constituents' needs and concerns, allowing foreign policies to align more with public interests.

Despite its potential benefits, reinforcement learning in international politics poses several difficulties. First, RL relies on massive volumes of data for training, and acquiring reliable, unbiased, and up-to-date data in international politics can be challenging. Concerns about data privacy and security complicate matters even more. Second, in RL, finding the correct balance between exploring new techniques and leveraging current knowledge is crucial. Finding the ideal balance in international politics, where the stakes are high, is critical to avoiding potentially costly blunders. Third, reinforcement learning models can be sophisticated and challenging to grasp, creating questions about openness and accountability in decision-making processes. Building procedures for keeping these systems responsible is critical, especially when RL-driven decisions have substantial implications for international relations.

RL frequently necessitates many samples (interactions with the environment) to develop successful policies. This inefficiency in sample size can result in lengthy learning processes and high processing costs, making it challenging to deploy RL in real-world applications with limited time and resources.

In many real-world problems, the agent does not have comprehensive state information about the environment, making learning optimal policies difficult. Furthermore, non-stationary environments with changing transition dynamics and reward functions present additional hurdles to RL algorithms.

Reinforcement learning must scale to high-dimensional states and action spaces to solve challenging real-world problems. Traditional RL approaches, however, frequently suffer from scalability. While deep reinforcement learning approaches have helped, they still have difficulty dealing with large state-action spaces and extended time horizons.

4.8   AI AND POLITICS

AI has made remarkable advances in recent years, impacting various fields ranging from healthcare to finance. However, AI's potential to restructure decision-making processes, improve diplomatic discussions, and transform global security has not gone unnoticed in international politics. This section investigates the implications of AI in international politics, diving into its current and potential applications, problems, and ethical concerns surrounding its use.

AI can scan massive volumes of data to detect patterns and trends, allowing policymakers to make well-informed decisions based on accurate forecasts. This could lead to a more effective international policy setup considering economic trends, social movements, and geopolitical dynamics.

AI-powered simulations can help negotiators prepare for complex debates and design ideal strategies by modelling diplomatic scenarios. Furthermore, by evaluating historical data and cultural nuances, these simulations can provide significant insights and encourage more effective dialogue between nations.

By recognizing dangers and vulnerabilities in areas such as cyber-security, terrorism, and weapons proliferation, AI has the potential to improve global security. AI systems can spot trends and abnormalities in massive amounts of data from multiple sources, leading to more effective prevention and reaction strategies.

AI can determine public mood on various international topics by evaluating social media data, news stories, and other sources. This data can help governments better understand their constituents' needs and concerns, allowing foreign policies to align more with public interests.

Despite the potential benefits, the use of AI in international politics poses several problems and ethical concerns. Because AI relies on massive volumes of data, data privacy and security become critical. Protecting sensitive information, such as diplomatic communications and national security data, is essential to preventing misuse and preserving international confidence.

AI systems are prone to biases in the data used for training. This could lead to biased or unfair foreign policy decisions, increasing tensions and wars. AI algorithms and computations can be complicated to comprehend, raising questions about openness and responsibility. Therefore, constructing processes for holding individuals for AI-driven decisions responsible is critical, especially when they have important implications for international relations.

The growing reliance on AI in international politics may diminish human involvement, prompting concerns about the autonomy that AI systems should be permitted. To ensure responsible and ethical use, we should balance taking advantage of AI capabilities and keeping human control.

4.9   Conclusion

AI has far-reaching consequences for international politics in its different incarnations, including Narrow AI, General AI, and Superintelligent AI. It impacts every facet of global affairs, from governance and diplomacy to security and power relations. AI technologies bring potential and challenges, demanding careful consideration and aggressive policymaking.

When used responsibly, AI technologies can transform global government and diplomacy by increasing efficiency and decision-making. They can, among other things, provide valuable insights to policymakers, create improved international communication, and enhance threat detection capabilities. However, the rise of AI brings with it significant concerns. It can potentially increase global power inequalities, raise ethical dilemmas, and put existing legal structures under strain.

Furthermore, the probable arrival of General AI and Superintelligent AI could cause a paradigm shift in international politics, needing new governance systems and ethical principles. The prospect of an AI weapons race, challenges of accountability and transparency, and the risk of misapplication highlight the importance of international cooperation and dialogue in shaping the future of AI.

Finally, AI is more than just a scientific advancement; it is a political phenomenon with the potential to transform the global order. We must navigate this digital revolution with a clear vision and shared responsibility. The goal should be to enhance AI technology and ensure that it promotes world peace, justice, and human well-being. This needs a global dialogue and concerted efforts to build AI governance frameworks that are inclusive, transparent, and fair.

REFERENCES

Abe, B. T., Gidudu, A., & Marwal, T. (2010). *Investigating the effects of ensemble classification on remotely sensed data for land cover mapping*. 2010 IEEE International Geoscience and Remote Sensing Symposium, pp. 2832–2835.

Abe, B. T., Olugbara, O. O., & Marwala, T. (2014). *Classification of hyperspectral images using machine learning methods*. IAENG Transactions on Engineering Technologies: Special Issue of the World Congress on Engineering and Computer Science 2012, pp. 555–569. Springer.

Amin, M. M., Cambria, E., & Schuller, B. W. (2023). Will affective computing emerge from foundation models and general artificial intelligence? A first evaluation of ChatGPT. *IEEE Intelligent Systems, 38*(2), 15–23.

Annaswamy, A. M. (2023). Adaptive control and intersections with reinforcement learning. *Annual Review of Control, Robotics, and Autonomous Systems, 6*, 65–93.

Auer, P., Jaksch, T., & Ortner, R. (2008). *Near-optimal regret bounds for reinforcement learning*. Advances in Neural Information Processing Systems, 21.

Brundage, M. (2015). Taking superintelligence seriously: Superintelligence: Paths, dangers, strategies by Nick Bostrom (Oxford University Press, 2014). *Futures, 72*, 32–35.

Davis, E. (2015). Ethical guidelines for a superintelligence. *Artificial Intelligence, 220*, 121–124.

Fernandes, M. A., Patel, P., & Marwala, T. (2015). Automated detection of human users in Twitter. *Procedia Computer Science, 53*, 224–231.

Fjelland, R. (2020). Why general artificial intelligence will not be realized. *Humanities and Social Sciences Communications, 7*(1), 1–9.

François-Lavet, V., Henderson, P., Islam, R., Bellemare, M. G., & Pineau, J. (2018). An introduction to deep reinforcement learning. *Foundations and Trends® in Machine Learning, 11*(3–4), 219–354.

Gidudu, A., Bolanle, A. T., & Marwala, T. (2009). *Random ensemble feature selection for land cover mapping*. 2009 IEEE International Geoscience and Remote Sensing Symposium, Vol. 2, pp. II–840.

Gidudu, A., Gregg, H., & Tshilidzi, M. (2007). *Image classification using SVMs: one-against-one vs one-against-all*. arXiv preprint arXiv:0711.2914

Hurwitz, E., & Marwala, T. (2007). *Learning to bluff*. 2007 IEEE International Conference on Systems, Man and Cybernetics, pp. 1188–1193.

Khoza, M., & Marwala, T. (2012). *Computational intelligence techniques for modelling an economic system*. The 2012 International Joint Conference on Neural Networks (IJCNN), pp. 1–5.

LeCun, Y., Bengio, Y., & Hinton, G. (2015). Deep learning. *Nature, 521*(7553), 436–444.

Leke, C. A., & Marwala, T. (2016, June 25–30). *Missing data estimation in high-dimensional datasets: A swarm intelligence-deep neural network approach*. Advances in Swarm Intelligence: 7th International Conference, ICSI 2016, Bali, Indonesia, Proceedings, Part I, pp. 259–270. Springer.

Leke, C. A., & Marwala, T. (2019). *Deep learning and missing data in engineering systems* (p. 179). Springer.

Leke, C. A., Ndjiongue, A. R., Twala, B., & Marwala, T., (2017a, July 27–August 1). *A deep learning-cuckoo search method for missing data estimation in high-dimensional datasets*. Advances in Swarm Intelligence: 8th International Conference, ICSI 2017, Fukuoka, Japan, Proceedings, Part I, pp. 561–572. Springer.

Leke, C. A., Ndjiongue, A. R., Twala, B., & Marwala, T. (2017b, October). *Deep learning-bat high-dimensional missing data estimator*. 2017 IEEE International Conference on Systems, Man, and Cybernetics (SMC), pp. 483–488.

Lunga, D., & Marwala, T. (2006, October 3–6). *Online forecasting of stock market movement direction using the improved incremental algorithm*. In Neural Information Processing: 13th International Conference, ICONIP 2006, Hong Kong, China. Proceedings, Part III, pp. 440–449. Springer.

Machowski, L. A., & Marwala, T. (2005). Using object oriented calculation process framework and neural networks for classification of image shapes. *International Journal of Innovative Computing, Information and Control, 1*(4), 609–623.

Marais, E., & Marwala, T. (2004). *Predicting global Internet instability caused by worms using neural networks*. Proceedings of the Annual Symposium of the Pattern Recognition Association of South Africa. Cape Town, pp. 81–85.

Marivate, V. N., & Marwala, T. (2008). *Social learning methods in board game agents*. 2008 IEEE Symposium on Computational Intelligence and Games, pp. 323–328.

Marwala, T. (2000a). Damage identification using committee of neural networks. *Journal of Engineering Mechanics, 126*(1), 43–50.

Marwala, T. (2000b). *Fault identification using neural networks and vibration data* (PhD Thesis). Cambridge University.

Marwala, T. (2001a). Probabilistic fault identification using a committee of neural networks and vibration data. *Journal of Aircraft, 38*(1), 138–146.

Marwala, T. (2001b). Scaled conjugate gradient and Bayesian training of neural networks for fault identification in cylinders. *Computers & Structures, 79*(32), 2793–2803.

Marwala, T. (2001c). Probabilistic fault identification using vibration data and neural networks. *Mechanical Systems and Signal Processing, 15*(6), 1109–1128.

Marwala, T. (2003). Fault classification using pseudomodal energies and neural networks. *AIAA Journal, 41*(1), 82–89.

Marwala, T. (2004). Fault classification using pseudomodal energies and probabilistic neural networks. *Journal of Engineering Mechanics, 130*(11), 1346–1355.

Marwala, T. (2009). *Computational intelligence for missing data imputation, estimation, and management: Knowledge optimization techniques.* IGI Global.

Marwala, T. (2010). *Finite element model updating using computational intelligence techniques: Applications to structural dynamics.* Springer.

Marwala, T. (2012). *Condition monitoring using computational intelligence methods.* Springer.

Marwala, T. (2013). *Economic modeling using artificial intelligence methods.* Springer.

Marwala, T. (2014). *Artificial intelligence techniques for rational decision making.* Springer.

Marwala, T. (2015). *Causality, correlation, and artificial intelligence for rational decision making.* World Scientific.

Marwala, T. (2018). *Handbook of machine learning: Foundation of artificial intelligence* (Vol. 1). World Scientific Publication.

Marwala, T. (2020). *Closing the gap: The Fourth Industrial Revolution in Africa.* Pan Macmillan.

Marwala, T., Boulkaibet, I., & Adhikari, S. (2016). *Probabilistic finite element model updating using Bayesian statistics: Applications to aeronautical and mechanical engineering.* Wiley.

Marwala, T., & Hurwitz, E. (2009). A multi-agent approach to bluffing. In *Multiagent systems.* IntechOpen.

Marwala, T., & Hurwitz, E. (2017). *Artificial intelligence and economic theory: Skynet in the market* (Vol. 1). Springer.

Marwala, T., & Lagazio, M. (2011). *Militarized conflict modeling using computational intelligence.* Springer.

Marwala, T., & Leke, C. A. (2019). *Handbook of machine learning: Optimization and decision making* (Vol. 2). World Scientific Publication.

Marwala, T., Mbuvha, R., & Mongwe, W. T. (2023). *Hamiltonian Monte Carlo methods in machine learning.* Elsevier.

McClelland, J. L., Rumelhart, D. E., & PDP Research Group. (1987). *Parallel distributed processing, Volume 2: Explorations in the microstructure of cognition: Psychological and biological models* (Vol. 2). MIT Press.

McCulloch, W. S., & Pitts, W. (1943). A logical calculus of the ideas immanent in nervous activity. *The Bulletin of Mathematical Biophysics, 5*, 115–133.

Mistry, J., Nelwamondo, F. V., & Marwala, T. (2009). *Investigating demographic influences for HIV classification using Bayesian autoassociative neural networks.* Advances in Neuro-Information Processing: 15th International Conference, ICONIP 2008, Auckland, New Zealand, November 25–28, 2008, Revised Selected Papers, Part II, pp. 752–759. Springer.

Moloi, T., & Marwala, T. (2020). *Artificial intelligence in economics and finance theories.* Springer.

Msiza, I. S., Nelwamondo, F. V., & Marwala, T. (2007). *Water demand forecasting using multi-layer perceptron and radial basis functions.* 2007 International Joint Conference on Neural Networks, pp. 13–18.

Ng, A. Y., & Russell, S. (2000). *Algorithms for inverse reinforcement learning.* ICML, Vol. 1, p. 2.

Ogunleye, A., Wang, Q. G., & Marwala, T. (2019). Integrated learning via randomized forests and localized regression with application to medical diagnosis. *IEEE Access, 7*, 18727–18733.

Patel, P. B., & Marwala, T. (2006, October 3–6). *Neural networks, fuzzy inference systems and adaptive-neuro fuzzy inference systems for financial decision making.* Neural Information Processing: 13th International Conference, ICONIP 2006, Hong Kong, China. Proceedings, Part III, pp. 430–439. Springer.

Pires, M. M., & Marwala, T. (2004). *Option pricing using neural networks and support vector machines.* IEEE International Conference on Systems, Man and Cybernetics, Vol. 2, No. 1, pp. 1279–1285.

Pires, M. M., & Marwala, T. (2005). *American option pricing using Bayesian multi-layer perceptrons and Bayesian support vector machines.* IEEE 3rd International Conference on Computational Cybernetics, 2005. ICCC 2005, pp. 219–224.

Roy, T., Marwala, T., & Chakraverty, S. (2020). *Speech emotion recognition using neural network and wavelet features.* Recent Trends in Wave Mechanics and Vibrations: Select Proceedings of WMVC 2018, pp. 427–438. Springer.

Russell, M. J., Rubin, D. M., Wigdorowitz, B., & Marwala, T. (2008, June 16–20). *The artificial larynx: A review of current technology and a proposal for future development.* 14th Nordic-Baltic Conference on Biomedical Engineering and Medical Physics: NBC, Riga, Latvia, pp. 160–163. Springer.

Russell, S. (2017). Artificial intelligence: The future is superintelligent. *Nature, 548*, 520–521.

Sewak, M. (2019). Deep Q Network (DQN), double DQN, and dueling DQN: A step towards general artificial intelligence. In *Deep reinforcement learning: Frontiers of artificial intelligence* (pp. 95–108). Springer.

Shetty, A., & Raj, N. (2022). *A study on recent advances in artificial intelligence and future prospects of attaining superintelligence.* Proceedings of Third International Conference on Communication, Computing and Electronics Systems: ICCCES 2021, pp. 879–892. Springer.

Spiller, J. M., & Marwala, T. (2007). Medical image segmentation and localization using deformable templates. In World Congress on Medical Physics and Biomedical Engineering 2006: August 27–September 1, 2006 COEX Seoul, Korea "Imaging the Future Medicine", pp. 2292–2295. Springer.

Sutton, R. S., & Barto, A. G. (2018). *Reinforcement learning: An introduction.* MIT Press.

Szegedy, C. (2020, July 26–31). *A promising path towards autoformalization and general artificial intelligence.* In Intelligent Computer Mathematics: 13th International Conference, CICM 2020, Bertinoro, Italy. Proceedings 13, pp. 3–20. Springer.

Tettey, T., & Marwala, T. (2007). *Conflict modelling and knowledge extraction using computational intelligence methods.* 2007 11th International Conference on Intelligent Engineering Systems, pp. 161–166.

Tim, T., & Marwala, T. M. (2007). *Computational intelligence methods for risk assessment of HIV.* World Congress on Medical Physics and Biomedical Engineering 2006: August 27–September 1, 2006 COEX Seoul, Korea "Imaging the Future Medicine", pp. 3717–3721. Springer.

Vilakazi, C. B., & Marwala, T. (2009). Computational its intelligence approach to condition monitoring: Incremental learning and application. In *Intelligent engineering systems and computational cybernetics* (pp. 161–171). Springer.

Werbos, P. J. (1994). *The roots of backpropagation: From ordered derivatives to neural networks and political forecasting* (Vol. 1). Wiley.

Xing, B., & Marwala, T. (2018). *Smart maintenance for human–robot interaction* (pp. 3–19). Studies in Systems, Decision and Control. Springer.

CHAPTER 5

Data in Politics

5.1 Introduction to Data and International Relations

Data has evolved as an important component in the twenty-first century, influencing practically every aspect of human life, from business and health to education and governance (Eisenstein, 2022; Tuomi, 2000). Furthermore, data has become increasingly important in international politics, altering power dynamics, conflict, and international collaboration. This chapter examines the use of data in international politics, including its consequences and challenges. Countries that can obtain, store, analyze, and use data effectively have a huge strategic edge in international affairs.

Nations can use data to make educated judgments on a wide range of topics. The efficient use of data can improve economic policies, healthcare methods, environmental programs, and national security measures. Real-time data, for example, can help manage global catastrophes such as pandemics, track disease progress, and properly allocate resources.

Furthermore, data plays an essential role in molding international public opinion. Thanks to the rise of social media platforms and digital diplomacy, countries can utilize data to assess and influence global sentiment, affecting their international reputation and soft power.

The emergence of data has far-reaching consequences for international politics. It is changing the character of global power dynamics, with data-rich countries gaining a competitive advantage in various industries. For example, the ongoing battle between the United States and China in the digital arena signals a new type of data-driven geopolitics.[1]

Data has also brought innovative tools and methods in international conflicts and negotiations. Cyber warfare, disinformation tactics, and data-driven propaganda have all become commonplace in the geopolitical environment. On a more positive note, data can aid international cooperation by facilitating joint endeavors in climate change and global health.

However, the abundance of data in international politics brings with it a number of issues. Data privacy and security have emerged as critical international problems, with data breaches and misuse on the rise. These challenges underscore the importance of strong international legislation and conventions to preserve individual privacy and national security.

Furthermore, data ethics is a critical topic. The possibility of using data to manipulate or coerce people, such as in disinformation campaigns or mass surveillance, presents severe ethical and human rights concerns.

5.2   DATA GATHERING AND INTERNATIONAL POLITICS

Data gathering is crucial in international politics for understanding and managing the global political scene (Crawford et al., 2014; Kitchin, 2014; Leskovec et al., 2014; Sánchez, 2020; Zwitter, 2015). It provides empirical evidence for trend analysis, theory testing, and policy decision-making. This section delves into the significance of data gathering in international politics, the methods employed, and the ramifications for policymaking and diplomatic relations.

Data gathering is the foundation of international politics study and analysis. To begin, gathering data is critical for understanding global patterns. Scholars and policymakers can use data on political events, economic indicators, social demographics, and environmental circumstances to better comprehend global patterns, compare countries, and forecast future changes. Second, data gathering makes it easier to test

---

[1] https://www.cfr.org/timeline/us-china-relations.

theories. Empirical data is critical for testing international relations theories such as realism, liberalism, and constructivism. It gives evidence to support or refute these beliefs. Third, data gathering helps policymakers make better decisions. Data gathering serves as the foundation for policymakers to make evidence-based decisions. It enables them to analyze the impact of previous policies, forecast the repercussions of possible acts, and track progress toward policy objectives.

In international politics, data gathering covers a wide range of methods and sources. Official Records is one of these. Governments and international organizations generate enormous data on various elements of international politics, such as trade figures, defense budgets, and treaty databases. Second, surveys and polls of public opinion provide information about people's attitudes regarding international issues, political leaders, and foreign policy. Third, news stories, social media posts, and broadcast transcripts can all be used to comprehend political discourses better, track political events, and gauge public opinion. Fourth, researchers may undertake interviews, focus groups, or direct observations to collect qualitative data on specific issues or circumstances.

The gathering and analysis of data in international politics have far-reaching consequences. By better understanding the challenges and forecasting the effects of policy choices, data-driven policymaking can lead to more effective and efficient solutions. Data on public opinion and political events can help shape diplomatic strategy and influence how countries communicate and negotiate. Data on conflict dynamics, peace accords, and post-conflict reconstruction can guide conflict resolution and peacebuilding initiatives. Data on international politics available to the public can improve government accountability, promote openness, and encourage informed public debate on foreign policy problems.

5.3   DATA AND GAME THEORY

Digitalization and Big Data have transformed several industries, including international politics. Simultaneously, game theory, a branch of mathematics that investigates strategic interactions, is increasingly being used to comprehend the intricacies of international relations. The purpose of this section is to investigate the role of data and game theory in international politics, emphasizing their implications and challenges (Bruce, 2013; Gao et al., 2022; Wu et al., 2017; Zheng et al., 2017a, 2018). Figure 5.1 depicts the importance of data in enriching game theory.

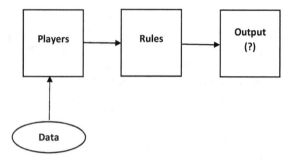

Fig. 5.1 Data-enhanced game theory

The players in the game in this figure can be made more realistic by applying data. For example, we could represent players using a neural network and then utilize genetic programming to help the players adapt (Marwala et al., 2007).

Data is gradually becoming a strong tool in international politics, giving governments that can properly exploit it a strategic advantage. Understanding public mood, anticipating economic trends, managing resources, and molding foreign policies are just a few examples of how data may be used in international politics.

The foundation for evidence-based policymaking is data. It allows a country to understand its domestic environment and international standing, as well as make educated decisions. Data about trade flows, tariffs, and domestic industries, for example, might help a country's negotiating strategy in international trade accords.

Data is also essential in diplomacy and changing public opinion. Countries use statistics to develop effective public diplomacy tactics and assess the influence of their activities on international public opinion.

Game theory, on the other hand, provides a framework for evaluating international strategic interactions. It uses mathematical models to forecast the behavior of participants in a variety of scenarios, ranging from economic talks to military clashes.

Policymakers can use game theory to better comprehend the likely outcomes of their decisions and the decisions of others in the international arena. Furthermore, it can provide insights into how diverse actors may react to specific policies, assisting countries in developing effective strategies. The Cuban Missile Crisis, for example, is frequently examined through game theory because it featured strategic decision-making under high risk and uncertainty.[2]

Data synthesis and game theory can potentially improve the predictive and analytical skills of international politics. With the increased availability of data, game-theoretical models can be given real-world information, improving the accuracy and reliability of their predictions. However, the use of statistics and game theory in international politics raises a number of difficulties. For example, data privacy and misuse are serious issues that necessitate worldwide conventions and policies to limit dangers. Similarly, while game theory can provide valuable insights, it is predicated on a number of assumptions, such as rational behavior, that may not always be true. Thus, infusing game theory with evidence and mitigating its limits is critical.

5.4   DATA AND MECHANISM DESIGN

Mechanism Design and Game Theory are two essential techniques for understanding and forecasting strategic behavior (Zhan et al., 2020; Zheng et al., 2017b). While game theory examines "games" based on a set of rules, mechanism design builds the "rules" or "mechanisms" to attain a desired result. These mathematical models have become essential in international politics, helping to understand and shape strategic relations among nations. This section investigates the roles of data infused mechanism design and game theory in international politics, as well as their potential consequences and problems. As seen in Fig. 5.2, data can help with mechanism design. In this case, data can be used to train a model that understands the link between inputs and outputs, and this input–output model can then be used to discover the rules that will produce the desired output. Data can also be utilized to define the parameters of the rule space that will be sampled.

As a part of mathematics, game theory investigates the strategic interactions of rational decision-makers. As a result, it provides a significant foundation for understanding how governments engage in international politics in many contexts, from diplomacy and negotiations to conflict and cooperation.

---

[2] https://history.state.gov/milestones/1961-1968/cuban-missile-crisis#:~:text=The% 20Cuban%20Missile%20Crisis%20of,came%20closest%20to%20nuclear%20conflict.

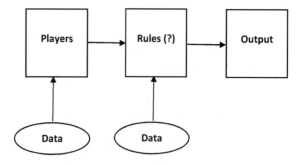

Fig. 5.2 Data-aided mechanism design

The notion of Nash Equilibrium, which states that no player can better their status unilaterally given the behaviors of other players, has been used to explain strategic stability among nations, such as the concept of mutually assured destruction in nuclear strategy. Game theory can provide significant insights to policymakers by forecasting alternative outcomes based on the strategic choices of actors.

Mechanism design, frequently referred to as the "reverse" of game theory, is the process of designing the "game" or "mechanism" to get desired results. This is especially beneficial when dealing with information asymmetry, where one party has more information than the other.

Mechanism design can be used in international politics to incentivize governments to operate in a certain way or divulge private information. In international trade treaties, for example, a mechanism can be devised to incentivize countries to declare their genuine preferences or costs, resulting in more efficient outcomes. Similarly, in climate change discussions, mechanism design might be used to motivate countries to declare their emissions accurately and work together to reduce global carbon output.

Interactions between game theory and mechanism design can yield robust models for analyzing and affecting international politics. Understanding countries' strategic behaviors through game theory allow us to build systems that guide these behaviors toward globally desirable results.

Despite its importance, applying game theory and mechanism design to international politics is difficult. One significant difficulty is the assumption of rationality, which may not always be accurate, given the many elements that might influence a country's decisions, such as domestic politics, historical biases, and cultural contexts.

Furthermore, ethical issues arise in the implementation of mechanism design. Manipulating rules to induce specific actions involves autonomy, justice, and equity issues. Therefore, it is critical to strike a balance between strategic goals and ethical issues.

5.5 DATA AND ARTIFICIAL INTELLIGENCE

We are experiencing an incredible transition in international politics, fueled by rapid data gathering, analysis, and AI breakthroughs (Elish & Boyd, 2018; Norori et al., 2021; O'Leary, 2013; Penchevaet al., 2020; Yang & Ying, 2022). These technological advancements are reshaping global power relations, creating new opportunities for improvement while posing new problems and ethical quandaries. This section examines the role and implications of data and artificial intelligence in international politics.

The first important topic to explore is the impact of statistics on international politics. Nations that capture, store, analyze, and use data effectively gain enormous advantages in economic growth, public policy, national security, and global influence.

Data allows governments to understand their inhabitants better, allowing them to make informed decisions that can influence economic policies, healthcare tactics, and other areas. For example, real-time data can help manage pandemic, disease tracking, and resource allocation. Furthermore, data can tremendously impact worldwide public opinion, as seen by the rise of social media platforms and digital diplomacy.

AI is another game-changer in international politics, fueled by unprecedented access to data. The ability of AI to automate jobs, improve decision-making, and even do predictive analysis is changing global geopolitical dynamics.

AI has transformed intelligence gathering and military technology in security, with breakthroughs such as autonomous weaponry and surveillance drones. However, this raises concerns about a hypothetical AI arms race, which could destabilize world peace and security.

AI also opens up new opportunities for economic competition and collaboration. Nations that lead in AI technology will acquire a competitive advantage in the global economy, ushering in a new era of digital geopolitics. For example, the United States and China compete to dominate the global AI environment.[3]

However, the abundance of data and AI poses a number of concerns. As a result, data privacy and security have emerged as crucial global concerns. Data breaches and misuse incidents underscore the need for strong international legislation and standards to protect individual privacy and prevent data exploitation.

Similarly, the use of AI in politics presents a slew of ethical and moral concerns. The potential for artificial intelligence to propagate disinformation, manipulate public opinion, or even automate conflict is frightening. These problems necessitate international cooperation to develop standards and legislation governing the use of AI in politics.

5.6   MISSING AND IMPERFECT DATA

In the information age, data has been essential in determining international politics. However, the reality of missing and poor data frequently complicates the dynamics of global political systems. Moreover, erroneous, incomplete, or entirely missing information creates new issues and ramifications for international relations. This section investigates the significance of missing and imperfect data in international politics, as well as various mitigation techniques.

In international politics, missing and incomplete data is a common problem. It can be caused by a variety of factors, including a lack of technology infrastructure, data-gathering capabilities, or intentional withholding or modification of information for strategic objectives. Yet, regardless of the origin, the lack of reliable and complete data can stymie decision-making, misguide policy execution, and even contribute to international tensions and conflicts.

Imperfect data can lead to inaccurate assumptions or misinterpretations, clouding understanding of critical issues, including economic growth, social development, and public health. For example, missing or imperfect data about a country's military capabilities or economic situations can lead to miscalculations or misperceptions about that country's intentions and capabilities, potentially exacerbating tensions or leading to wrong measures.

---

[3] https://www.brookings.edu/research/us-china-relations-in-the-age-of-artificial-intelligence/.

The consequences of missing and inaccurate data affect every aspect of international politics. For example, it might jeopardize the efficiency of international aid by causing resource misallocation due to erroneous data on poverty, health, or education levels. In addition, it can destabilize global economic systems since untrustworthy economic data can mislead investors and affect market views.

Missing or altered data in security and diplomacy can contribute to misunderstandings or mistrust among states. Inadequate information regarding a country's nuclear program or emissions levels, for example, might lead to charges of non-compliance with international treaties, thus straining diplomatic relations.

Addressing the problem of missing and incomplete data demands a global effort. Improved data-gathering procedures, data-sharing agreements, and international data standards can all contribute to better data quality and availability.

Using robust statistical models and data analysis approaches might be beneficial for missing or imperfect data. For example, data imputations and probabilistic modelling can assist in estimating missing values and accounting for uncertainty.

Furthermore, promoting a culture of transparency and accountability in international politics might deter willful data withholding or manipulation. Finally, international conventions and agreements can encourage states to use responsible data practices.

5.7 Missing Data Estimation

Researchers and analysts in a variety of sectors, including social sciences, economics, and medical, frequently encounter missing data (Mohamed & Marwala, 2005; Nelwamondo & Marwala, 2008a; Nelwamondo et al., 2013). Incomplete or missing observations in datasets can result in skewed or inconsistent results, lowering the reliability and validity of statistical studies. As a result, dealing with missing data has become critical in assuring the accuracy and robustness of study findings. To address this difficulty, missing data estimate and imputation approaches have been developed, which fill in missing values and provide a complete dataset for analysis (Abdella & Marwala, 2005b; Leke & Marwala, 2006; Marivate et al., 2008; Ssali & Marwala, 2007).

Mbuvha et al. (2022) imputed missing streamflow data from numerous Benin Republic river gauging sites. Abdella and Marwala (2005a, 2005b) approximated missing data in a database using evolutionary algorithms and neural networks. In contrast, Nelwamondo et al. (2007) estimated missing data using auto-associative neural networks and expectation maximization techniques. Furthermore, Nelwamondo and Marwala (2007a) employed fuzzy logic and neural networks to estimate missing data in real time, whereas Nelwamondo and Marwala (2008b) used missing data estimation for online condition monitoring. Missing data estimating techniques have also been used successfully in financial data (Duma et al., 2010, 2012b; Nelwamondo & Marwala, 2007b), medical applications (Pantanowitz & Marwala, 2009a), and engineering systems (Leke et al., 2014; Mistry et al., 2008a; Mohamed et al., 2008).

This section examines the significance of dealing with missing data, the numerous estimation and imputation approaches, and their practical uses in research and analysis. Missing data can occur for various reasons, including nonresponse in surveys, data entry errors, or record loss. However, ignoring missing data might result in many problems.

For starters, it can lead to skewed estimations. When data is persistently missing, the estimates obtained from the available data may be biased because they may not adequately represent the underlying population. Second, it may result in a reduction in statistical power. Missing data can diminish a dataset's effective sample size, resulting in a loss of statistical power and the ability to identify significant effects or connections. Third, it may result in inefficient data consumption. Ignoring missing data can lead to wasteful use of accessible data, as full cases may be ignored due to missing values in other variables.

Various methods have been developed to estimate and impute missing data, ranging from simple procedures to more advanced strategies. Mean imputation is one of these. This entails substituting the mean of the available data for the same variable for missing values. While simple to apply, this strategy may result in underestimating data variability. Regression imputation is the second type. This method uses a regression model to estimate missing values based on the observed data for other variables. Although it produces more accurate estimates than mean imputation, it may still underestimate data variability. The third type of imputation is multiple imputations. By selecting random samples from the estimated distribution of missing values, this technique provides several imputed datasets (Duma et al., 2012a; Mistry et al., 2008b). The outcomes are combined to get a final estimate and measure of uncertainty. The multiple imputation techniques is thought to be more robust because it accounts for the variability and uncertainty associated with missing data.

Missing data estimate and imputation approaches have been widely used to overcome the issues of missing data in various sectors. Imputation procedures are frequently employed to assure the validity and reliability of research findings while avoiding estimation biases. For example, missing values in economic data are common due to nonresponse, data entry errors, or discrepancies in data gathering. Imputation procedures produce more precise and trustworthy estimations of economic indicators such as GDP and unemployment rates. Missing data in clinical research might result from participant dropout or loss of follow-up. Imputation strategies are used to deal with missing data and increase the accuracy and generalizability of clinical trial and observational study findings (Pantanowitz & Marwala, 2009b).

5.8   Cross-Border Data Flow

Cross-border data flows have become an intrinsic aspect of the current world economy as a result of the rapid rise of digital technology and globalization (Chaisse, 2023; Chen, 2019; Jara & Bocchi, 2019; Mitchell & Mishra, 2019; Pepper et al., 2016). Global communication, collaboration, and economic progress have all benefited from this interconnection. However, data flow across boundaries has added new difficulties to international politics. In this section, we look at the role of cross-border data flows in international politics and their challenges and consequences for future policymaking.

The transmission of digital information across national borders is referred to as cross-border data flow. This interchange of information has become an essential component of international politics. It encourages economic integration. The cross-border data flow has become critical for the seamless running of global supply chains and the expansion of e-commerce as firms increasingly rely on digital technologies for their operations. Countries' interconnectedness can enhance cooperation and lessen disputes.

The ever-increasing data flow across borders has created several issues in the worldwide political scene. First, privacy, security, and monitoring concerns have grown as more data is collected and transported globally. As a result, countries with opposing perspectives on privacy rights have clashed, resulting in political difficulties and trade disagreements. Second, data flowing across borders is increasingly vulnerable to theft, espionage, and manipulation. The growing frequency of cyberattacks against governments, organizations, and individuals has raised the stakes in international affairs, stoking distrust and potentially igniting conflict. Finally, the reliance on cross-border data flow has created concerns about nations' digital sovereignty, with some governments seeking greater control over data within their borders. This can lead to digital protectionism, stifling innovation and impeding international cooperation.

Addressing the issues of cross-border data flow in international politics will necessitate robust policymaking that balances the need for global connectedness with national interest protection. Developing worldwide standards and frameworks for data privacy, protection, and cybersecurity is critical for fostering international trust and collaboration. Multilateral agreements, international organizations, and coordinated efforts between governments and the private sector can help achieve this. Improving countries' technological capacity to manage and secure their digital infrastructure is critical for maintaining data security and combating cybersecurity threats. This can be accomplished through international collaboration, research and development initiatives, and the exchange of best practices. Diplomacy must adapt in the digital age to accommodate the problems and opportunities posed by cross-border data flow. Governments should invest in digital diplomacy initiatives that encourage international cooperation, dialogue, and mutual understanding.

5.9 Data Ethics

The digital age and the growth of Big Data have not only altered the dynamics of international relations, but have also presented new ethical concerns. In international relations, ethical data processing is critical for sustaining confidence, ensuring openness, and upholding human rights. This section investigates the ethical implications of data used in international relations and suggests ways to maintain ethical standards.

Data has become essential in international relations, impacting policymaking, diplomacy, conflict resolution, and international collaboration. It aids in the analysis of global trends, the forecasting of potential scenarios, and the formation of strategic decisions. However, data misuse or unethical data processing can have profound effects, ranging from invading individual privacy to jeopardizing national security.

Keeping data private and secret is one of international relations' most challenging ethical concerns. Individual privacy rights must be respected during data gathering, storage, and processing, particularly personal data. Moreover, personal data misuse for political goals, such as influencing elections or disseminating misinformation, can weaken democratic processes and violate human rights.

Data security is another major ethical concern. Unauthorized access to sensitive information can result from data breaches, jeopardizing national security and international stability. Furthermore, cyberattacks on data infrastructure can impair critical services, posing serious societal hazards.

Finally, data correctness and integrity are critical considerations. Manipulation of data or incorrect presentation of facts can alter perceptions, misguide policy choices, and aggravate disputes.

Maintaining ethical norms in data use in international relations necessitates a multifaceted strategy. It starts with building strong data governance frameworks that define unambiguous data gathering, storage, processing, and sharing policies. Individual privacy rights should be respected, data security should be ensured, and data accuracy and integrity should be promoted.

Another critical component of ethical data practices is transparency. Nations' data practices should be transparent, with clear information on what data is collected, how it is used, and who has access to it. Transparency can increase trust, discourage unethical behavior, and improve accountability.

International cooperation is also required to promote ethical data practices. For example, the General Data Protection Regulation (GDPR), a comprehensive data protection law adopted by the European Union (EU), harmonizes and strengthens data protection regulations across EU member states and gives individuals more control over their personal data.[4] The GDPR applies to all organizations that process the personal data of EU residents, regardless of their location within or outside of the EU. It establishes rights and principles regarding acquiring, using, storing, and sharing personally identifiable information. Given the global nature of data flows, states should collaborate to develop international data ethical rules and regulations. Data protection, cybersecurity, and digital rights agreements are examples of this.

---

[4] https://gdpr-info.eu/.

Furthermore, building an ethical culture in data use is critical. This includes teaching and training data workers, supporting responsible behavior, and fostering a broader public knowledge of data ethics.

5.10   DATA GOVERNANCE

Data has become a vital resource in the age of digital globalization, affecting several areas, including international politics. However, the proliferation of data creates new issues, demanding robust governance frameworks to effectively and ethically oversee its usage. This section examines the role and significance of data governance in international politics, the issues involved, and prospective data governance initiatives.

Data governance is the set of processes, policies, standards, and technology used to manage, secure, and ensure data quality. Data governance is critical in international politics to maintain data integrity, ensure data security, protect privacy rights, and promote effective and ethical data use.

Effective data governance can improve decision-making processes in international politics by assuring access to accurate, reliable, and timely data. It can help with policy formation, strategic planning, and diplomatic talks, making international relations more informed and effective.

Data governance is fraught with difficulties in international politics. First, the global nature of data flows makes governance initiatives more difficult. Data frequently cross national borders, making enforcing national rules and regulations challenging.

Second, the rapid speed of technological progress makes keeping governance frameworks current difficult. As new technologies arise, such as artificial intelligence and blockchain, new data types and usage possibilities emerge, necessitating ongoing adaption of data governance policies.

Third, data privacy and security are major problems in data governance. Data governance requires ensuring the confidentiality of sensitive data, protecting against data breaches, and honoring individual privacy rights.

In international politics, effective data governance necessitates a multifaceted strategy. First and foremost, effective data governance rules must be established at the national level. These should include explicit procedures for data gathering, storage, processing, and sharing, as well as maintaining data integrity and security and protecting individuals' privacy rights.

Given the worldwide nature of data, international cooperation is also required, and the global version of the GDPR must be developed. Countries should work together to develop global data governance norms and rules that address challenges such as cross-border data flows, data protection, and digital rights. International organizations can be critical in facilitating this collaboration.

Furthermore, technology solutions can help with data governance. For example, advances in encryption, anonymization, and blockchain technology can improve data security and privacy, while data management systems can maintain data quality and integrity.

Finally, cultivating an ethical data culture is critical. This includes supporting responsible data practices, providing data governance education and training, and fostering transparency and responsibility in data use.

5.11 CONCLUSION

The intersection of data and international politics has transformed the global political scene, changing the dynamics of power, conflict, and collaboration. Data has evolved into a strategic asset, impacting policy-making, diplomacy, and international relations in unprecedented ways. The ability to successfully gather, analyze, and use data has emerged as a crucial predictor of a country's influence and competitiveness in the global arena.

However, the expanding use of data in international politics has created many issues, including privacy concerns, data security problems, and ethical quandaries. Furthermore, concerns with missing and incomplete data confuse the picture, potentially affecting the accuracy of decision-making processes and the effectiveness of policy execution.

Addressing these issues requires robust data governance systems at both the national and international levels. It takes coordinated efforts to develop global data-use norms and rules, promote openness and accountability, and foster a data ethics culture. Enhancing data integrity, security, and privacy requires technological solutions and capacity-building activities.

The interplay between data and international politics will continue to grow as we go further into the era of digital globalization. The international political system's future security and profitability rely heavily on our capacity to successfully, responsibly, and ethically manage the data-driven world. The work at hand is not easy, but the potential advantages—improved decision-making, better openness, and a more equal global order—make it a worthwhile endeavor.

REFERENCES

Abdella, M., & Marwala, T. (2005a). *Treatment of missing data using neural networks and genetic algorithms*. Proceedings. 2005 IEEE International Joint Conference on Neural Networks, Vol. 1, pp. 598–603.

Abdella, M., & Marwala, T. (2005b). *The use of genetic algorithms and neural networks to approximate missing data in database*. IEEE 3rd International Conference on Computational Cybernetics, 2005 ICCC, pp. 207–212.

Bruce, L. M. (2013). *Game theory applied to big data analytics in geosciences and remote sensing*. 2013 IEEE International Geoscience and Remote Sensing Symposium-IGARSS, pp. 4094–4097.

Chaisse, J. (2023). 'The black pit:' Power and pitfalls of digital FDI and cross-border data flows. *World Trade Review, 22*(1), 73–89.

Chen, L. (2019). ASEAN in the digital era: Enabling cross-border E-commerce. In *Developing the digital economy in ASEAN* (pp. 259–275). Routledge.

Crawford, K., Gray, M. L., & Miltner, K. (2014). Big Data| critiquing Big Data: Politics, ethics, epistemology| special section introduction. *International Journal of Communication, 8*, 10.

Duma, M., Twala, B., Marwala, T., & Nelwamondo, F. V. (2010). *Classification performance measure using missing insurance data: A comparison between supervised learning models*. International Conference on Computer and Computational Intelligence, Nanning, China, pp. 550–555.

Duma, M., Twala, B., Marwala, T., & Nelwamondo, F. V. (2012a). *Classification with missing data using multi-layered artificial immune systems*. 2012 IEEE Congress on Evolutionary Computation, pp. 1–8.

Duma, M., Twala, B., Nelwamondo, F., & Marwala, T. (2012b). Predictive modeling with missing data using an automatic relevance determination ensemble: A comparative study. *Applied Artificial Intelligence, 26*(10), 967–984.

Eisenstein, M. (2022). In pursuit of data immortality. *Nature, 604*(7904), 207–208.

Elish, M. C., & Boyd, D. (2018). Situating methods in the magic of Big Data and AI. *Communication Monographs, 85*(1), 57–80.

Gao, Y., Chen, L., Wu, G., Li, Q., & Fu, T. (2022). A game theory study of Big Data analytics in Internet of Things. *IEEE Transactions on Network and Service Management, 20*, 1707–1716.

Jara, A. J., & Bocchi, Y. (2019). *GEO-trust: Geo-aware security protocol for enabling cross-border trustable operations and data exchange in a global digital economy*. 2019 IEEE 1st Sustainable Cities Latin America Conference (SCLA), pp. 1–6.

Kitchin, R. (2014). *The data revolution*. Sage.

Leke, B. B., & Marwala, T. (2006). *Ant colony optimization for missing data estimation*. Proceeding of the Pattern Recognition of South Africa, pp. 183–188.

Leke, C., Twala, B., & Marwala, T. (2014). *Modeling of missing data prediction: Computational intelligence and optimization algorithms*. 2014 IEEE International Conference on Systems, Man, and Cybernetics (SMC), pp. 1400–1404.

Leskovec, J., Rajaraman, A., & Ullman, J. D. (2014). *Mining of massive datasets*. Cambridge University Press.

Marivate, V. N., Nelwamondo, F. V., & Marwala, T. (2008). Investigation into the use of autoencoder neural networks, principal component analysis and support vector regression in estimating missing HIV data. *IFAC Proceedings Volumes, 41*(2), 682–689.

Marwala, T., De Wilde, P., Correia, L., Mariano, P., Ribeiro, R., Abramov, V., Szirbik, N., & Goossenaerts, J. (2007). *Scalability and optimization of a committee of agents using genetic algorithm*. arXiv preprint arXiv:0705.1757

Mbuvha, R., Adounkpe, J. Y. P., Mongwe, W. T., Houngnibo, M., Newlands, N., & Marwala, T. (2022). *Imputation of missing streamflow data at multiple gauging stations in Benin Republic*. arXiv preprint arXiv:2211.11576

Mistry, J., Nelwamondo, F., & Marwala, T. (2008a). *Estimating missing data and determining the confidence of the estimate data*. 2008 Seventh International Conference on Machine Learning and Applications, pp. 752–755.

Mistry, J., Nelwamondo, F., & Marwala, T. (2008b). *Using principal component analysis and autoassociative neural networks to estimate missing data in a database*. Proceedings of the 12th World Multi-Conference on Systemics, Cybernetics and Informatics: WMSCI 2008, Orlando, FL, pp. 24–29.

Mitchell, A. D., & Mishra, N. (2019). Regulating cross-border data flows in a data-driven world: How WTO Law can contribute. *Journal of International Economic Law, 22*(3), 389–416.

Mohamed, A. K., Nelwamondo, F. V., & Marwala, T. (2008). *Estimation of missing data: Neural networks, principal component analysis and genetic algorithms*. Proceedings of the 12th World Multi-Conference on Systemics, Cybernetics and Informatics, Orlando, FL, pp. 36–41.

Mohamed, S., & Marwala, T. (2005). *Neural network-based techniques for estimating missing data in databases*. Proceedings of the 16th Annual Symposium of the Pattern Recognition Society of South Africa, Langebaan, South Africa, pp. 27–32.

Nelwamondo, F. V., Golding, D., & Marwala, T. (2013). A dynamic programming approach to missing data estimation using neural networks. *Information Sciences, 237*, 49–58.

Nelwamondo, F. V., & Marwala, T. (2007a). Fuzzy artmap and neural network approach to online processing of inputs with missing values. *SAIEE Africa Research Journal, 98*(2), 45–51.

Nelwamondo, F. V., & Marwala, T. (2007b, June 3–7). *Handling missing data from heteroskedastic and nonstationary data.* Advances in Neural Networks–ISNN 2007: 4th International Symposium on Neural Networks, ISNN 2007, Nanjing, China, Proceedings, Part I, pp. 1293–1302. Springer.

Nelwamondo, F. V., & Marwala, T. (2008a, June 29–July 2). *Key issues on computational intelligence techniques for missing data imputation—A review.* Proceedings of the 12th World Multi-Conference on Systemics, Cybernetics and Informatics: WMSCI 2008, Orlando, FL, pp. 36–41.

Nelwamondo, F. V., & Marwala, T. (2008b). Techniques for handling missing data: Applications to online condition monitoring. *International Journal of Innovative Computing, Information and Control, 4*(6), 1507–1526.

Nelwamondo, F. V., Mohamed, S., & Marwala, T. (2007). Missing data: A comparison of neural network and expectation maximization techniques. *Current Science, 93*, 1514–1521.

Norori, N., Hu, Q., Aellen, F. M., Faraci, F. D., & Tzovara, A. (2021). Addressing bias in big data and AI for health care: A call for open science. *Patterns, 2*(10), 100347.

O'Leary, D. E. (2013). Artificial intelligence and big data. *IEEE Intelligent Systems, 28*(2), 96–99.

Pantanowitz, A., & Marwala, T. (2009a). Evaluating the impact of missing data imputation. In *ADMA* (Vol. 5678, pp. 577–586). Springer.

Pantanowitz, A., & Marwala, T. (2009b). Missing data imputation through the use of the random forest algorithm. In *Advances in computational intelligence* (pp. 53–62). Springer.

Pencheva, I., Esteve, M., & Mikhaylov, S. J. (2020). Big Data and AI—A transformational shift for government: So, what next for research? *Public Policy and Administration, 35*(1), 24–44.

Pepper, R., Garrity, J., & LaSalle, C. (2016). *Cross-border data flows, digital innovation, and economic growth* (The Global Information Technology Report 2, pp. 39–47).

Sánchez, J. L. M. (2020). Big Data and international politics. *Baltic Yearbook of International Law Online, 18*(1), 52–71.

Ssali, G., & Marwala, T. (2007). *Estimation of missing data using computational intelligence and decision trees.* arXiv preprint arXiv:0709.1640

Tuomi, I. (2000). Data is more than knowledge. *Journal of Management Information Systems, 6*(3), 103–117.

Wu, X., Wu, T., Khan, M., Ni, Q., & Dou, W. (2017). Game theory based correlated privacy preserving analysis in big data. *IEEE Transactions on Big Data, 7*(4), 643–656.

Yang, T., & Ying, Y. (2022). AUC maximization in the era of big data and AI: A survey. *ACM Computing Surveys, 55*(8), 1–37.

Zhan, Y., Li, P., Wang, K., Guo, S., & Xia, Y. (2020). Big data analytics by crowdlearning: Architecture and mechanism design. *IEEE Network, 34*(3), 143–147.

Zheng, Z., Song, L., & Han, Z. (2017a). *Bridging the gap between big data and game theory: A general hierarchical pricing framework.* 2017 IEEE International Conference on Communications (ICC), pp. 1–6.

Zheng, Z., Song, L., & Han, Z. (2017b). Bridge the gap between ADMM and Stackelberg game: Incentive mechanism design for big data networks. *IEEE Signal Processing Letters, 24*(2), 191–195.

Zheng, Z., Song, L., Han, Z., Li, G. Y., & Poor, H. V. (2018). Game theory for big data processing: Multileader multifollower game-based ADMM. *IEEE Transactions on Signal Processing, 66*(15), 3933–3945.

Zwitter, A. (2015). Big data and international relations. *Ethics & International Affairs, 29*(4), 377–389.

CHAPTER 6

Deep Learning in Politics

6.1 Deep Learning and Politics Overview

Deep learning, a subset of artificial intelligence (AI), is making historic advances in various fields, including international politics. Deep learning transforms how political actors comprehend, influence, and engage with the global political scene by allowing machines to learn from massive volumes of data (Leke & Marwala, 2016, 2019; Leke et al., 2015, 2017). This chapter investigates the impact of deep learning on international politics and its possible uses, problems, and ethical implications.

The power of deep learning to evaluate complicated and large-scale datasets holds enormous promise for international politics. It can forecast economic trends, social unrest, disinformation dissemination, and even violence or election outcomes. This predictive capability can help policymakers and diplomats make decisions, plan strategically, and manage crises.

Furthermore, deep learning can evaluate and comprehend global public sentiment, providing insights into political alignment, public opinion on policy concerns, and reactions to international events. Diplomatic initiatives, public communication efforts, and policy creation can all benefit from this.

While deep learning has enormous potential, it also has drawbacks. Data integrity is one of the critical problems. Deep learning models rely

T. Marwala, *Artificial Intelligence, Game Theory and Mechanism Design in Politics*, https://doi.org/10.1007/978-981-99-5103-1_6

on vast volumes of data, and any errors in the data can result in incorrect results. This is especially true in international politics, where wrong forecasts or interpretations can have devastating implications.

Another issue is the "black box" nature of deep learning models, which makes it difficult to understand how they reach specific results. This lack of transparency can be problematic in politics, where accountability and decision-making rationale are essential.

Deep learning in international politics brings essential ethical concerns. One critical concern is privacy. Deep learning frequently requires the analysis of personal data, which raises concerns about spying and individual privacy rights.

Furthermore, the potential for abuse of deep learning technology is a significant problem. It could, for example, be used to disseminate misinformation, alter public opinion, or launch cyberattacks. Because of these possible abuses, stringent rules and ethical guidelines for applying deep learning in international politics are required.

As deep learning evolves and pervades international politics, it is critical to navigate its ramifications properly. This entails establishing robust data governance mechanisms to protect data integrity and privacy. It is also necessary to improve the transparency and interpretability of deep learning models to assure accountability.

Furthermore, international cooperation is essential in developing ethical standards and rules for using deep learning in politics. This includes preventing misuse, supporting fair practices, and ensuring that technology is utilized to improve rather than threatening the public good.

6.2   Deep Learning Types

Deep learning uses neural networks with multiple layers (thus the name 'deep') to extract higher-level features from raw input data. While the notion of deep learning is well established, its different forms, each with its architecture and applications, offer a wide range of options for problem-solving and decision-making. This section looks at the many types of deep learning, such as feedforward neural networks (FFNs), convolutional neural networks (CNNs), recurrent neural networks (RNNs), and generative adversarial networks (GANs), as well as their specific applications (Xiang et al., 2023).

FNNs, sometimes called the multi-layer perceptrons (MLPs), are the most basic type of artificial neural network (Dhlamini & Marwala, 2004a, b; Dhlamini et al., 2006; Patel & Marwala, 2009). In an FNN, information flows in just one direction: from the input layer to the output layer via the hidden layers. The network has no loops; data is processed in a 'feedforward' fashion. Because of its efficiency and simplicity, FNNs are commonly utilized in pattern recognition and classification issues.

CNNs are a type of neural network with a grid-like topology that is well suited for image recognition tasks (Ajit et al., 2020; Cong & Zhou, 2023; O'Shea & Nash, 2015; Qin et al., 2023; Wu et al., 2023). CNNs' distinct architecture enables them to handle high-dimensionality raw images. Convolutional layers function as automatic feature extractors, identifying images' edges, gradients, textures, and other components. They are common in facial recognition systems, self-driving automobiles, and other computer vision applications.

RNNs, unlike FNNs and CNNs, can analyze sequences of inputs using their internal state (memory), making them suitable for evaluating time-series data or any other sequential data (Eltouny & Liang, 2023; Khanduzi & Sangaiah, 2023; Zhong et al., 2023). Because of this property, RNNs are extremely useful in natural language processing, speech recognition, and time-series prediction tasks. Traditional RNNs, on the other hand, suffer from vanishing and exploding gradient issues, limiting their ability to handle extended sequences. This problem has been chiefly addressed by variants such as long short-term memory (LSTM) networks and gated recurrent unit (GRU) networks.

In the field of deep learning, GANs are a relatively new idea (Bethencourt-Aguilar et al., 2023; Marwala, 2021; Ngo et al., 2023; Sidogi et al., 2022; Wang et al., 2023). They are made up of two neural networks that are trained together: a generator and a discriminator. The generator attempts to generate data similar to real data, whereas the discriminator attempts to discern between real and fake data. The training procedure consists of a two-player minimax game in which the generator tries to mislead the discriminator while the discriminator tries to avoid being tricked. GANs have been used to create realistic images, transform images, improve image resolution, etc.

6.3   FEEDFORWARD NEURAL NETWORKS

Neural networks, a crucial AI type, have revolutionized our ability to analyze and comprehend complex data. These computer models, inspired by biological neural networks in the human brain, can learn from and interpret data in a human-like manner. This section delves into neural networks, their uses, problems, and future ramifications. Many sectors use neural networks (Leke et al., 2006; Marwala, 2007; Marwala & Chakraverty, 2006; Mbuvha et al., 2021; Soares et al., 2006). They are used in healthcare to diagnose diseases, predict patient outcomes, and personalize therapies. They aid in identifying fraud, credit scoring, and algorithmic trading in finance. They also play an essential role in natural language processing, enabling translation services, chatbots, and sentiment analysis tools.

Neural networks, also known as artificial neural networks (ANNs), are computational models that imitate the architecture of the human brain. The architecture of an ANN is made up of three layers: an input layer, one or more hidden layers, and an output layer. Each layer is made up of many interconnected nodes known as neurons. The raw data or features are received by the input layer, which is then processed, typically nonlinearly, by the hidden layers, and the output layer provides the final result. During training, the strength of the connections between neurons, known as weights, is modified, allowing the network to 'learn' from the input.

Neural networks with numerous layers (deep neural networks) may learn complicated patterns in enormous datasets, giving rise to the subject of deep learning. Figure 6.1 depicts a multi-layer perceptron neural network as an example.

Here, there is an input layer, three hidden layers, and an output layer. Deep learning network is if there is more than one hidden layer. Data preparation, model initialization, forward propagation, backpropagation,

Fig. 6.1 A feedforward system having three input units, one hidden layer with four nodes, and one output unit

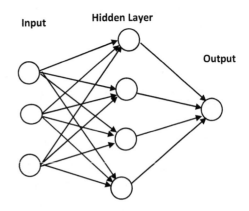

and model tuning are all steps in training a feedforward neural network. A complete guide to training a feedforward neural network is provided below:

Step 1: Gathering Data

Before beginning the training process, the first step is to prepare the data. This entails gathering the data, cleaning it, addressing missing values, and normalizing it. Following that, the data is usually divided into three sets: training, validation, and testing.

Step 2: Model Initialization

After preparing the data, the neural network model must be initialized. This entails establishing the network's topology, which includes the number of layers, the number of nodes in each layer, and the activation functions for each layer. The neural network's weights are typically initialized with modest random numbers.

Step 3: Propagation Forward

The training data is fed into the network. By transmitting the input data through each network layer, the network determines an output for each input. Each layer's output is computed by taking the weighted total of the inputs, adding a bias, and then applying an activation function.

Step 4: Loss Calculation

A loss function is applied after the forward propagation stage to calculate the difference between the network's prediction and output. This loss indicates the model's performance. The training process's purpose is to reduce this loss.

Step 5: Backpropagation

The method of modifying the network weights to reduce loss is called backpropagation. This is accomplished by computing the gradient of the loss function with respect to each weight in the network and then adjusting the weights to lower the loss. This entails calculating the derivative of the loss function with respect to the weights and then modifying the weights in the direction that lowers the loss by a tiny step.

Step 6: Iteration

Steps 3–5 (forward propagation, loss computation, and backpropagation) are repeated until the model's performance is acceptable. An epoch is a pass over the complete training dataset. The number of epochs is a programmable hyperparameter.

Step 7: Model Tuning

Following the initial training, the model may require tuning to increase its performance. Various hyperparameters must be adjusted, such as the learning rate, the number of epochs, the batch size, and others.

Step 8: Validation and Testing

Testing the model on unseen data after training and adjusting it is critical. To avoid overfitting, the validation set is used during the tuning phase, and the final model is tested on the test set to evaluate its performance.

Training a feedforward neural network aims to produce a model that can generalize successfully. However, this frequently necessitates a delicate balance between fitting the training data well and not too well to avoid overfitting.

Despite their transformational promise, neural networks are fraught with difficulties. One primary source of concern is their opacity, also known as the 'black box' problem. As a result, it is frequently difficult to grasp how neural networks arrive at a given choice or prediction, posing difficulties in cases where explainability is critical.

Furthermore, neural networks require enormous amounts of data to learn successfully, raising concerns regarding data privacy and security. The training data's quality and representativeness also substantially impact the network's performance, potentially leading to bias and fairness issues.

The future of neural networks includes exciting possibilities. Efforts are now underway to improve their transparency and interpretability. Furthermore, strategies such as attention processes and explainable AI are being developed to make these models less of a 'black box.'

Furthermore, combining neural networks with other technologies, such as quantum computing, may result in quantum neural networks dramatically improving processing power and efficiency. In designing and deploying neural networks, there is also a rising emphasis on ethical aspects, such as ensuring fairness, privacy, and security.

6.4   Deep Learning

Deep learning is a sort of neural network that has made significant advances in recent years, revolutionizing a variety of sectors and industries around the world. This sophisticated technology models and understands complex patterns in data using artificial neural networks with multiple layers (known as 'deep' networks). This section delves into deep learning and its uses, problems, and potential future implications.

Deep learning is inspired by the human brain's neural networks, aiming to replicate its ability to learn and process information. These artificial neural networks comprise interconnected layers of nodes or 'neurons,' with each layer learning to transform input data into a more abstract and composite representation. As illustrated in Fig. 6.2, deep learning algorithms can learn and represent data at multiple levels of abstraction by employing multiple layers, allowing them to make sense of complex data and deliver high accuracy in tasks such as image and speech recognition, natural language processing, and predictive analytics.

Deep learning has made significant contributions in a variety of fields. Deep learning algorithms, for example, can scan medical pictures to detect diseases, forecast patient outcomes, and tailor treatment regimens in healthcare (Aslani & Jacob, 2023; Azadi et al., 2023; Bhat

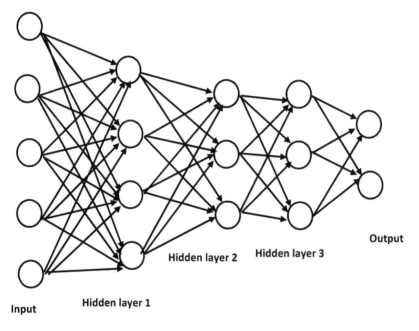

Fig. 6.2 A three-layer deep learning network

et al., 2023; Kumar et al., 2023; Soni et al., 2023). Deep learning models in autonomous vehicles enable real-time processing and decision-making, interpreting sensor data to navigate highways safely (Choi & Kim, 2023; Saleh & Fathy, 2023). Deep learning powers chatbots, translation services, and sentiment analysis tools in natural language processing (Diwan, 2023; McMaster et al., 2023). Deep learning has also made significant contributions to the entertainment industry, allowing for producing realistic video game worlds and powering recommendation algorithms in streaming platforms (Jiang & Zheng, 2023; Su & Sun, 2023).

Deep learning, although its transformative promise, also poses considerable limitations. One of the main concerns is the requirement for massive amounts of data. To ensure accuracy and generalizability, deep learning models require large datasets for training, which are not always available or ethically sourced.

Furthermore, deep learning models frequently lack interpretability. As a result, it is difficult to understand why a particular model made a specific conclusion, which is crucial in industries such as healthcare or finance, where explainability is required.

Furthermore, deep learning models are computationally intensive, necessitating sophisticated hardware and, in many cases, enormous energy resources, raising environmental issues.

Deep learning's future is anticipated to see breakthroughs and more integration with other technologies. For example, deep learning models are being made more visible and interpretable by developing approaches such as attention mechanisms and explainable AI. In addition, converging deep learning with technologies like the Internet-of-Things (IoT) and edge computing may also enable more efficient, real-time decision-making in devices with limited computational resources.

Furthermore, as we gain a better understanding of the ethical and environmental consequences of deep learning, future advancements are likely to focus on developing more efficient algorithms, lowering dependency on enormous training datasets, and assuring the ethical use of AI.

6.5   CONVOLUTIONAL NEURAL NETWORKS (CNNs)

CNNs have established themselves as a dominant architecture in deep learning, particularly in image processing. CNNs, which are inspired by the structure of the animal visual cortex, provide a novel and efficient technique for processing grid-like data such as photographs. This section goes into the construction, principles of operation, and various applications of CNNs, demonstrating their enormous impact on artificial intelligence.

CNNs are made up of several hidden layers, an input layer, and an output layer. In contrast to traditional neural networks, CNN's hidden layers typically include convolutional layers, pooling layers, and fully connected layers. Convolutional layers add filters to the input data, pooling layers minimize spatial dimensions, and fully linked layers do classification. Figure 6.3 depicts this.

To build a feature map, CNNs apply a series of filters to an image's raw pixel data. This is accomplished in the convolutional layer using a mathematical technique known as convolution. First, each convolutional layer produces a set of feature maps that a non-linear activation function has processed. Following that, the pooling layers lower the dimensionality of the feature maps while keeping the vital information. This procedure, known as down-sampling, aids in making the network insensitive to minor

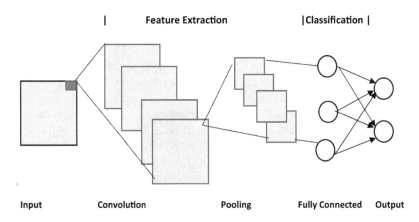

Fig. 6.3 Convolution neural network

changes or distortions in the input image while also reducing computing complexity.

A CNN's final layers are typically fully connected layers that employ the high-level characteristics created by the convolutional and pooling layers to classify the image into one of several predefined categories.

CNNs have a wide range of applications because they can extract and learn characteristics automatically from input data. CNNs have been employed in facial recognition systems, object detection, and scene labelling (Tsai et al., 2023). For example, they are used to detect people, other vehicles, and traffic signs in self-driving automobiles (Moorthy et al., 2023; Nadeem et al., 2023). CNNs have demonstrated exceptional success in disease diagnosis by interpreting medical images like MRIs, CT scans, and X-rays, often matching or outperforming human experts (Arvind et al., 2023). CNNs may distinguish actions in films by analyzing frame sequences (Dewil et al., 2023; Uchiyama et al., 2023). CNNs have been effectively adapted for text analysis, sentiment analysis, and other natural language processing tasks despite being built for image processing (Li et al., 2018; Yin et al., 2017).

6.6   Generative Adversarial Networks (GANs)

GANs have emerged as an exciting discovery in deep learning, enabling the generation of remarkably realistic synthetic data. GANs, which were introduced in 2014 by Ian Goodfellow and his colleagues, are composed of two neural networks—a generator and a discriminator—that are trained concurrently (Alqahtani et al., 2021; Lu et al., 2022; Pan et al., 2019; Saxena & Cao, 2021; Wang et al., 2017). This section delves into the architecture, operation principles, and applications of GANs, emphasizing their disruptive potential in AI.

GANs are made up of two main components: the generator and the discriminator, which are both neural networks. The generator's job is to make synthetic data that looks like real data, while the discriminator's job is to distinguish between generated and real data. GANs' distinct architecture encourages competition between these two networks, resulting in the development of increasingly realistic synthetic data. Figure 6.4 depicts this.

In Fig. 6.4, the generator network inputs a random noise signal and outputs synthetic data. This generated, and real data are put into the discriminator network, which determines whether it is real or fake.

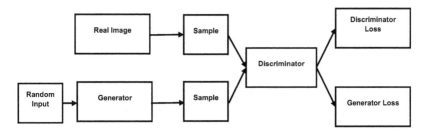

Fig. 6.4 Generative adversarial network

During the training process, both networks improve over time: the generator aims to generate data that is so realistic that the discriminator cannot distinguish it from actual data. On the other hand, the discriminator improves its capacity to distinguish real data from fake data. This procedure generates a dynamic feedback loop, which forces the generator to produce increasingly higher-quality synthetic data.

A generator and a discriminator are the two main components of the training process. GANs are trained in the following ways:

Step 1: Set up the Network
   Set up the generator and discriminator networks. The generator creates new data instances, whereas the discriminator validates them.

Step 2: Generate Synthetic Samples
   The generator generates synthetic data by taking in random noise and returning synthetic data. Typically, the noise is a random vector sampled from a predetermined latent space with a Gaussian distribution.

Step 3: Discriminator Training
   The discriminator is trained to distinguish between actual and fake data in the first half of each training iteration. It is given real data samples from the training set and synthetic data generated by the generator. The discriminator is trained to categorize real data as 1 and fake data as 0.

Step 4: Generator Training
   The generator is trained to deceive the discriminator in the second half of each training cycle. Again, the generator generates new synthetic data, which the discriminator evaluates. This time,

though, the labels are reversed. The goal is to change the generator's parameters so that the discriminator recognizes the synthetic data as real.

Step 5: Backpropagation and Optimization

The gradients of the loss function with respect to the model parameters are calculated via backpropagation, and an optimizer is used to adjust these parameters to minimize the loss.

Step 6: Iterate Until Convergence

Steps 2–5 are repeated until the generator and discriminator have reached equilibrium. Then, when the generator generates realistic synthetic data, the discriminator can no longer tell the difference between actual and synthetic data.

Training GANs can be difficult owing to concerns such as mode collapse, which occurs when the generator generates only a few types of samples, and vanishing gradients, which occur when the discriminator becomes so good that the generator can no longer learn. Therefore, monitoring the loss for the generator and the discriminator during training is critical. Moreover, monitoring provides valuable insights into the training process, such as whether one of the generators or discriminators outperforms the other, perhaps leading to bad results.

GANs' ability to produce realistic synthetic data has many applications. GANs can generate remarkably realistic images, including artificial faces, and fill in image gaps, a technique known as inpainting (Sorin et al., 2020). Second, GANs can convert low-resolution images to high-resolution versions, which is helpful in various domains, such as medical imaging and video streaming (Wang et al., 2020). Finally, GANs can improve machine learning model performance by augmenting datasets with synthetic datasets (Sidogi et al., 2022; Wu et al., 2022).

6.7   Deep Learning and International Politics

Deep learning is transforming several fields, including international politics, by allowing computers to learn from massive amounts of data. This section investigates deep learning's impact on politics and its possible uses, problems, and ramifications.

The ability of deep learning to examine complicated and large-scale datasets has immense potential in international politics. It can, for example, be used to forecast economic trends, forecast wars, and even simulate election outcomes. This predictive power can help policymakers and diplomats make decisions, plan strategically, and manage crises.

The ability to predict political events and electoral outcomes is one of the most promising applications of deep learning in politics. By analyzing historical data, social media trends, and public sentiment, deep learning algorithms can predict electoral outcomes, political crises, and policy impacts with increasing precision. This can aid political campaigns in allocating their resources more effectively and assist governments in preparing for and mitigating crises.

Deep learning can also facilitate the decision-making procedure. Deep learning can inform policy decisions, making them more evidence-based and potentially more effective by providing legislators and policymakers with data-driven insights. Thus, deep learning could lead to more strategic and informed political decision-making.

Deep learning can revolutionize international security by aiding in identifying hazards and opportunities in real time. From cyber threats to terrorist plotting, the technology can assist in analyzing a large volume of intelligence data, detecting patterns, and accurately assessing threats. This enhanced capacity to monitor and respond to security threats has the potential to alter the global balance of power significantly.

Threat Detection is one of the most critical applications of deep learning in international security. Deep learning algorithms can filter through vast amounts of data in real time to identify abnormal behaviors or patterns that may indicate the presence of potential threats. This includes identifying signs of terrorism or emerging geopolitical tensions as well as predicting cyberattacks.

Deep learning-powered surveillance technologies have the potential to revolutionize international security. Deep learning can process and interpret massive amounts of surveillance data faster and more accurately than human analysts, making it easier to identify and respond to security threats in real time.

Deep learning algorithms can forecast crime hotspots, assisting law enforcement agencies with proactive measures and resource allocation. This predictive capability can strengthen international cooperation in the fight against transnational illicit activity.

Deep learning can aid in bolstering cybersecurity, a vital element of international security. It can predict and detect cyber threats, safeguard critical infrastructure, and respond to cyberattacks effectively.

Diplomatic communication frequently depends on a nuanced understanding of language, context, and attitude. Combining deep learning and natural language processing (NLP) can assist in deciphering and interpreting these nuances in diplomatic discourses, facilitating a better understanding and more effective communication. Deep learning can power sophisticated translation tools that translate languages and comprehend cultural nuances, enabling diplomats to communicate more effectively in multilingual and multicultural contexts.

Deep learning can predict the potential effects of diplomatic actions or statements by analyzing past diplomatic exchanges and outcomes, thereby assisting in decision-making and strategy formulation. Deep learning analyzes social media trends and public sentiment regarding specific diplomatic issues, providing valuable insights that can influence diplomatic strategies.

Deep learning can predict market trends by analyzing vast quantities of historical data. These forecasts can give businesses and nations a competitive edge, resulting in more strategic business decisions and policies. Unusual patterns that may indicate fraudulent activity can be identified using deep learning, facilitating the detection and prevention of fraud. Similarly, it can forecast potential hazards, enabling financial institutions to manage their portfolios more effectively. Deep learning can automate routine duties, which increases productivity and efficiency. This can lead to cost reductions and competitive advantages in manufacturing and supply chain management industries.

Deep learning can provide insight into the causes and potential solutions of economic inequality by identifying patterns in economic data. This could aid in developing policies to reduce income disparities and foster economic growth.

While deep learning has enormous potential, it also has drawbacks. Data integrity is one of the critical problems. Deep learning models rely on vast volumes of data, and any errors in the data can result in incorrect results. This is especially true in international politics, where wrong forecasts or interpretations can have devastating implications.

Another issue is the "black box" nature of deep learning models, which makes it difficult to understand how they reach specific results. This lack of transparency can be problematic in politics, where accountability and decision-making rationale are essential.

One critical concern is privacy. Deep learning frequently requires the analysis of personal data, which raises concerns about spying and individual privacy rights.

Furthermore, the potential to abuse deep learning technology is a significant problem. It could, for example, disseminate misinformation, manipulate public opinion, or launch cyberattacks. Because of these possible abuses, stringent rules and ethical guidelines for applying deep learning in international politics are required.

6.8 Conclusions

To summarize, deep learning has the potential to transform international politics in various ways due to its ability to handle and evaluate massive volumes of complex data. Deep learning can improve diplomatic strategies and global governance, from forecasting economic and political trends to gauging the public mood and informing policy decisions. However, implementing these technologies is not without difficulties. Data integrity difficulties, the 'black box' nature of deep learning algorithms, privacy concerns, and the potential for exploitation all require careful consideration. As we continue incorporating deep learning into international politics, we must address these concerns with solid legislation, ethical principles, and a dedication to transparency and accountability. By doing so, we may ensure that applying deep learning in politics strengthens democratic processes, boost international collaboration, and eventually contribute to the benefit of global society.

References

Ajit, A., Acharya, K., & Samanta, A. (2020). *A review of convolutional neural networks*. 2020 International Conference on Emerging Trends in Information Technology and Engineering (ic-ETITE), pp. 1–5.

Alqahtani, H., Kavakli-Thorne, M., & Kumar, G. (2021). Applications of generative adversarial networks (GANs): An updated review. *Archives of Computational Methods in Engineering, 28*, 525–552.

Arvind, S., Tembhurne, J. V., Diwan, T., & Sahare, P. (2023). Improvised light weight deep CNN based U-Net for the semantic segmentation of lungs from chest X-rays. *Results in Engineering, 17*, 100929.

Aslani, S., & Jacob, J. (2023). Utilization of deep learning for COVID-19 diagnosis. *Clinical Radiology, 78*(2), 150–157.

Azadi, M., Yousefi, S., Saen, R. F., Shabanpour, H., & Jabeen, F. (2023). Forecasting sustainability of healthcare supply chains using deep learning and network data envelopment analysis. *Journal of Business Research, 154*, 113357.

Bethencourt-Aguilar, A., Castellanos-Nieves, D., Sosa-Alonso, J. J., & Area-Moreira, M. (2023). Use of generative adversarial networks (GANs) in educational technology research. *Journal of New Approaches in Educational Research, 12*, 153.

Bhat, R., Mannarswamy, S., & Shreyas, N. C. (2023). *DL4HC: Deep learning for healthcare.* Proceedings of the 6th Joint International Conference on Data Science & Management of Data (10th ACM IKDD CODS and 28th COMAD), pp. 327–329.

Choi, J. D., & Kim, M. Y. (2023). A sensor fusion system with thermal infrared camera and LiDAR for autonomous vehicles and deep learning based object detection. *ICT Express, 9*(2), 222–227.

Cong, S., & Zhou, Y. (2023). A review of convolutional neural network architectures and their optimizations. *Artificial Intelligence Review, 56*(3), 1905–1969.

Dewil, V., Courtois, A., Rodríguez, M., Ehret, T., Brandonisio, N., Bujoreanu, D., Facciolo, G., & Arias, P. (2023). *Video joint denoising and demosaicing with recurrent CNNs.* Proceedings of the IEEE/CVF Winter Conference on Applications of Computer Vision, pp. 5108–5119.

Dhlamini, S. M., & Marwala, T. (2004a). *Bushing monitoring using MLP and RBF.* 2004 IEEE AFRICON (7th Africon Conference in Africa).

Dhlamini, S. M., & Marwala, T. (2004b). *An application of SVM, RBF and MLP with ARD on bushings.* IEEE Conference on Cybernetics and Intelligent Systems, Vol. 2, pp. 1254–1259.

Dhlamini, S. M., Marwala, T., & Majozi, T. (2006). *Fuzzy and multilayer perceptron for evaluation of HV bushings.* 2006 IEEE International Conference on Systems, Man and Cybernetics, Vol. 2, pp. 1331–1336.

Diwan, S. A. (2023). Implementation patterns of natural language processing using pre-trained deep learning models. *International Journal of Intelligent Systems and Applications in Engineering, 11*(1), 33–38.

Eltouny, K. A., & Liang, X. (2023). Large-scale structural health monitoring using composite recurrent neural networks and grid environments. *Computer-Aided Civil and Infrastructure Engineering, 38*(3), 271–287.

Jiang, Y., & Zheng, L. (2023). Deep learning for video game genre classification. *Multimedia Tools and Applications, 82*, 21085–21099.

Khanduzi, R., & Sangaiah, A. K. (2023). An efficient recurrent neural network for defensive Stackelberg game. *Journal of Computational Science, 67*, 101970.

Kumar, P., Kumar, R., Gupta, G. P., Tripathi, R., Jolfaei, A., & Islam, A. N. (2023). A blockchain-orchestrated deep learning approach for secure data transmission in IoT-enabled healthcare system. *Journal of Parallel and Distributed Computing, 172*, 69–83.

Leke, C. A., & Marwala, T. (2016, June 25–30). *Missing data estimation in high-dimensional datasets: A swarm intelligence-deep neural network approach.* Advances in Swarm Intelligence: 7th International Conference, ICSI 2016, Bali, Indonesia, Proceedings, Part I, pp. 259–270. Springer.

Leke, B. B., Marwala, T., Tim, T. & Lagazio, M. (2006, October). *Prediction of HIV status from demographic data using neural networks.* In 2006 IEEE International Conference on Systems, Man and Cybernetics, Vol. 3, pp. 2339–2344.

Leke, C. A., & Marwala, T. (2019). *Deep learning and missing data in engineering systems* (p. 179). Springer.

Leke, C. A., Marwala, T., & Paul, S. (2015). *Proposition of a theoretical model for missing data imputation using deep learning and evolutionary algorithms.* arXiv preprint arXiv:1512.01362

Leke, C. A., Ndjiongue, A. R., Twala, B., & Marwala, T. (2017, July 27–August 1). *A deep learning-cuckoo search method for missing data estimation in high-dimensional datasets.* Advances in Swarm Intelligence: 8th International Conference, ICSI 2017, Fukuoka, Japan, Proceedings, Part I, pp. 561–572. Springer.

Li, P., Li, J., & Wang, G. (2018). *Application of convolutional neural network in natural language processing.* 2018 15th International Computer Conference on Wavelet Active Media Technology and Information Processing (ICCWAMTIP), pp. 120–122.

Lu, Y., Chen, D., Olaniyi, E., & Huang, Y. (2022). Generative adversarial networks (GANs) for image augmentation in agriculture: A systematic review. *Computers and Electronics in Agriculture, 200*, 107208.

Marwala, T. (2007). Bayesian training of neural networks using genetic programming. *Pattern Recognition Letters, 28*(12), 1452–1458.

Marwala, T. (2021). *Rational machines and artificial intelligence.* Academic Press.

Marwala, T., & Chakraverty, S. (2006). Fault classification in structures with incomplete measured data using autoassociative neural networks and genetic algorithm. *Current Science, 90*, 542–548.

Mbuvha, R., Mongwe, W. T., & Marwala, T. (2021). Separable shadow Hamiltonian hybrid Monte Carlo for Bayesian neural network inference in wind speed forecasting. *Energy and AI, 6*, 100108.

McMaster, C., Chan, J., Liew, D. F., Su, E., Frauman, A. G., Chapman, W. W., & Pires, D. E. (2023). Developing a deep learning natural language processing algorithm for automated reporting of adverse drug reactions. *Journal of Biomedical Informatics, 137*, 104265.

Moorthy, A., Sivashanmugam, B., Sriram, R., & Swathi, M. (2023). Real time image and video semantic segmentation for self-driving cars. *Journal of Survey in Fisheries Sciences, 10*(2S), 3208–3216.

Nadeem, H., Javed, K., Nadeem, Z., Khan, M. J., Rubab, S., Yon, D. K., & Naqvi, R. A. (2023). Road feature detection for advance driver assistance system using deep learning. *Sensors, 23*(9), 4466.

Ngo, T. A., Nguyen, T., & Thang, T. C. (2023). A survey of recent advances in quantum generative adversarial networks. *Electronics, 12*(4), 856.

O'Shea, K., & Nash, R. (2015). *An introduction to convolutional neural networks.* arXiv preprint arXiv:1511.08458

Pan, Z., Yu, W., Yi, X., Khan, A., Yuan, F., & Zheng, Y. (2019). Recent progress on generative adversarial networks (GANs): A survey. *IEEE Access, 7,* 36322–36333.

Patel, P. B., & Marwala, T. (2009, November 25–28). *Caller interaction classification: A comparison of real and binary coded GA-MLP techniques.* Advances in Neuro-Information Processing: 15th International Conference, ICONIP 2008, Auckland, New Zealand, Revised Selected Papers, Part II, pp. 728–735. Springer.

Qin, C., Huang, G., Yu, H., Wu, R., Tao, J., & Liu, C. (2023). Geological information prediction for shield machine using an enhanced multi-head self-attention convolution neural network with two-stage feature extraction. *Geoscience Frontiers, 14*(2), 101519.

Saleh, S. N., & Fathy, C. (2023). A novel deep-learning model for remote driver monitoring in SDN-based internet of autonomous vehicles using 5G technologies. *Applied Sciences, 13*(2), 875.

Saxena, D., & Cao, J. (2021). Generative adversarial networks (GANs) challenges, solutions, and future directions. *ACM Computing Surveys (CSUR), 54*(3), 1–42.

Sidogi, T., Mongwe, W. T., Mbuvha, R., & Marwala, T. (2022). *Creating synthetic volatility surfaces using generative adversarial networks with static arbitrage loss conditions.* 2022 IEEE Symposium Series on Computational Intelligence (SSCI), pp. 1423–1429.

Soares, F., Burken, J., & Marwala, T. (2006, October 3–6). *Neural network applications in advanced aircraft flight control system, a hybrid system, a flight test demonstration.* Neural Information Processing: 13th International Conference, ICONIP 2006, Hong Kong, China. Proceedings, Part III, pp. 684–691. Springer.

Soni, V., Yadav, H., Semwal, V. B., Roy, B., Choubey, D. K., & Mallick, D. K. (2023). *A novel smartphone-based human activity recognition using deep learning in health care.* Machine Learning, Image Processing, Network Security and Data Sciences: Select Proceedings of 3rd International Conference on MIND 2021, pp. 493–503. Springer.

Sorin, V., Barash, Y., Konen, E., & Klang, E. (2020). Creating artificial images for radiology applications using generative adversarial networks (GANs)—A systematic review. *Academic Radiology, 27*(8), 1175–1185.

Su, Y., & Sun, W. (2023). Classification and interaction of new media instant music video based on deep learning under the background of artificial intelligence. *The Journal of Supercomputing, 79*(1), 214–242.

Tsai, T. H., Lu, J. X., Chou, X. Y., & Wang, C. Y. (2023). Joint masked face recognition and temperature measurement system using convolutional neural networks. *Sensors, 23*(6), 2901.

Uchiyama, T., Sogi, N., Niinuma, K., & Fukui, K. (2023). *Visually explaining 3D-CNN predictions for video classification with an adaptive occlusion sensitivity analysis.* Proceedings of the IEEE/CVF Winter Conference on Applications of Computer Vision, pp. 1513–1522.

Wang, J., Deng, X., Xu, M., Chen, C., & Song, Y. (2020, August 23–28). *Multi-level wavelet-based generative adversarial network for perceptual quality enhancement of compressed video.* Computer Vision–ECCV 2020: 16th European Conference, Glasgow, UK, Proceedings, Part XIV, pp. 405–421. Springer.

Wang, K., Gou, C., Duan, Y., Lin, Y., Zheng, X., & Wang, F. Y. (2017). Generative adversarial networks: Introduction and outlook. *IEEE/CAA Journal of Automatica Sinica, 4*(4), 588–598.

Wang, R., Bashyam, V., Yang, Z., Yu, F., Tassopoulou, V., Chintapalli, S. S., Skampardoni, I., Sreepada, L. P., Sahoo, D., Nikita, K., & Abdulkadir, A. (2023). Applications of generative adversarial networks in neuroimaging and clinical neuroscience. *NeuroImage, 269*, 119898.

Wu, A. N., Stouffs, R., & Biljecki, F. (2022). Generative Adversarial Networks in the built environment: A comprehensive review of the application of GANs across data types and scales. *Building and Environment, 223*, 109477.

Wu, T. W., Zhang, H., Peng, W., Lü, F., & He, P. J. (2023). Applications of convolutional neural networks for intelligent waste identification and recycling: A review. *Resources, Conservation and Recycling, 190*, 106813.

Xiang, H., Zou, Q., Nawaz, M. A., Huang, X., Zhang, F., & Yu, H. (2023). Deep learning for image inpainting: A survey. *Pattern Recognition, 134*, 109046.

Yin, W., Kann, K., Yu, M., & Schütze, H. (2017). *Comparative study of CNN and RNN for natural language processing.* arXiv preprint arXiv:1702.01923

Zhong, Z., Gao, Y., Zheng, Y., Zheng, B., & Sato, I. (2023). Real-world video deblurring: A benchmark dataset and an efficient recurrent neural network. *International Journal of Computer Vision, 131*(1), 284–301.

CHAPTER 7

Natural Language Processing in Politics

7.1 Natural Language Processing (NLP) and Politics Overview

NLP, a subfield of artificial intelligence, is revolutionizing our approach to data analysis across numerous disciplines (Johnson & Lerner, 2023; Mahmud et al., 2023; Németh, 2022; Shaik et al., 2023; Torregrosa et al., 2023). NLP alters international politics by reshaping how we evaluate, comprehend, and engage with political speech. This chapter investigates the impact of NLP on politics, focusing on its applications, benefits, and ethical implications.

At its foundation, politics is concerned with understanding a considerable array of unstructured textual data, such as diplomatic communications, speeches, news stories, and social media debates. Unfortunately, the old method of manual analysis is time-consuming and prone to human error. NLP provides a potent solution to these difficulties because it can understand, interpret, and generate human language.

The uses of NLP in politics are numerous. Sentiment analysis, for example, might use social media posts to gauge public opinion and attitudes regarding governmental decisions, geopolitical events, or diplomatic ties (Matalon et al., 2021). Topic modelling can help us discover important political discourse topics and track political narrative changes across time (Bagozzi & Berliner, 2018). Text categorization can sift through large datasets to find relevant papers for policy study or intelligence

T. Marwala, *Artificial Intelligence, Game Theory and Mechanism Design in Politics*, https://doi.org/10.1007/978-981-99-5103-1_7

investigation (Grimmer & Stewart, 2013). Another important NLP technology is machine translation, which can bridge language barriers and allow for speedy comprehension of foreign language documents.

The incorporation of NLP into politics has various advantages. First, it enables real-time analysis of global political dialogue. Staying current is critical in an ever-changing political context. In addition, NLP can rapidly process and analyze massive volumes of data, delivering critical real-time insights for decision-making.

Second, NLP can detect changes in mood or policy that are not always obvious. Subtle alterations in the wording used in a series of speeches or documents, for example, could suggest an impending policy shift, offering an early warning system for analysts and decision-makers.

Third, NLP can aid in the detection of emerging trends or dangers. NLP systems can spot trends or potential risks by analyzing social media speech, news reports, or other publicly available text data, offering vital information to policymakers, intelligence agencies, and diplomats.

Finally, NLP has the potential to democratize access to information. For example, NLP breaks down communication barriers by translating foreign language texts and making massive text dataset analysis possible, allowing more individuals to engage in international politics.

Despite its merits, using NLP in politics creates ethical and practical issues. For example, privacy and consent are critical when evaluating personal data, such as social media posts. A crucial difficulty is balancing the need for data analysis with individual privacy rights.

Another source of concern is the possibility of algorithmic bias. If the data used to train NLP models contains prejudice, the models can perpetuate and amplify that bias, resulting in skewed or biased results.

Furthermore, NLP models' interpretations and predictions are probabilistic and may be erroneous. Therefore, over-reliance on NLP without human monitoring and comprehension might result in misinterpretations and blunders.

Finally, the availability and misuse of NLP technologies for harmful reasons, such as disinformation or propaganda dissemination, are a continuing worry. As a result, adopting norms and regulations that encourage the responsible use of NLP is an urgent need.

7.2   Topic Modelling

Political science has undergone a digital revolution, resulting in an abundance of textual data encapsulating political speech (Carmichael and Eaton, 2023; Fu and Shao, 2023; Jafery et al., 2023; Ogunleye et al., 2023; Osnabrügge et al., 2023; Paul et al., 2019). Traditional analytical approaches can be demanding and time-consuming when dealing with this vast, unstructured data. However, topic modelling, an NLP technique, can give a highly efficient, automated approach to evaluating and interpreting political narratives. This section dives into subject topic modelling in politics, including its benefits, problems, and ethical implications.

Topic modelling is an unsupervised machine learning technique for discovering latent thematic structures in documents. This can be utilized for various types of text data in politics, such as legislative papers, political speeches, social media posts, or news articles, to successfully identify the predominant themes or issues under discussion.

Topic modelling can detect important topics and trends in various text sources, including diplomatic communications, international treaties, speeches by world leaders, news stories, and social media posts. Analyzing foreign policy speech is one of the principal uses of topic modelling in international politics. For example, analysts might discover major topics and priorities in a country's foreign policy by applying topic modelling to policy documents or leaders' speeches.

Topic modelling can also examine international treaties and agreements to uncover similar themes and patterns. It can evaluate news stories or social media conversations on global events, providing insights into public opinion and mood.

The advantages of topic modelling are numerous. As a result, it allows for the efficient study of massive datasets that would be impossible to analyze manually. Identifying essential themes in international political discourse provides an overview of the global political scene. Furthermore, identifying hidden patterns and trends might provide helpful information to policymakers, diplomats, and researchers.

In political science, topic modelling has numerous uses. It can, for example, evaluate political manifestos to discover major themes that various political parties emphasize. It can also trace the evolution of political speech across time by noting trends in parliamentary debates or media coverage of political themes.

The analysis of social media speech is an application of topic modelling. For example, researchers can evaluate popular mood and interest in various political issues by detecting trending topics on sites like Twitter or Facebook.

The advantages of topic modelling are numerous. To begin with, it allows for the examination of massive text corpora that would be too large for manual evaluation. Second, it offers a bird's-eye view of the political scene, highlighting significant topics and trends. Finally, discovering underlying trends or shifts in political discourse can provide policymakers, political analysts, and researchers with important information.

However, subject modelling is not without difficulties. Topic interpretation, albeit computerized, frequently requires human judgment. The discovered word clusters may sometimes be confusing or overlapping, challenging assigning unambiguous, unique labels. Input data quality and variety are also key challenges. For example, text preparation, model parameter selection, and text data quality all impact topic modelling results.

Ethical concerns about privacy and permission emerge when analyzing personal data such as social media posts. As a result, topic modelling procedures must respect individual privacy rights and follow ethical principles.

7.3   SENTIMENT ANALYSIS

Political discourse has expanded beyond traditional media to include social media, blogs, and online forums as digital communication platforms have proliferated (Diaz, 2023; del Valle & de la Fuente, 2023; Park et al., 2023; Samih et al., 2023; Vahdat-Nejad et al., 2023). This transition has resulted in massive amounts of text data ideal for analysis. Sentiment analysis, an NLP approach, has emerged as a valuable tool for understanding this data, providing unique insights into political opinions and behaviors. This section discusses the role of sentiment analysis in political science, including its uses, benefits, problems, and ethical implications.

The computational study of people's opinions, sentiments, assessments, appraisals, and feelings regarding entities, individuals, situations, events, themes, and qualities is known as sentiment analysis, sometimes known as opinion mining. Sentiment analysis, for example, can be used in politics to gauge popular opinion on political issues, candidates, or events using text data from social media, news articles, or other digital platforms.

Providing a snapshot of public opinion on global issues is one of the critical ways sentiment analysis influences international politics. Governments and international organizations can use sentiment analysis to evaluate public opinion on international treaties, conflicts, humanitarian crises, and foreign policy choices. This data can be used to drive diplomatic efforts, forecast political trends, and inform policymakers' decisions.

Sentiment analysis, for example, can assist in identifying trends in public opinion toward foreign affairs. For example, sentiment analysis can reveal an unexpectedly negative shift in attitude toward a given country or international agreement. In that instance, policymakers can explore and address the underlying reasons before they become diplomatic concerns.

Sentiment analysis can also be helpful in crisis management. For example, sentiment analysis can help identify public fears and concerns during an international crisis by monitoring social media discussions and news broadcasts. This can lead governments and international organizations to address public concerns and sustain societal stability appropriately.

Furthermore, sentiment research can help with electoral forecasts in democratic countries. Sentiment analysis can uncover trends and prospective shifts in voter behavior by measuring sentiment surrounding candidates or policy concerns, providing significant insights into political campaigns.

Election forecasting is a fundamental use of sentiment analysis in political science. For example, studying social media opinions toward various candidates might assist in anticipating election outcomes or highlight critical issues that impact voters. It can also monitor the public's reaction to political events or policy decisions, providing politicians with real-time feedback.

Furthermore, sentiment analysis can assist in identifying political polarization and echo chambers in online places. For example, analyzing political opinions across several social media platforms or user groups might reveal patterns of political isolation and ideological echo chambers.

The advantages of sentiment analysis are substantial. First, it provides a more direct gauge of public opinion than traditional surveys or polls, reducing difficulties such as social desirability and non-response bias. Second, it allows for real-time monitoring of public sentiment, which allows for quick solutions to emergent problems or crises. Finally, uncovering trends in public mood can help shape political strategies, legislative decisions, and communication initiatives.

Despite its potential, sentiment analysis presents unique problems. The nuance and complexity of human sentiment can be difficult to convey using automated procedures. Sarcasm, irony, and cultural references, which are ubiquitous in political speech, might be particularly difficult. Another critical issue is the data's quality and representativeness. For example, social media data, a popular source for sentiment analysis, may not represent the larger population, resulting in biased or skewed conclusions.

From an ethical standpoint, sentiment analysis poses concerns about privacy and permission, particularly when dealing with personal data such as social media posts. As a result, it is critical to ensure that sentiment analysis adheres to individual privacy rights and data protection rules.

7.4   Text Classification

The expansion of digital text data has created new opportunities for political science study and analysis (Bestvater & Monroe, 2023; Chang & Masterson, 2020; Osnabrügge et al., 2023; Rao & Spasojevic, 2016; Terechshenko et al., 2020). As a result, text classification, an NLP approach, has emerged as an effective tool for evaluating political speech. This section details text classification's function in political science, highlighting its uses, benefits, problems, and ethical concerns.

Text classification entails categorizing text based on its content into specified classes. It uses machine learning algorithms to discover patterns from labelled examples and apply them to new, previously unknown text. For example, text classification in political science can categorize textual data, such as news stories, social media posts, political speeches, or policy documents, according to various political themes, attitudes, or ideologies.

Text classification has numerous substantial uses in international politics. First, it can aid in monitoring global news and social media to discover and categorize key events, public opinions, and developing trends. This can give policymakers real-time insight into international political processes, allowing them to make more educated decisions. Second, text classification is useful in diplomatic communications, such as official mail and speeches. This can aid in identifying different countries' important interests, attitudes, and methods, resulting in a more sophisticated knowledge of international relations. Third, text classification can monitor and anticipate conflict. Text classification can detect increasing tensions or potential confrontations by examining news headlines and social media activity. This can enable proactive responses by providing early notice of future catastrophes. Fourth, it can detect and track political falsehoods on the internet. Researchers can track the spread of political misinformation and its impact on the public debate by training text classifiers to discern between reputable and untrustworthy material. Fifth, it enables efficient analysis of vast amounts of text data that would be impossible to analyze manually. Sixth, it provides a systematic and reproducible approach to text analysis, reducing the subjectivity and prejudice inherent in manual analysis. Seventh, text classification can offer valuable insights to policymakers, political analysts, and campaign strategists by revealing patterns and trends in political discourse. Finally, text classification can help with election analysis. Text classification can reveal insights into voter behavior and election outcomes by classifying public dialogue surrounding electoral campaigns, issues, and candidates. This can be very valuable in predicting election results and understanding their influencing elements.

Despite its potential benefits, text classification in international politics is difficult. Language complexity, such as sarcasm, cultural nuances, and context-specific meanings, is among the most significant barriers.

There are also ethical considerations about privacy and data security. Using text categorization to evaluate public dialogue, for example, raises concerns regarding the appropriate use of personal data. As a result, legislators must ensure that such technologies are used in accordance with privacy and data protection regulations.

Furthermore, the vagueness and nuance of political discourse can make text classification difficult. For example, text classifiers may struggle to interpret sarcasm, cultural references, or coded language, which is typical in political debate.

Ethically, privacy considerations occur when dealing with personal data, such as social media posts, and ensuring that text classification respects individual privacy rights and data protection requirements. Furthermore, given the potential impact of text classification results on political decision-making or public opinion, guaranteeing the classification process's transparency and impartiality is critical.

7.5   Machine Translation

The automated translation of text or speech from one language to another is called machine translation, a subfield of computational linguistics and artificial intelligence. Over the years, technology has progressed from rule-based systems to statistical approaches and neural networks. While its impact is acknowledged in many fields, including commerce and education, its impact on politics is substantial and growing. This section examines the role of machine translation in politics and its potential consequences (Asscher & Glikson, 2021; Cabrera, 2022; KhudaBukhsh et al., 2021; Weber & Mehandru, 2022).

Machine translation ranges from simple word-for-word translations to more sophisticated systems that attempt to grasp and translate the original text's context and grammar. Furthermore, the introduction of neural machine translation, which utilizes deep learning algorithms to translate text, has resulted in more accurate and natural-sounding translations, broadening the technology's potential applications.

Machine translation is essential in politics for various reasons. First, it can improve communication and understanding between nations that speak multiple languages. This can result in more effective diplomacy, cooperation, and mutual understanding. Machine translation can examine foreign language news items, social media posts, and other information sources. This can assist politicians and policymakers in understanding global trends and public mood better, offering valuable insights for decision-making.

In politics, machine translation can help politicians reach out to voters who speak different languages, allowing them to broaden their support base. It can also assist voters in understanding foreign politicians' perspectives and ideas, contributing to a more internationally informed electorate.

Machine translation is also helpful in multinational organizations like the United Nations, where documents must be translated into various languages. It can help to speed up the translation process and improve the efficiency of international cooperation.

Despite the apparent benefits, utilizing machine translation in politics is fraught with difficulties. Even the most sophisticated machine translation systems are susceptible to errors, resulting in misunderstandings or misinterpretations.

Furthermore, machine translation systems may struggle with cultural nuances and context-specific interpretations, which could result in erroneous translations. This can be a significant issue in a political situation where language clarity is critical.

There are other ethical issues to consider when using machine translation. For example, relying on machine translation can marginalize skilled human translators. Furthermore, if machine translation is utilized to convey political propaganda or misinformation, it could have far-reaching societal consequences.

7.6 Under-Resourced Languages

NLP has transformed the way we engage with technology. NLP has enabled computers to interpret, generate, and respond to human language, from translation services to voice assistants (Besacier et al., 2014; Cunliffe et al., 2022; Karim et al., 2020; Kumar et al., 2023). However, much of this development has been focused on a few widely spoken languages, leaving numerous under-resourced ones in the dust. This section investigates the role of NLP in bridging the digital language divide and the possible benefits for under-resourced language communities.

The gap in digital resources and services available for different languages is referred to as the digital language divide. For example, significant languages such as English, Mandarin, and Spanish have considerable support in digital resources and NLP technologies. However, many under-resourced languages, particularly those spoken by tiny or marginalized communities, do not have this kind of support.

The lack of digital resources for under-resourced languages can exacerbate social and economic inequities, limiting speakers' access to information and opportunities. By developing tools and systems that serve under-resourced languages, NLP has the potential to help overcome this gap.

There are various hurdles to developing NLP tools for under-resourced languages. The most significant issue is a shortage of labelled data, which is essential for training NLP algorithms. Machine learning models use human-labelled text or speech data to learn linguistic patterns. Unfortunately, this information is rare or non-existent for many under-resourced languages. Another problem is that many under-resourced languages have distinctive linguistic properties, such as complicated grammar or phonetics, which might be difficult to capture using standard NLP techniques.

Building NLP tools for under-resourced languages can yield significant benefits despite these obstacles. It can help preserve and promote these languages in the digital era by improving access to information and services for speakers of these languages. Several efforts are currently in the works to solve these issues. Among these are attempts to generate and distribute linguistic data for under-resourced languages, research into low-resource NLP approaches that can learn from small quantities of data, and learning transfer tools. Transfer learning is one example in which models trained on high-resource languages are converted to augment low-resource languages.

7.7   African Languages

While NLP has made tremendous progress in many languages, developing and implementing it for African languages present distinct opportunities and obstacles. This section investigates the importance of NLP in the context of African languages and its potential to promote linguistic inclusion and cultural preservation (England, 1998; Riza, 2008; Turin, 2007; Zhang et al., 2022). With nearly 2000 unique languages, the African continent is linguistically diverse. However, most NLP research and applications have concentrated on a few major languages, such as English, French, Spanish, and Chinese. As a result, African languages are vastly underrepresented in the digital world. This provides a unique opportunity for NLP to play a critical role in promoting linguistic diversity and inclusivity.

First, NLP can help with machine translation for African languages, allowing for greater communication across diverse language speakers on the continent and abroad. This can potentially improve social cohesiveness, economic integration, and mutual understanding.

Second, NLP can create language-based applications in African languages, such as virtual assistants and chatbots. This can help bridge the digital gap and make technology accessible to African language speakers.

Third, NLP can conserve and document African languages, many of which are on the verge of extinction. NLP can contribute to cultural preservation and linguistic variety by generating digital resources for these languages.

Despite its potential benefits, applying NLP to African languages poses several difficulties. The most significant barrier for these languages is a lack of available data, as NLP systems often require substantial amounts of data to train.

Furthermore, Africa's high linguistic diversity is a barrier to NLP. Many African languages have complicated grammar systems; some are tonal, adding another layer of complexity to NLP systems.

Despite these obstacles, there is an increasing interest in expanding NLP research to include African languages. Initiatives such as the Masakhane project seek to develop machine translation for African languages and to promote NLP research in Africa.[1] Such efforts can aid in promoting linguistic diversity, preserving cultural legacy, and advancing technology to make it more accessible and inclusive.

7.8 Language Preservation

Language is both a means of communication and a repository of cultural legacy and identity. Unfortunately, many languages worldwide are in danger of extinction, which can result in the loss of cultural diversity and historical information. NLP is a promising technology for helping to preserve endangered languages. This section delves into the role of NLP in this endeavor, its applications, problems, and future possibilities.

NLP techniques could collect, document, and analyze endangered languages. The linguistic data gathered can construct digital resources such as online dictionaries, language learning aids, and even translation systems, thereby assisting in preserving and revitalizing these languages. NLP can help save endangered languages in a variety of ways. Speech recognition techniques, for example, can be used to transcribe spoken language data, assisting in the documentation of languages having a strong oral tradition but little written material. In addition, machine translation and cross-lingual transfer learning can translate between endangered and commonly spoken languages, increasing the visibility and accessibility to the former (Mbuvha et al., 2023).

Several projects are already using NLP to preserve languages. For example, Google-backed Endangered Languages Project employs NLP

---

[1] https://www.masakhane.io/.

to provide a comprehensive online resource for endangered languages.[2] Another effort, the Universal Dependencies Project, is working on generating treebanks for low-resource languages, which will be useful in developing NLP tools.[3]

While NLP has enormous potential for language preservation, it also faces considerable problems. One of the most significant issues is a lack of data for many endangered languages. NLP techniques rely on vast amounts of annotated data, which is rarely available for endangered languages.

The diversity and complexity of many endangered languages are another barriers. These languages frequently have linguistic traits not found in other widely spoken languages, making them difficult to model using standard NLP techniques.

Despite these obstacles, NLP has significant potential to preserve endangered languages. Recent improvements in NLP, such as unsupervised and low-resource learning, may aid in the resolution of several data-related issues. Collaborations between linguists, local communities, and NLP academics could also help collect and annotate data and ensure that NLP tools are culturally sensitive and acceptable.

7.9   Hate Speech

Communication platforms have increased tremendously in the digital era, offering millions of people throughout the world a voice (Ghosal et al., 2023; Govers et al., 2023; Halevy, 2023; Lee et al., 2023; Poletto et al., 2021). Unfortunately, this greater ease of communication has also facilitated negative communication, notably hate speech. This problem is being addressed using NLP. This section goes into the role of NLP in hate speech prevention, covering its applications, concerns, and future potential.

Hate speech, defined as expressions of hate, discrimination, or violence directed against individuals or groups based on characteristics such as race, religion, ethnic origin, or sexual orientation, has become an increasingly serious issue on the internet. Given the number of online contacts, manual

---

[2] https://blog.google/outreach-initiatives/arts-culture/endangered-languages-project-supporting/.

[3] https://universaldependencies.org/.

monitoring and moderation of hate speech are impractical, necessitating automated approaches. NLP provides the foundation for automated solutions because it can understand, interpret, and produce human language.

To fight hate speech, NLP can be used in various ways. Text classification, for example, can determine whether a text is hate speech depending on its content. Another NLP application, sentiment analysis, can detect unfavorable sentiments and emotions frequently accompanying hate speech. Finally, topic modelling can uncover recurring themes in hate speech, providing insights into the underlying conditions that motivate such behavior.

Several social media networks and online communities are starting to use NLP-based algorithms to detect and filter out hate speech. These algorithms can automatically scan and analyze large amounts of text, finding potential hate speech more effectively than human moderators.

While NLP has enormous potential to prevent hate speech, substantial hurdles exist. One of the most challenging issues is language's intrinsic intricacy and subtlety. Hate speech, for example, frequently employs innuendo, euphemism, and coded language, which can be difficult for NLP systems to identify. Furthermore, context is critical for effectively comprehending language, and existing NLP algorithms may struggle to understand the context in which words are employed.

There are also ethical problems, such as the possibility of false positives leading to censorship or violation of free expression. Finding a happy medium between suppressing hate speech and maintaining free speech is a difficult task we must carefully address.

Despite the difficulties, using NLP to combat hate speech offers enormous promise. Machine learning and AI are improving, allowing more accurate detection and understanding of hate speech.

NLP is an effective method in combating hate speech. By enabling the automated detection and analysis of hate speech, NLP can assist in establishing safer and more inclusive online places. However, as we continue to improve these technologies, we must also ensure they are ethically and responsibly used, balancing the need to protect free expression with preventing harm.

7.10   Conclusion

The interaction of NLP and international politics creates a new frontier of potential and difficulties. NLP's ability to comprehend, analyze, and interpret large amounts of linguistic data can transform how we approach international relations. NLP provides a unique lens for examining the dynamics of international relations, from tracking and altering political feelings to recognizing significant topics in political speech. However, it is critical to address the issues that come with it, such as the complexity and ambiguity of political language and its cultural nuances. As the field progresses, more advanced NLP tools capable of overcoming these problems will be required. Furthermore, as with any technology, ethical considerations must guide its use. While NLP can considerably improve openness and understanding of international politics, its possible misuses, such as invasion of privacy or information abuse, must be carefully avoided.

Nonetheless, NLP holds enormous promise for improving our understanding of international affairs. It is a great resource for researchers, policymakers, and political analysts, providing new perspectives on the intricacies of international relations. As these technologies are refined and expanded, the interplay between NLP and international politics will play an essential role in shaping the future of global discourse.

References

Asscher, O., & Glikson, E. (2021). Human evaluations of machine translation in an ethically charged situation. *New Media & Society*, 14614448211018833.

Besacier, L., Barnard, E., Karpov, A., & Schultz, T. (2014). Automatic speech recognition for under-resourced languages: A survey. *Speech Communication, 56*, 85–100.

Bestvater, S. E., & Monroe, B. L. (2023). Sentiment is not stance: Target-aware opinion classification for political text analysis. *Political Analysis, 31*(2), 235–256.

Bagozzi, B. E., & Berliner, D. (2018). The politics of scrutiny in human rights monitoring: Evidence from structural topic models of US State Department human rights reports. *Political Science Research and Methods, 6*(4), 661–677.

Cabrera, L. (2022). Babel Fish Democracy? Prospects for addressing democratic language barriers through machine translation and interpretation. *American Journal of Political Science.*

Carmichael, J. J., & Eaton, S. E. (2023). Security risks, fake degrees, and other fraud: A topic modelling approach. In *Fake degrees and fraudulent credentials in higher education* (pp. 227–250). Springer International Publishing.

Chang, C., & Masterson, M. (2020). Using word order in political text classification with long short-term memory models. *Political Analysis, 28*(3), 395–411.

Cunliffe, D., Vlachidis, A., Williams, D., & Tudhope, D. (2022). Natural language processing for under-resourced languages: Developing a Welsh natural language toolkit. *Computer Speech & Language, 72*, 101311.

del Valle, E., & de la Fuente, L. (2023). Sentiment analysis methods for politics and hate speech contents in Spanish language: A systematic review. *IEEE Latin America Transactions, 100* (in press).

Diaz, M. O. (2023). A domain-specific evaluation of the performance of selected web-based sentiment analysis platforms. *International Journal of Software Engineering and Computer Systems, 9*(1), 1–09.

England, N. C. (1998). Mayan efforts toward language preservation. In *Endangered languages: Current issues and future prospects* (pp. 99–116).

Fu, H. Z., & Shao, L. (2023). Telling our own story: A bibliometrics analysis of mainland China's influence on Chinese politics research, 2001–2020. *PS: Political Science & Politics, 56*(1), 18–28.

Grimmer, J., & Stewart, B. M. (2013). Text as data: The promise and pitfalls of automatic content analysis methods for political texts. *Political Analysis, 21*(3), 267–297.

Ghosal, S., Jain, A., Tayal, D. K., Menon, V. G., & Kumar, A. (2023). Inculcating context for Emoji powered Bengali hate speech detection using extended fuzzy SVM and text embedding models. In *ACM transactions on Asian and low-resource language information processing*.

Govers, J., Feldman, P., Dant, A., & Patros, P. (2023). Down the Rabbit Hole: Detecting online extremism, radicalisation, and politicised hate speech. *ACM Computing Surveys*.

Halevy, K. (2023). *A group-specific approach to NLP for hate speech detection*. arXiv preprint arXiv:2304.11223.

Jafery, N. N., Keikhosrokiani, P., & Asl, M. P. (2023a). An artificial intelligence application of theme and space in life writings of Middle Eastern women: A topic modelling and sentiment analysis approach. In *Handbook of research on artificial intelligence applications in literary works and social media* (pp. 19–35). IGI Global.

Johnson, T., & Lerner, J. Y. (2023). Environmentalism among poor and rich countries: Using natural language processing to handle perfunctory support and rising powers. *Review of International Political Economy, 30*(1), 127–152.

Karim, M. R., Chakravarthi, B. R., McCrae, J. P., & Cochez, M. (2020). Classification benchmarks for under-resourced Bengali language based on multichannel convolutional-lstm network. In *2020 IEEE 7th International Conference on Data Science and Advanced Analytics* (DSAA) (pp. 390–399).

KhudaBukhsh, A. R., Sarkar, R., Kamlet, M. S., & Mitchell, T. (2021). We don't speak the same language: Interpreting polarization through machine translation. In *Proceedings of the AAAI Conference on Artificial Intelligence* (Vol. 35, No. 17, pp. 14893–14901).

Kumar, M., Kim, J., Gowda, D., Garg, A., & Kim, C. (2023). Self-supervised accent learning for under-resourced accents using native language data. In *ICASSP 2023–2023 IEEE International Conference on Acoustics, Speech and Signal Processing (ICASSP)* (pp. 1–5)

Lee, N., Jung, C., & Oh, A. (2023). Hate speech classifiers are culturally insensitive. In *Proceedings of the First Workshop on Cross-Cultural Considerations in NLP (C3NLP)* (pp. 35–46).

Mahmud, M. A. I., Talukder, A. T., Sultana, A., Bhuiyan, K. I. A., Rahman, M. S., Pranto, T. H., & Rahman, R. M. (2023). Toward news authenticity: Synthesizing Natural Language Processing and human expert opinion to evaluate news. *IEEE Access, 11*, 11405–11421.

Matalon, Y., Magdaci, O., Almozlino, A., & Yamin, D. (2021). Using sentiment analysis to predict opinion inversion in Tweets of political communication. *Scientific Reports, 11*(1), 1–9.

Mbuvha, R., Adelani, D. I., Mutavhatsindi, T., Rakhuhu, T., Mauda, A., Maumela, T. J., Masindi, A., Rananga, S., Marivate, V., & Marwala, T. (2023). MphayaNER: Named Entity Recognition for Tshivenda. arXiv preprint arXiv: 2304.03952.

Németh, R. (2022). A scoping review on the use of natural language processing in research on political polarization: Trends and research prospects. *Journal of Computational Social Science*, 1–25.

Ogunleye, B., Maswera, T., Hirsch, L., Gaudoin, J., & Brunsdon, T. (2023). Comparison of topic modelling approaches in the banking context. *Applied Sciences, 13*(2), 797.

Osnabrügge, M., Ash, E., & Morelli, M. (2023). Cross-domain topic classification for political texts. *Political Analysis, 31*(1), 59–80.

Park, S., Strover, S., Choi, J., & Schnell, M. (2023). Mind games: A temporal sentiment analysis of the political messages of the Internet Research Agency on Facebook and Twitter. *New Media & Society, 25*(3), 463–484.

Paul, S., Hasija, M., Mangipudi, R. V., & Marwala T. (2019). Early estimation of protest time spans: A novel approach using topic modelling and decision trees. In J. Nayak, A. Abraham, B. Krishna, G. Chandra Sekhar, & A. Das (Eds.), *Soft Computing in Data Analytics. Advances in Intelligent Systems and Computing* (Vol. 758). Springer.

Poletto, F., Basile, V., Sanguinetti, M., Bosco, C., & Patti, V. (2021). Resources and benchmark corpora for hate speech detection: A systematic review. *Language Resources and Evaluation, 55,* 477–523.

Rao, A., & Spasojevic, N. (2016). *Actionable and political text classification using word embeddings and LSTM.* arXiv preprint arXiv:1607.02501.

Riza, H. (2008). Indigenous languages of Indonesia: Creating language resources for language preservation. In *Proceedings of the IJCNLP-08 Workshop on NLP for Less Privileged Languages.*

Samih, A., Ghadi, A., & Fennan, A. (2023). Enhanced sentiment analysis based on improved word embeddings and XGboost. *International Journal of Electrical and Computer Engineering, 13*(2), 1827.

Shaik, M. A., Sree, M. Y., Vyshnavi, S. S., Ganesh, T., Sushmitha, D., & Shreya, N. (2023). Fake news detection using NLP. In *2023 International Conference on Innovative Data Communication Technologies and Application (ICIDCA)* (pp. 399–405).

Terechshenko, Z., Linder, F., Padmakumar, V., Liu, M., Nagler, J., Tucker, J. A., & Bonneau, R. (2020). *A comparison of methods in political science text classification: Transfer learning language models for politics.* Available at SSRN 3724644.

Torregrosa, J., D'Antonio-Maceiras, S., Villar-Rodríguez, G., Hussain, A., Cambria, E., & Camacho, D. (2023). A mixed approach for aggressive political discourse analysis on Twitter. *Cognitive Computation, 15*(2), 440–465.

Turin, M. (2007). *Linguistic diversity and the preservation of endangered languages: A case study from Nepal.* International Centre for Integrated Mountain Development (ICIMOD).

Vahdat-Nejad, H., Akbari, M. G., Salmani, F., Azizi, F., & Nili-Sani, H. R. (2023). *Russia-Ukraine war: Modelling and clustering the sentiments trends of various countries.* arXiv preprint arXiv:2301.00604.

Weber, S., & Mehandru, N. (2022). The 2020s political economy of machine translation. *Business and Politics, 24*(1), 96–112.

Zhang, S., Frey, B., & Bansal, M. (2022). *How can NLP help revitalize endangered languages? A case study and roadmap for the Cherokee language.* arXiv preprint arXiv:2204.11909.

CHAPTER 8

Evolutionary Programming in Politics

8.1 Evolutionary Programming and Politics Overview

Exploring new ways to understand, predict, and respond to global issues is critical in the ever-changing political landscape. As the world grows increasingly interconnected, the complexity and unpredictability of international relations have become increasingly evident. Understanding these dynamics has traditionally been the domain of political scientists, diplomats, and international relations scholars. However, new interdisciplinary fields have begun to emerge due to advanced computational techniques. One of these fields, evolutionary programming (EP), combines computer science and international politics.

Evolutionary programming is artificial intelligence (AI) that uses mechanisms inspired by biological evolution, such as reproduction, mutation, recombination, and selection. It represents an innovative approach to problem-solving and prediction, where potential solutions evolve based on their fitness or suitability to a particular task. For example, in international politics, it can be used to model and simulate various scenarios, offering insights into potential outcomes and strategies that might not be immediately apparent to human observers (Mutalib et al., 2014; Marwala & Lagazio, 2011a; Xing & Marwala, 2018).

Evolutionary programming in politics is a new but rapidly expanding field. By developing dynamic models and simulations, it is possible to

T. Marwala, *Artificial Intelligence, Game Theory and Mechanism Design in Politics*, https://doi.org/10.1007/978-981-99-5103-1_8

investigate various scenarios, from conflict resolution and trade negotiations to climate policy and humanitarian crises. As a result, researchers and policymakers can better understand the complexities of global politics and make more informed decisions by incorporating evolutionary programming.

Combining these fields—evolutionary programming and international politics—provides a new perspective and novel solutions to long-standing problems. In this chapter, we will look at the fundamental concepts of evolutionary programming, investigate its potential applications in international politics, and consider the implications of this novel approach for the future of global relations.

8.2   Evolutionary Programming and Politics

The domain of international politics, characterized by its complex dynamics and intricate relationships, presents significant challenges for scholars and policymakers alike. Unfortunately, traditional models frequently fail to capture this. EP is one such tool emerging from the intersection of computer and biological sciences. Inspired by biological evolution, this computational strategy offers a unique perspective and approach to understanding and negotiating the complexity of international politics (Boulkaibet et al., 2014; Leke & Marwala, 2016; Mthembu et al., 2011).

EP operates through mutation, recombination, and selection mechanisms, gradually evolving a population of candidate solutions to a problem. EP can then effectively search complex solution spaces and adapt to changing environments by iteratively evaluating and refining these solutions based on their fitness or suitability.

The potential for EP in international politics is vast, offering a new approach to understanding and managing complex global dynamics. It can be used to resolve conflicts. EP can assist in identifying effective paths to peace by modelling international conflicts and simulating various strategies and potential resolutions. It can be used in commercial negotiations. Trade agreements are the result of complicated talks involving several elements. EP can provide a way to explore this complexity, simulating potential agreements and optimizing negotiation strategies. It can be applied to climate change policies. EP can be used to simulate how nations interact as they develop and implement climate change policies, assisting in identifying strategies that balance national interests and global environmental needs. It can be applied to diplomacy and international relations: The complex web of international relationships can be simulated and analyzed through EP, providing insights into the dynamics of diplomatic interactions and helping to devise effective strategies for maintaining and enhancing international relations. The application of EP can improve the prediction of future political trends and events by providing a deeper understanding of the potential impacts of policy decisions through its ability to simulate and analyze complex dynamics. This enables proactive and effective governance. Furthermore, it can promote international cooperation, fostering more effective global problem-solving and leading to more amicable international relations.

8.3   Genetic Algorithms and Politics

The complexities of international politics present a significant challenge for researchers and policymakers seeking to comprehend and navigate the ever-changing landscape of global relations. The complexity of international affairs grows exponentially as the world becomes more interconnected, making traditional models and methods less effective. In response to this challenge, interdisciplinary approaches have emerged that combine computer science and political science, seeking innovative ways to understand and address the complexities of global politics.

The use of genetic algorithms in international politics is one such technique, which provides new insights and answers to age-old problems (Bacao et al., 2005; Borji, 2007; Chou et al., 2007; Ivanova & Tagarev, 2000; Šetinc et al., 2015). Genetic algorithms are a subset of evolutionary algorithms and are computational models inspired by biological evolution principles (Abdella & Marwala, 2005; Duma et al., 2013; Marwala, 2002; Marwala & Chakraverty, 2006; Marwala et al., 2007; Perez & Marwala, 2012). Genetic algorithms employ a variety of evolutionary mechanisms, including selection, crossover, mutation, and reproduction, to search for optimal solutions to complex problems. As a result, even in complicated and dynamic contexts, genetic algorithms can create highly effective tactics and outcomes by iteratively refining potential solutions through generations.

Understanding complex, dynamic systems through genetic algorithms in international politics is intriguing. While the specific implementation in global politics may vary depending on the particular problem, here is a general framework that could be used:

Step 1: Generate an initial population of potential solutions. Each solution in international politics may represent a specific strategy or policy. The representation could be a string of binary or real numbers, each representing a feature of the strategy or policy.

Step 2 Fitness Evaluation: Use a fitness function to evaluate each solution. The fitness function should be constructed to assess how well a strategy or program performs in a simulated political environment. The fitness function, for example, may assess how much a policy reduces conflict, promotes cooperation, or achieves a balance of power.

Step 3: Based on their fitness scores, choose solutions for reproduction. Solutions with greater fitness scores are more likely to be chosen, indicating more effective methods or policies.

Step 4 Crossover (Recombination): Pair selected solutions and combine them to create new solutions. This could entail combining features from each parent solution to create offspring solutions.

Step 5: Introduce random changes to the offspring solutions to maintain diversity and prevent premature convergence on suboptimal solutions. This could entail changing aspects of the strategy or policy at random.

Step 6: Replace the old solution population with the new population of offspring solutions.

Step 7: Check to see if a termination condition has been met. This could be reaching the maximum number of iterations, achieving a satisfactory fitness score, or observing no significant improvement over a long period.

Step 8: If the termination condition is met, the algorithm comes to a halt and returns the best solution found. According to the fitness function, the best solution, in this context, would be the most effective strategy or policy.

Remember that in any application of genetic algorithms, including international politics, the representation of solutions, the fitness function, and the genetic operators (selection, crossover, mutation), must be carefully designed to suit the specific problem and ensure meaningful results.

Genetic algorithms can transform international politics by revealing new insights into the behavior of states, non-state actors, and global institutions. Conflict resolution is a key area where genetic algorithms can be applied. By modelling conflicts and simulating various negotiation strategies, genetic algorithms can help identify optimal solutions for peaceful resolution and prevent the escalation of hostilities. In trade and economic policy, genetic algorithms can provide insights into the most beneficial arrangements for participating nations and predict the potential outcomes of various policy decisions by simulating trade agreements and economic policies. We can use genetic algorithms to simulate the complex interactions between nations in developing and implementing climate change policies, assisting in identifying cooperative strategies that maximize global environmental benefits. In diplomacy and coalition building, genetic algorithms can help uncover effective strategies for fostering cooperation and collaboration among nations, even in the face of deep disagreements and diverging interests, by simulating diplomatic interactions and alliance formation. Incorporating genetic algorithms into the study and practice of international politics has far-reaching implications. Improved decision-making through offering a fuller awareness of the potential consequences of policy actions is one of the potential benefits. Decision-makers can use genetic algorithms to develop more effective solutions for addressing global concerns. Genetic algorithms enhance predictive capabilities and offer more accurate predictions of future events and trends, allowing nations to anticipate better and respond to emerging threats and opportunities. Genetic algorithms identify mutually advantageous techniques and foster a shared knowledge of complicated situations by encouraging collaboration. Genetic algorithms can help nations cooperate and approach global challenges more collaboratively.

8.4 Ant Colony Optimization and Politics

With its intricate dynamics and often unpredictable outcomes, international politics presents an ongoing challenge for understanding, managing, and predicting global interactions. The field is marked by complex problems requiring high-level decision-making strategies, often under time pressure and with incomplete information. As the world becomes more interconnected, the demand for creative problem-solving methods has never been greater. In response, an interdisciplinary approach that combines computer science principles with international politics has emerged. One such promising technique is the application of Ant Colony Optimization (ACO) algorithms to global political dynamics

(Leke & Marwala, 2019; Ranjan et al., 2018; Mpanza & Marwala, 2011; Selvaraj et al., 2016; Xing et al., 2010).

Ant Colony Optimization is a probabilistic technique for solving computational problems that mimic the behavior of ants in finding paths from the colony to food sources. Despite their simple individual behavior, ants use pheromone trails to identify an optimized network of paths. The ACO algorithm applies this principle to find optimal solutions to complex problems by exploring multiple paths and gradually favoring the most successful ones. When applied to international politics, it could be used to optimize decision-making processes or strategies. Here is a general framework:

Step 1 Initialization: Define the problem space. This could be a set of international policy decisions, strategies, or policies. Initialize pheromone levels on all paths. Pheromone levels represent the desirability of a path (decision, strategy, or policy).

Step 2 Ant Deployment: Distribute the "ants" (simulated agents) along various decision points (paths). Each ant symbolizes a possible solution or decision-making process.

Step 3 Construction of Solutions: Each ant constructs a solution by moving through the decision space according to some heuristic information (the problem-specific knowledge) and pheromone levels (the collective knowledge). The movement typically favors paths with higher pheromone levels, simulating the way real ants prefer paths marked by more pheromones.

Step 4: Update Pheromone Levels: Once all ants have built their solutions, update the pheromone levels on the paths. Pheromone evaporation occurs initially, lowering the level of pheromones on all pathways to replicate natural evaporation. Then, ants deposit pheromones on their paths, with more successful ants (those with better solutions) depositing more pheromones.

Step 5 Solution Assessment: Evaluate the solutions constructed by the ants using a problem-specific fitness function. The fitness function in international politics could assess the effectiveness of a strategy, policy, or decision based on various factors such as conflict resolution, cooperation promotion, or power balance.

Step 6: Check to see if a termination condition has been met. This could be a set number of iterations, a good fitness score, or a lack of significant improvement over several iterations.

Step 7: If the termination condition is met, the algorithm terminates and returns the best solution found.

In an international politics context, ACO could be used to explore a wide variety of potential solutions to complex problems, considering both the collective wisdom of past solutions (pheromone trails) and problem-specific knowledge (heuristics). Of course, the specific implementation would depend on the exact nature of the problem.

Applying the principles of ACO to international politics has the potential to revolutionize our understanding of global dynamics and provide innovative solutions to complex problems (Hou et al., 2014; Kumar et al., 2018; Mi et al., 2015; Toksarı, 2007). Key areas where ACO can be applied include conflict resolution, where ACO algorithms can help discover optimal approaches to peaceful outcomes, aiding in conflict avoidance and peace-building projects. Furthermore, trade agreements can be considered complex optimization problems in trade negotiations—each party seeking to maximize its benefits. ACO provides new insights into achieving mutually beneficial agreements by simulating different negotiation strategies and outcomes. Furthermore, in diplomatic strategy, countries must navigate complex networks of relationships and interests. ACO algorithms can simulate these networks and recommend optimal diplomatic methods, helping to establish alliances and manage international relations.

8.5   Particle Swarm Optimization and Politics

International politics is a complex and dynamic system defined by various actors, interests, and forces interacting randomly. Traditional methods of analysis and prediction often struggle to capture the nuanced intricacies of this system, necessitating innovative approaches that can handle such complexity. The implementation of Particle Swarm Optimization (PSO) algorithms is one strategy that has developed from the cross-pollination of computer science, biological and political sciences (Boulkaibet et al., 2015, 2017; Mthembu et al., 2011; Marwala et al., 2018). This interdisciplinary method can revolutionize our understanding of international politics and provide novel solutions to some of the world's most pressing issues.

Particle Swarm Optimization is a computational method that optimizes a problem by iteratively trying to improve a candidate solution. Inspired by the social behavior of bird flocking or fish schooling, PSO involves a group (or swarm) of potential solutions (particles) moving in the search space to find the best outcome. Each particle's movement is influenced by its personal best-known position and the overall best-known position of the swarm. Through this process, the swarm gradually converges toward the optimal solution. Here are the steps to apply PSO in the context of international politics:

> *Step 1:* Define the problem that has to be optimized in international politics. This could be optimizing diplomatic strategies, resource allocation, policy decisions, etc.
>
> *Step 2 Solution Representation*: Determine how the potential solutions will be represented in the system. This could be vectors, strings, or other data structures representing political strategies or decisions.
>
> *Step 3:* Create a random population of particles (potential solutions). Each particle represents a potential strategy or decision in the political scenario. Initialize the velocity for each particle.
>
> *Step 4 Objective Function Definition*: Define an objective function that quantifies the quality or fitness of a solution. This could be a measure of the effectiveness of a strategy or policy in achieving a desired outcome.
>
> *Step 5:* Using the objective function, assess the fitness of each particle.
>
> *Step 6 Update Personal and Global Bests*: For each particle, compare its fitness with its personal best fitness. If the current fitness is better, then update the personal best position. Also, compare the fitness of each particle with the global best fitness. If the fitness of any particle improves, the global best position is updated.
>
> *Step 7*: Update each particle's velocity by taking into account its previous velocity, the distance from its personal best location, and the global best position. Use this velocity to update each particle's position.
>
> *Step 8:* Check to see if a termination condition has been met. This could be due to a maximum number of iterations, a satisfactory fitness score, or a lack of significant improvement across multiple iterations.
>
> *Step 9:* If the termination condition is met, the algorithm is terminated, and the global best position found thus far is returned. This reflects the optimized strategy or decision.

The specific implementation of PSO would depend on the exact nature of the problem in international politics. The design of the solution representation, the objective function, and the parameters utilized to update the velocity and position are critical to the PSO algorithm's efficacy.

PSO has enormous potential in international politics, bringing novel ways to many complex challenges. In conflict resolution, PSO can be used to model conflicts and simulate various resolution strategies, identifying potential paths toward peaceful outcomes. Trade agreements frequently involve several variables and interests. By treating each prospective agreement as a particle in the swarm, PSO may simulate and optimize negotiation processes, aiding in forging mutually advantageous agreements. In the face of global climate change, countries must collaborate to reduce greenhouse gas emissions. PSO can simulate the numerous possibilities and consequences, assisting in identifying optimal methods that balance environmental sustainability and economic growth. Finally, PSO can be used to simulate diplomatic strategies and the complex web of international relationships, allowing for insights into effective policymaking and alliance-building.

8.6   SIMULATED ANNEALING AND POLITICS

Understanding and predicting the outcomes of various actions are critical in the complex world of international politics. However, as global dynamics become more intertwined and complicated, traditional models and methodologies fail to keep up. However, the cross-disciplinary fusion of computer science and physical science has given rise to innovative approaches that can handle such complexity. Simulated annealing (SA), a probabilistic strategy, has been applied to international politics (Patel & Marwala, 2012; Perez & Marwala, 2012; Marwala, 2010; Marwala & Lagazio, 2011b; Siddique & Adeli, 2016). This method can potentially transform our knowledge of global politics and give novel answers to important issues.

SA is a probabilistic technique used to approximate the solution to an optimization problem. The idea was inspired by the metallurgical process of annealing, which involves heating and controlled cooling of a material to increase the size of its crystals and reduce defects. Similarly, the SA algorithm examines a problem's solution space, accepting not just better but also, on occasion, worse solutions in order to avoid becoming caught in local minima. This provides a natural law explanation of the concept of strategic retreat in order to succeed. Furthermore, this approach allows for a more thorough examination of potential solutions, increasing the likelihood of discovering the global optimum. Here are some examples of how it might be used in international politics:

Step 1: Clearly define the optimization problem within international politics. This could include increasing diplomatic achievement, reducing conflict, or improving resource allocation.

Step 2 Initial Solution: At random, generate an initial solution. This solution will be used to kick off the search process.

Step 3 Objective Function: Define an objective function that can measure the quality or fitness of a solution. The objective function could, for example, quantify the effectiveness of a diplomatic approach or a policy choice.

Step 4 Temperature Schedule: Create a temperature schedule. The temperature in SA represents the algorithm's willingness to accept less desirable solutions during the search process. It usually starts out hot (to encourage solution space exploration) and gradually cools down (to focus the search on the best-found solutions).

Step 5: Create a neighborhood function that creates new potential solutions based on the present one. This could entail minor changes to the current solution.

Step 6 Iterative Process: Generate a neighbor solution for each iteration and calculate its fitness using the objective function. Move to the new solution if it is better or if a randomly generated number is less than the acceptance probability (calculated using the current temperature and the fitness difference).

Step 7 Cooling Schedule: Reduce the temperature in accordance with the *cooling* schedule and repeat the process iteratively.

Step 8: The algorithm terminates when the temperature reaches a predetermined minimum value, after a certain number of iterations without improvement, or when a solution meeting the requirements is found.

Step 9 Result: The best solution found during the search process is the final solution. This is an optimum strategy or decision for the problem defined in *Step 1.*

This procedure outlines how to use SA in international politics. Specific details can be fine-tuned according to the complexity and requirements of the specific political problem at hand. The use of simulated annealing in international politics offers a transformative approach to understanding and addressing complex global challenges. First, SA can be used to model and simulate various conflict scenarios and resolution processes, providing insights into potential approaches toward peaceful outcomes. A trade agreement, for example, necessitates complex negotiations with numerous variables. SA can be used to evaluate each possible agreement, and negotiation strategies can be optimized to reach a mutually beneficial agreement. Second, SA can be used to model the complex interactions between nations when developing and implementing climate policies, assisting in identifying strategies that maximize global benefits while balancing national interests. Third, using SA, the web of international ties can be replicated, providing insights into diplomatic interaction dynamics and assisting in developing effective diplomatic tactics. Fourth, by better comprehending the probable repercussions of policy actions, SA can strengthen global political decision-making processes. Using SA to predict future political dynamics can provide more accurate predictions, allowing for more proactive and effective responses. Finally, by identifying mutually beneficial strategies, SA can promote international cooperation and contribute to more effective global problem-solving.

8.7 Artificial Immune System and Politics

The Artificial Immune System (AIS) is a computational system inspired by human immune system principles and processes. It is designed to adapt and learn from its surroundings to identify and eliminate risks, just like the biological immune system does. Using AIS in international politics opens up intriguing possibilities, ranging from predictive modelling to policy optimization. This section explores AIS's potential role and political implications (Duma et al., 2012, 2013; Duma & Twala, 2018; Huang et al., 2013; Muhammad Nasir et al., 2009).

AIS can model complex political situations due to its ability to learn, adapt, and remember. It can analyze massive amounts of data from various sources, identify patterns, and forecast future political trends. This can provide policymakers with valuable insights and assist them in making informed decisions.

For example, by analyzing various data sources such as news reports, social media feeds, and economic indicators, an AIS model could be trained to detect early warning signs of political instability or conflict. By recognizing these patterns, the model could potentially predict the outbreak of conflict, allowing for early intervention and conflict prevention.

Moreover, AIS could be utilized to optimize policy decisions. Policies can be thought of as a set of constantly tested and evaluated strategies, much like the immune system tests different antibodies to combat pathogens. Using AIS, policies might be regularly changed and improved based on their effectiveness in obtaining intended results. Here is an example of how AIS might be used in politics:

> *Step 1:* Define the issue or decision-making process that must be optimized in the context of politics. This could be predicting political instability, optimizing policy decisions, or any other relevant problem.
>
> *Step 2 Representation*: Determine how political strategies, policies, or decisions are represented in the system. This could be a string of numbers, each representing a feature of the strategy or policy.
>
> *Step 3 Initialization*: Generate a population of random solutions (antibodies). Each solution is a possible strategy or policy.
>
> *Step 4:* Create an affinity *measure* (akin to the fitness function in evolutionary algorithms) to assess how well each solution answers the problem. This measure could assess the effectiveness of a strategy or policy in achieving a desired outcome.
>
> *Step 5*: Based on the affinity measure, select a subset of the best cloning solutions. The chosen solutions are then cloned (replicated), with the number of clones increasing in direct proportion to their affinity.
>
> *Step 6*: Hypermutate the copied solutions. The mutation rate is usually inversely proportional to the affinity of the solution; solutions with lower affinity have higher mutation rates.
>
> *Step 7*: Select the best solutions from the original and the modified clones for the next generation.
>
> *Step 8 Maintain variation (Optional):* To maintain variation in the population and avoid early convergence to suboptimal solutions, add new random solutions into the population.

Step 9 Termination Check: Check if a termination condition has been met. This could be a maximum number of iterations, a satisfactory affinity score, or a lack of significant improvement over time.
Step 10: If the termination condition is met, the algorithm terminates and returns the best solution discovered.

This basic approach can be tweaked and extended to suit the individual political challenge. The AIS, for example, might combine other immunological-inspired techniques such as immune network theory or negative selection. To ensure meaningful results, the representation of solutions, the affinity measure, and the AIS operators must be carefully designed.

The use of AIS in politics has serious consequences. On the one hand, it has the potential to lead to more effective and responsive policymaking, thereby improving international stability and collaboration. On the other hand, it creates serious ethical and security concerns. Ethically, using AIS in international politics requires careful consideration of transparency, accountability, and data privacy. Like other AI systems, AIS models can be opaque, making it difficult to grasp how they generate predictions or choices. This could raise questions of accountability, especially if AIS-based choices considerably impact international relations.

8.8 CONCLUSION

Traditional models and approaches frequently fail to represent and forecast the complicated dynamics of international politics. Incorporating evolutionary programming, a computational technique inspired by the mechanisms of biological evolution, offers a powerful new tool for understanding and navigating these complexities. As a result, EP can increase decision-making processes, boost predictive capacities, and promote international cooperation by modelling and assessing an extensive range of prospective situations and strategies. The use of EP in fields such as conflict resolution, trade negotiations, climate change policy, and diplomacy demonstrates this approach's revolutionary potential. Combining EP and politics could provide invaluable insights and facilitate more effective, proactive governance as we grapple with pressing global issues and challenges. The intersection of computer science and political science, exemplified by the application of EP to international politics, represents a promising and exciting frontier in our quest to understand and shape our interconnected world. As we move forward, researching further and utilizing the potential of such interdisciplinary approaches are crucial. By doing so, we can arm ourselves with the cutting-edge tools and perspectives required to navigate the changing landscape of global politics and work toward a more peaceful and sustainable future.

References

Abdella, M., & Marwala, T. (2005). The use of genetic algorithms and neural networks to approximate missing data in database. *In IEEE 3rd International Conference on Computational Cybernetics, ICCC 2005* (pp. 207–212)

Bacao, F., Lobo, V., & Painho, M. (2005). Applying genetic algorithms to zone design. *Soft Computing, 9*, 341–348.

Borji, A. (2007). A new global optimization algorithm inspired by parliamentary political competitions. In *Proceedings of the 6th Mexican International Conference on Artificial Intelligence, MICAI 2007: Advances in Artificial Intelligence, November 4–10, 2007, Aguascalientes, Mexico* (pp. 61–71). Springer Berlin Heidelberg.

Boulkaibet, I., Mthembu, L., De Lima Neto, F., & Marwala, T. (2015). Finite element model updating using fish school search and volitive particle swarm optimization. *Integrated Computer-Aided Engineering, 22*(4), 361–376.

Boulkaibet, I., Mthembu, L., Marwala, T., Friswell, M. I., & Adhikari, S. (2014). Finite element model updating using the separable shadow hybrid Monte Carlo technique. In *Proceedings of the 32nd IMAC a Conference and Exposition on Structural Dynamics 2014 Topics in Modal Analysis II, Volume 8* (pp. 267–275). Springer International Publishing.

Boulkaibet, I., Marwala, T., Friswell, M. I., Khodaparast, H. H., & Adhikari, S. (2017). Fuzzy finite element model updating using metaheuristic optimization algorithms. In *Proceedings of the 35th IMAC a Conference and Exposition on Structural Dynamics 2017 Special Topics in Structural Dynamics, Volume 6* (pp. 91–101). Springer International Publishing.

Chou, C. I., Chu, Y. L., & Li, S. P. (2007). Evolutionary strategy for political districting problem using genetic algorithm. In *Proceedings of the 7th International Conference on Computational Science–ICCS 2007, Beijing, China, May 27–30, 2007, Part IV 7* (pp. 1163–1166). Springer Berlin Heidelberg.

Duma, M., Marwala, T., Twala, B., & Nelwamondo, F. (2013). Partial imputation of unseen records to improve classification using a hybrid multi-layered artificial immune system and genetic algorithm. *Applied Soft Computing, 13*(12), 4461–4480.

Duma, M., & Twala, B. (2018). Optimizing latent features using artificial immune system in collaborative filtering for recommender systems. *Applied Soft Computing, 71*, 183–198.

Duma, M., Twala, B., Marwala, T., & Nelwamondo, F. V. (2012). Classification with missing data using multi-layered artificial immune systems. In *2012 IEEE Congress on Evolutionary Computation* (pp. 1–8)

Hou, J., Mi, W., & Sun, J. (2014). Optimal spatial allocation of water resources based on Pareto ant colony algorithm. *International Journal of Geographical Information Science, 28*(2), 213–233.

Huang, K., Liu, X., Li, X., Liang, J., & He, S. (2013). An improved artificial immune system for seeking the Pareto front of land-use allocation problem in large areas. *International Journal of Geographical Information Science, 27*(5), 922–946.

Ivanova, P. I., & Tagarev, T. D. (2000). Indicator space configuration for early warning of violent political conflicts by genetic algorithms. *Annals of Operations Research, 97*, 287–311.

Kumar, P. M., Manogaran, G., Sundarasekar, R., Chilamkurti, N., & Varatharajan, R. (2018). Ant colony optimization algorithm with internet of vehicles for intelligent traffic control system. *Computer Networks, 144*, 154–162.

Leke, C. A., & Marwala, T. (2019). *Deep learning and missing data in engineering systems* (p. 179). Springer International Publishing.

Leke, C., & Marwala, T. (2016). Missing data estimation in high-dimensional datasets: A swarm intelligence-deep neural network approach. In *Proceedings of the 7th International Conference and Advances in Swarm Intelligence, ICSI 2016, Bali, Indonesia, June 25–30, 2016, Part I 7* (pp. 259–270). Springer International Publishing.

Marwala, T. (2010). *Finite-element-model updating using computational intelligence techniques*. Springer.

Marwala, T. (2002). Finite element model updating using wavelet data and genetic algorithm. *Journal of Aircraft, 39*(4), 709–711.

Marwala, T., & Chakraverty, S. (2006). Fault classification in structures with incomplete measured data using autoassociative neural networks and genetic algorithm. *Current Science*, 542–548.

Marwala, T., De Wilde, P., Correia, L., Mariano, P., Ribeiro, R., Abramov, V., Szirbik, N., & Goossenaerts, J. (2007). *Scalability and optimization of a committee of agents using genetic algorithm*. arXiv preprint arXiv:0705.1757.

Marwala, T., & Lagazio, M. (2011a). *Militarized conflict modeling using computational intelligence*. Springer Science & Business Media.

Marwala, T., & Lagazio, M. (2011b). Simulated annealing optimized rough sets for modeling interstate conflict. In *Militarized conflict modeling using computational intelligence* (pp. 165–182).

Mbuvha, R., Boulkaibet, I., Marwala, T., & de Lima Neto, F. B. (2018). A hybrid ga-pso adaptive neuro-fuzzy inference system for short-term wind power prediction. In *Proceedings of the 9th International Conference on Advances in Swarm Intelligence, ICSI 2018, Shanghai, China, June 17–22, 2018, Part I 9* (pp. 498–506). Springer International Publishing.

Mi, N., Hou, J., Mi, W., & Song, N. (2015). Optimal spatial land-use allocation for limited development ecological zones based on the geographic information system and a genetic ant colony algorithm. *International Journal of Geographical Information Science, 29*(12), 2174–2193.

Mpanza, L. J., & Marwala, T. (2011). Ant colony optimization of rough set for HV bushings fault detection. In *The Fourth International Workshop on Advanced Computational Intelligence* (pp. 97–102)

Mthembu, L., Marwala, T., Friswell, M. I., & Adhikari, S. (2011). Finite element model selection using Particle Swarm Optimization. In *Dynamics of Civil Structures, Volume 4: Proceedings of the 28th IMAC, A Conference on Structural Dynamics, 2010* (pp. 41–52). Springer New York.

Muhammad Nasir, A. N., Selamat, A., & Selamat, M. H. (2009). Web mining for Malaysia's political social networks using artificial immune system. In *Knowledge Acquisition: Approaches, Algorithms and Applications: Pacific Rim Knowledge Acquisition Workshop, PKAW 2008, Hanoi, Vietnam, December 15–16, 2008, Revised Selected Papers 10* (pp. 137–146). Springer Berlin Heidelberg.

Mutalib, N. H. A., Dahlan, N. Y., Abon, S. A., Rajemi, M. F., Nawi, M. N. M., & Baharum, F. (2014). Optimum generation mix for Malaysia's additional capacity using evolutionary programming. In *2014 IEEE International Conference on Power and Energy (PECon)* (pp. 65–70).

Patel, P. B., & Marwala, T. (2012). Optimization of fuzzy inference system field classifiers using genetic algorithms and simulated annealing. In *Proceedings of the 13th International Conference on Engineering Applications of Neural Networks, EANN 2012, London, UK, September 20–23, 2012* (pp. 21–30). Springer Berlin Heidelberg.

Perez, M., & Marwala, T. (2012, November). Microarray data feature selection using hybrid genetic algorithm simulated annealing. In *2012 IEEE 27th Convention of Electrical and Electronics Engineers in Israel* (pp. 1–5).

Ranjan, A., Selvaraj, R., Kuthadi, V. M., & Marwala, T. (2018). Stealthy attacks in MANET to detect and counter measure by ant colony optimization. In *Advances in Electronics, Communication and Computing: ETAEERE-2016* (pp. 591–603). Springer Singapore.

Selvaraj, R., Madhav Kuthadi, V., & Marwala, T. (2016). Ant-based distributed denial of service detection technique using roaming virtual honeypots. *IET Communications, 10*(8), 929–935.

Šetinc, M., Gradišar, M., & Tomat, L. (2015). Optimization of a highway project planning using a modified genetic algorithm. *Optimization, 64*(3), 687–707.

Siddique, N., & Adeli, H. (2016). Simulated annealing, its variants and engineering applications. *International Journal on Artificial Intelligence Tools, 25*(6), 1630001.

Toksarı, M. D. (2007). Ant colony optimization approach to estimate energy demand of Turkey. *Energy Policy, 35*(8), 3984–3990.

Xing, B., Gao, W. J., Nelwamondo, F. V., Battle, K., & Marwala, T. (2010). Ant colony optimization for automated storage and retrieval system. In *IEEE Congress on Evolutionary Computation* (pp. 1–7)

Xing, B., & Marwala, T. (2018). Smart maintenance for human–robot interaction. In *Studies in systems, decision and control* (pp. 3–19). Springer.

CHAPTER 9

Cybersecurity in Politics

9.1 What is Cybersecurity?

As we progress into the twenty-first century, our reliance on technology grows, weaving a complex web of digital interconnectivity that permeates nearly every aspect of our lives. Yet, while driving extraordinary development and comfort, this digital transition raises several security vulnerabilities (Tonge et al., 2013). Cybersecurity, the practice of protecting our digital infrastructure, data, and online activities from malicious attacks, has thus become a critical concern in this era of pervasive digital connectivity (see Fig. 9.1).

The importance of cybersecurity cannot be overstated. With governments, corporations, and individuals storing vast amounts of sensitive data digitally, the potential consequences of a cyberbreach can be catastrophic. As a result, cyberattacks represent substantial hazards to our privacy, economic stability, and national security, from the theft of personal identities to the interruption of essential infrastructure.

Cybersecurity threats range from relatively harmless pranks to dangerous cybercrime. Viruses, malware, phishing, ransomware, and denial-of-service attacks are among the threats, with more sophisticated methods constantly emerging. Furthermore, state-sponsored cyber warfare and espionage complicate an already complex threat landscape.

Businesses, in particular, face significant cybersecurity risks. With financial transactions, confidential business information, and customer data

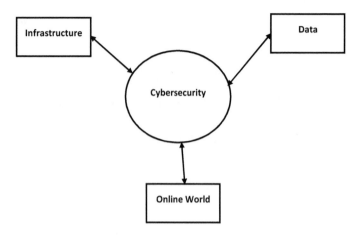

Fig. 9.1 Critical issues that necessitate cybersecurity

mainly occurring online, corporations are attractive targets for cybercriminals. The economic ramifications of a breach can be enormous in terms of financial loss as well as reputational and customer trust damage.

Governments must deal with threats to national infrastructure and state security in the meantime. However, cybersecurity is a personal concern as well as a business and government concern. With social media, online banking, and digital communications forming integral parts of our daily lives, we must all take steps to safeguard our personal information from potential attacks.

Combating cyber threats is a multifaceted endeavor. It all starts with strong technological defenses like firewalls, encryption, and intrusion detection systems. However, technology alone is insufficient. Good cybersecurity hygiene, including regular updates and patches, strong passwords, and vigilant behavior regarding suspicious emails or links, is equally important. As a result, education about common cyber threats and how to avoid them is an essential component of a comprehensive cybersecurity strategy.

Moreover, effective cybersecurity requires global cooperation. Because of the internet's transnational nature, cyber threats can originate anywhere and affect anyone. To address this global challenge, international collaborations and agreements are required.

9.2   CYBERSECURITY AND POLITICS

In the contemporary political landscape, cybersecurity has emerged as a critical element. With the rising reliance on digital platforms for government, diplomacy, and elections, the need for comprehensive cybersecurity measures has never been greater (Kuthadi et al., 2018; Marais & Marwala, 2004; Ranjan et al., 2018; Selvaraj et al., 2015a, 2015b; 2016a). This chapter addresses the role of cybersecurity in politics, its ramifications, and the issues states confront in maintaining the digital security of their political processes (Backman, 2023; Egloff & Shires, 2023; Kalra & Tanwar, 2023; Sharikov, 2023).

Cybersecurity has become increasingly important in international politics. States increasingly use cyber operations to achieve strategic goals, ranging from cyber espionage to cyber warfare. State-sponsored cyber operations include the infamous Stuxnet attack on Iran's nuclear facilities[1] and alleged Russian meddling in the 2016 US presidential election.[2] Such actions have far-reaching political consequences, affecting diplomatic relations, national security, and the balance of power among governments.

Furthermore, cybersecurity is a significant concern in administering free and fair elections. Election processes are becoming more vulnerable to cyber threats as they become more digitized. Cyberattacks can be used to influence election results, spread disinformation, or disrupt the voting process, weakening election integrity and public trust in democratic institutions. During the 2016 US presidential election, for example, hacking the Democratic National Committee's email system demonstrated how cyber threats could influence political discourse and public opinion.[3]

Cybersecurity also plays a vital role in internal politics. Governments increasingly rely on digital infrastructure to deliver public services, necessitating strong cybersecurity measures to safeguard sensitive data and ensure service continuity. Cyber threats can potentially disrupt these services, compromise citizens' data, and erode public trust in government.

---

[1] https://www.trellix.com/en-us/security-awareness/ransomware/what-is-stuxnet. html.

[2] https://www.fbi.gov/wanted/cyber/russian-interference-in-2016-u-s-elections.

[3] https://www.washingtonpost.com/world/national-security/how-the-russians-hacked-the-dnc-and-passed-its-emails-to-wikileaks/2018/07/13/af19a828-86c3-11e8-8553-a3c e89036c78_story.html.

Despite growing recognition of cybersecurity's importance in politics, states face significant challenges in ensuring cybersecurity. Cybersecurity is challenging due to the global nature of cyber threats, the rapid rate of technical change, and the complexity of digital ecosystems. Furthermore, the absence of international norms and agreements on state behavior in cyberspace makes preventing and responding to cyberattacks more difficult.

As a result, governments are grappling with developing comprehensive cybersecurity strategies. These strategies must strike a balance between the need for security, respect for individual privacy rights, and the internet's openness. They must also include measures to strengthen cybersecurity capacity, raise public awareness, and foster international cooperation.

Furthermore, states must work to establish international norms and agreements governing state behavior in cyberspace. Such norms can provide a framework for cooperation, deterrence, and conflict resolution in cyberspace, contributing to stability in international relations.

In the digital age, cybersecurity is inextricably linked to the political landscape. As states traverse the complicated cyber-political environment, a comprehensive knowledge of cybersecurity in politics is vital. Cybersecurity is not just a technical issue; it is a political issue that requires political solutions. Therefore, policymakers must engage with cybersecurity as a critical component of their political and diplomatic strategies, focusing on building resilience, fostering cooperation, and promoting responsible behavior in cyberspace.

9.3   TYPES OF CYBERSECURITY

In today's political context, cybersecurity has become critical to national security, public policy, and global relations. As the digital sphere increasingly permeates all aspects of society, understanding the types of cybersecurity relevant to politics is crucial (Li & Liu, 2021). This study provides a comprehensive understanding of how cybersecurity measures protect the integrity of political processes, protect national interests, and keep international relations stable.

Network security is critical for maintaining network and data integrity and usability. It comprises both hardware and software systems that prevent illegal infiltration. Network security is essential to a political context for protecting sensitive government data and ensuring the smooth operation of digital infrastructure. It is also crucial in protecting electoral systems from cyber threats and ensuring the integrity and reliability of democratic processes.

Application security is concerned with keeping software and devices safe from threats. As more government services move online, application security has become a critical political concern. Secure applications are essential to protect citizens' data and maintain public trust. Furthermore, application security can aid in preventing cyberattacks that exploit software flaws, a common tactic in cyber warfare.

Information security seeks to secure data confidentiality, integrity, and availability. This type of cybersecurity is critical in the political sphere for protecting sensitive information such as classified government documents, intelligence reports, and citizen data. Information security also plays a vital role in maintaining the secrecy of diplomatic communications and protecting against information warfare tactics such as disinformation campaigns.

Operational security refers to the processes and decisions for handling and securing digital assets. For example, operational security is critical in politics for managing sensitive information, especially during political campaigns or sensitive diplomatic negotiations. Access controls, network monitoring, and incident response planning are all part of it.

Disaster recovery and business continuity plans ensure systems can swiftly return to normal following a cyberattack. These plans are crucial for political institutions and processes where downtime can have serious consequences such as public unrest, loss of trust, or strategic advantage to adversaries.

9.4   Network Security and Politics

In the interconnected world of the twenty-first century, network security and international politics have become inextricably linked (Stevens, 2016). With nations becoming more dependent on digital networks for their infrastructure, communication, and defense systems, the importance of network security in the international political landscape cannot be overstated. This chapter delves into network security's role in international politics, examining its implications, challenges, and the need for global cooperation.

Network security protects a computer network and its network-accessible resources from unwanted access, misuse, or damage. In international politics, network security is crucial for protecting state secrets, maintaining the integrity of political processes, ensuring secure diplomatic communications, and defending against cyber warfare.

Conflicts between nations are fought on physical battlefields and in cyberspace in the digital age. As a result, network security is crucial in defending a country's digital infrastructure against cyberattacks ranging from data breaches and denial-of-service attacks to complex campaigns aimed at disrupting a country's economic or defense systems. Additionally, cyber espionage activities, where states attempt to infiltrate other nations' networks to gather intelligence, underscore the need for robust network security measures.

With the growing use of digital platforms for diplomatic communications and negotiations, network security is becoming increasingly important to ensure the privacy and integrity of these communications. In addition, safeguarding these channels is vital for sustaining trust and guaranteeing the smooth functioning of international relations.

As the internet grows more vital to global commerce, communication, and government, control over its infrastructure and standards has become a sensitive subject in international politics. Network security plays a crucial role in these conversations, as states must balance the need for security with considerations of privacy, freedom of expression, and economic prosperity.

Given the worldwide character of digital networks, international cooperation is essential for effective network security. This can involve sharing information about threats, coordinating responses to large-scale attacks, and establishing international norms and agreements for responsible behavior in cyberspace.

9.5   APPLICATION SECURITY AND POLITICS

In international politics, the rise of digital technology has created a new arena for interaction, negotiation, and conflict. As governments, institutions, and individuals increasingly rely on digital apps for various purposes, application security has become critical in international politics. This section discusses the significance and implications of application security in international politics, underlining the importance of this vital cybersecurity component in sustaining global stability and confidence (Enck et al., 2011; Sharma et al., 2023; Yip et al., 2009).

Application security refers to measures taken during the development lifecycle to protect applications from threats that can lead to unauthorized access, data breaches, and other vulnerabilities. In the international political landscape, application security is instrumental in ensuring the integrity and confidentiality of digital communications, protecting sensitive data, and preventing cyber threats that could undermine national security or international relations.

Digital diplomacy has emerged as an essential aspect of international relations, with applications critical in allowing nations to communicate and interact with one another. Ensuring these applications' security is vital to maintaining the privacy and integrity of diplomatic communications and fostering trust between countries.

Cyber warfare and espionage constitute substantial risks in the digital era, with state-sponsored actors often targeting apps to enter networks or access critical information. Ensuring comprehensive application security can protect against such threats, ensuring national security and international relations stability.

Many governments increasingly rely on digital applications to provide public services and engage citizens. As a result, the security of these applications is critical for protecting sensitive data and maintaining public trust and ensuring the smooth operation of government services.

Given the global nature of digital applications and the internet, international cooperation is crucial to ensure effective application security. This includes sharing information about risks, agreeing on security standards, and defining worldwide norms for responsible behavior in cyberspace.

9.6   Information Security and Politics

The proliferation of digital technologies and the world's increasing interconnectedness has increased the volume of data generated, stored, and transmitted across borders. As such, the function of information security within international politics has become critical. In this dynamic terrain, preserving sensitive data, ensuring privacy, and sustaining trust are crucial to the stability of international relations. This section explores the implications of information security in international politics and the evolving challenges that lie ahead (Eriksson & Giacomello, 2006; Tseruashvili, 2023; Wu et al., 2023).

Information security guards against unauthorized access, use, disclosure, disruption, modification, inspection, recording, or destruction of digital and analog data. In international politics, information security is essential for safeguarding state secrets, protecting citizens' privacy, ensuring the integrity of political processes, and defending against information warfare.

Cyber espionage and warfare are now commonplace in modern international conflicts, with states increasingly employing digital techniques to gain strategic advantages over their rivals. As a result, information security is critical to prevent unauthorized access to sensitive government data, military secrets, or intellectual property.

As diplomatic contacts and talks increasingly move online, the necessity for safe routes has never been more vital. Information security plays a critical role in ensuring the integrity and secrecy of these interactions, creating confidence between nations, and facilitating successful diplomacy in the digital age.

Because of the global nature of the internet and the increasing cross-border flow of data, data privacy has become a pressing issue in international politics. Nations must navigate complex questions around data sovereignty, privacy regulations, and international data-sharing agreements, making information security a central concern in these discussions.

Given the global character of the digital ecosystem, international cooperation is essential for adequate information security. This involves sharing threat intelligence, coordinating responses to large-scale cyberattacks, and establishing international norms and regulations for data privacy and security.

9.7   Operational Security and Politics

Operational security, a vital component of cybersecurity, is important in international politics, particularly in an era when digital technology supports political processes and interactions. The protection of sensitive political information from potential threats is a critical determinant in the execution of political strategies, the maintenance of national security, and the stability of international relations. This chapter explores the implications of operational security within international politics, illustrating its growing significance and the challenges it presents.

Operational security entails discovering and securing sensitive information that, if known, could be exploited to the advantage of adversaries. Operational security is critical in international politics for safeguarding diplomatic communications, protecting intelligence information, and ensuring the integrity of electoral processes, among other things (Whyte & Mazanec, 2023).

In the arena of international politics, intelligence plays a key role. Therefore, the secure handling and distribution of intelligence information are of utmost importance. In addition, operational security measures prevent intelligence leakage that could compromise national security or international relations. Furthermore, operations security includes actions against potential adversary counterintelligence efforts.

Digital diplomacy involves using digital tools and platforms for diplomatic communications and negotiations. Ensuring the operational security of these digital channels is critical to maintaining their integrity, confidentiality, and availability.

In the digital age, technology often helps electoral processes, making them possible targets for cyber threats to disrupt democratic processes. Therefore, operational security is essential to protect these processes and maintain public trust in democratic institutions.

Given the global nature of digital technologies and cyber threats, international cooperation is essential for adequate operational security. This includes working together to share threat intelligence, reach a consensus on cyber norms and standards, and coordinate responses to significant cyber incidents.

9.8   DISASTER RECOVERY, BUSINESS CONTINUITY, AND POLITICS

With its far-reaching connectivity and reliance on technology, the digital age has brought new challenges to international politics (Jiang et al., 2023; Vanichchinchai, 2023; Viveka, 2023; Young-Geun & Minjung, 2023). Among these challenges, ensuring disaster recovery and business continuity in the face of cyber threats has emerged as a critical concern. As political processes increasingly shift online and nations become more interconnected, maintaining the resilience of digital systems is paramount. This section explores the importance of disaster recovery and business continuity in international politics, focusing on safeguarding political stability and fostering international cooperation.

Disaster recovery (DR) is the strategy and measures to restore critical systems and operations after a disaster or interruption. On the other hand, business continuity (BC) involves maintaining essential functions during and after a disaster. In international politics, DR and BC are critical to ensuring the continuity of governmental operations, the support of public services, the integrity of democratic processes, and the protection of national security.

In the cyber warfare and espionage era, digital disruption threats have become integral to international conflicts. Therefore, nations must ensure robust DR and BC strategies to recover from cyberattacks and minimize their impact quickly. This involves technical measures, strategic planning, personnel training, and international cooperation.

As digital platforms become increasingly crucial for diplomatic communication and negotiation, ensuring DR and BC is vital. Any disruption to these platforms might have huge political ramifications, weakening trust and potentially leading to misinterpretation or confrontation.

With the growing use of digital applications for delivering public services, ensuring the continuity of these services is essential for maintaining public trust and social stability. This is especially important during times of crisis, when disruptions in public services can exacerbate existing problems and lead to public unrest.

Because digital systems and cyber threats are global in nature, multinational cooperation is critical for effective DR and BC. This can include sharing best practices, coordinating responses to large-scale cyberattacks, and developing international cyber resilience standards and agreements.

9.9   FIREWALLS AND INTRUSION DETECTION/PREVENTION SYSTEMS

Cyberattacks in the contemporary digital context have substantially threatened corporations, governments, and individuals. These attacks can result in financial loss, operational disruption, the compromise of sensitive information, and reputational harm. Therefore, implementing robust measures to counter cyberattacks is of utmost importance. This chapter investigates the many tools and tactics available for effectively countering cyberattacks.

One of the fundamental tools for countering cyber threats is a firewall (Bellovin & Cheswick, 1994; Bauböck & Permoser, 2023; Liang et al., 2023; Rajkumar & Arunakranthi, 2023; Saputra et al., 2023). Firewalls are a security gatekeeper between an internal network and the external internet. They monitor and control network traffic based on predefined security rules, preventing unauthorized access and malicious content.

Intrusion Detection Systems (IDS) and Intrusion Prevention Systems (IPS) are also essential. IDS tools monitor network traffic and send alerts when suspicious activity is detected. These assaults are detected, prevented, or mitigated by intrusion prevention systems (IPS) (Selvaraj et al., 2014; 2016b, 2016c; Marais & Marwala, 2007; Vilakazi & Marwala, 2006).

In international politics, the application of AI in Firewalls and Intrusion Detection/Prevention Systems is increasingly crucial (Alrajeh & Lloret, 2013; Khan et al., 2022). These technologies are central to the defense of digital infrastructure, forming the first line of defense against cyberattacks launched by state and non-state actors.

Nations' governmental, economic, and military operations increasingly rely on digital infrastructure. As a result, cybersecurity has become a top priority on a global scale. In this context, enhanced by AI, firewalls and IDS/IPS systems are critical tools, protecting against complex cyber threats that could disrupt national security, the economy, and international relations.

AI enables these systems to surpass traditional rule-based approaches and adapt to an ever-changing threat landscape. AI, for example, can learn from previous data, detect patterns, identify unusual behavior, and predict outcomes. This makes AI-powered firewalls and IDS/IPS capable of discovering new, previously undetected cyber dangers that could be employed in cyber warfare or cyber espionage activities.

Incorporating AI into cybersecurity tools has implications for cyber diplomacy and the development of international cyber norms. As AI-powered cybersecurity solutions grow more ubiquitous, it is vital to set rules and norms controlling their use, including transparency, responsibility, privacy, and the potential for misuse. This might be crucial for debates and negotiations in international forums and diplomatic interactions.

Using AI in firewalls and IDS/IPS raises concerns about cyber sovereignty. As AI-powered systems become more sophisticated, they may be able to infiltrate other countries' digital spaces, blurring the lines of cyber sovereignty. This could become a thorny problem in international relations, necessitating the creation of rules and agreements that respect and preserve cyber sovereignty.

The ability to build and deploy AI-enhanced firewalls and IDS/IPS can considerably impact worldwide power dynamics. Nations with advanced artificial intelligence capabilities may have an advantage in cyberspace, contributing to their overall strategic advantage. This could result in a cyberspace AI arms race, with nations competing to outperform each other in AI capabilities.

In conclusion, using AI in firewalls and IDS/IPS has important consequences for international politics. While it can potentially improve states' abilities to secure their digital infrastructure, it also poses issues with developing international norms, respect for cyber sovereignty, and influence on power dynamics. Policymakers and diplomats must deal with these problems to negotiate the complicated landscape of AI and cybersecurity in international politics.

9.10   Encryption and Virtual Private Networks (VPNs)

Encryption turns data into a format that can only be read with a decryption key, safeguarding the confidentiality of data both at rest and in transit (Bhanot & Hans, 2015; Davis, 1978; Fontaine & Galand, 2007; Ma & Wang, 2023; Singh & Singh, 2023). VPNs also enable an encrypted internet connection, ensuring secure communication and protecting users' privacy (Forbacha & Agwu, 2023; Naas & Fesl, 2023; Neto, 2023; Shneyderman & Casati, 2003).

AI is becoming more prevalent in cybersecurity, including encryption and VPNs (Lipp et al., 2019; Massaro et al., 2020; Nekovee et al., 2020). These developments have far-reaching consequences for international politics, affecting state security, diplomacy, privacy, and the digital economy. AI can significantly improve the effectiveness of encryption and VPNs, both of which are critical tools for securing digital communications. For instance, AI can generate and manage encryption keys more efficiently, detect anomalies in encrypted traffic, or optimize VPN routes for better performance and security. Improved encryption and VPN technology can help a state safeguard its communications, shielding vital governmental, military, and economic data from foreign opponents. However, AI can also be used by those trying to break through firewalls more effectively.

AI can influence the dynamics of cyber diplomacy as it improves the capabilities of encryption and VPN technologies. To address the challenges and opportunities presented by these advanced technologies, states may need to negotiate new international agreements. For instance, states may need to balance using AI to enhance their security and respecting individuals' and other nations' privacy and digital rights.

AI-enhanced encryption and VPNs have substantial privacy and surveillance consequences. On the one hand, they can provide individuals and organizations with more robust tools for protecting their online privacy, which could support broader digital technology adoption and the growth of the digital economy. However, the same technologies can be used for surveillance by states, potentially leading to power abuses and human rights violations.

The ability to create and deploy AI-enhanced encryption and VPN technologies can have economic consequences. States that excel in these technologies will have a competitive advantage in the expanding cybersecurity sector. Furthermore, strong encryption and VPN technologies can make e-commerce transactions safer and increase consumer trust in digital services, all of which contribute to the growth of the digital economy.

The advent of AI in encryption and VPN can potentially lead to an AI arms race in cyberspace. As these technologies advance, states may feel obligated to continuously improve their digital security capabilities in order to maintain a defensive advantage or attain superiority over prospective enemies.

Incorporating AI into encryption and VPN technologies has significant implications for international politics. While it can improve state security and help the digital economy grow, it raises concerns about privacy, surveillance, and the possibility of an AI arms race in cyberspace. States must handle these problems with caution, considering their security requirements and their responsibility to uphold digital rights and international conventions.

9.11 Security Information and Event Management Systems (SIEM)

SIEM systems consolidate and analyze log data created across the IT environment, discover abnormalities that might signal a cyberattack, and provide real-time analysis of security warnings. AI improves SIEM systems, which aggregate and analyze network activity data to provide comprehensive insights into security events and incidents within an IT environment (Bhatt et al., 2014; Muhammad et al., 2023; Novikova & Kotenko, 2013; Radoglou-Grammatikis et al., 2021; Setiawan, 2023). The application of AI in SIEM systems, and its ramifications, extends to international politics, touching upon state security, cyber diplomacy, economic interactions, and the digital arms race.

AI-enhanced SIEM solutions enable states to safeguard their digital infrastructure against cyber threats better. By leveraging machine learning algorithms, these systems can identify patterns, detect anomalies, and predict potential cyberattacks far more efficiently than traditional, rule-based systems. This capability is critical in today's international political landscape, where state-sponsored cyberattacks are an increasingly common form of aggression.

Integrating artificial intelligence into SIEM systems has implications for cyber diplomacy, particularly in developing international norms and regulations. As these technologies mature, there is a rising need for international cooperation to establish norms, share best practices, and formulate legislation that governs the use of AI in cybersecurity.

AI-enhanced SIEM systems can also impact economic relations between states. Advanced AI capabilities may give countries a competitive advantage in the global cybersecurity market, influencing international trade dynamics. Furthermore, a strong cybersecurity infrastructure supported by AI-enhanced SIEM systems can foster trust in digital services, promoting digital economy growth.

The increasing sophistication of AI-enhanced SIEM systems may contribute to a digital arms race in which states compete to outperform one another in cybersecurity capabilities. This race can lead to the development of even more advanced AI technologies but raises concerns about potential misuse and the risks of escalating cyber conflicts.

The ability to implement and use AI-enhanced SIEM systems may be restricted to wealthy states, thereby aggravating global digital disparities. Addressing these disparities through international cooperation and assistance is critical to ensuring that all states can effectively defend their digital infrastructure.

The application of AI in SIEM systems has far-reaching ramifications for international politics. While it provides significant benefits regarding increased state security and economic growth, it also raises concerns about cyber diplomacy, prospective digital weapons races, and global digital disparities. International players must traverse these hurdles and leverage the promise of AI-enhanced SIEM systems in ways that promote global security and collaboration. AI improves SIEM systems, which aggregate and analyze network activity data to provide comprehensive insights into security events and incidents within an information technology environment. The application of AI in SIEM systems, and its ramifications, extends to international politics, touching upon state security, cyber diplomacy, economic interactions, and the digital arms race.

9.12   INVESTMENT IN CYBERSECURITY

Investing in Multi-factor Authentication (MFA) technology is one way to ensure cybersecurity. MFA enhances security by requiring users to give two or more verification factors to access a resource, such as an application, online account, or VPN (Paul & Rao, 2023; Titus et al., 2023). Another option is to invest in Endpoint Protection Platforms, which provide features such as firewalls, antivirus, data encryption, and intrusion detection capabilities to protect endpoints such as desktops, laptops, and mobile devices from threats. A further option is to spend money on security awareness training. Security awareness training is essential because humans are frequently the weakest link in cybersecurity. Users can be educated on the importance of security, the threats they may face, and the best practices for maintaining security through regular training.

Institutions should create an incident response plan and instructions to detect, respond to, and recover from network security issues. It is an essential tool for mitigating the effects of a cyberattack and preventing future ones. Furthermore, it is critical to maintain systems, software, and devices up to date with the most recent updates. This is a simple but effective tool for defending against cyberattacks. Many attacks leverage known vulnerabilities already patched in later software versions. Furthermore, organizations should invest in threat intelligence platforms. Platforms for threat intelligence provide real-time information about emerging threats and actors, assisting organizations in anticipating, preparing for, and mitigating potential attacks.

Countering cyberattacks necessitates a multi-layered approach that combines tools ranging from firewalls and antivirus software to encryption, multi-factor authentication, and user education. Unfortunately, no single tool can guarantee comprehensive security against cyberattacks. As a result, organizations must use a combination of these tools, constantly assess their cybersecurity posture, and adapt their defenses to the changing threat landscape. The goal should be to develop a robust security environment to prevent attacks, identify them quickly when they happen, and react effectively to minimize damage and recover.

9.13   Conclusion

The interaction between cybersecurity and international politics has emerged as a defining feature of our modern, interconnected world. Furthermore, the shift toward a more digital global infrastructure has increased the importance of cybersecurity, which now permeates every aspect of international politics. As a result, the elements of cybersecurity are intricately woven into the fabric of international relations, from operational and information security to disaster recovery and business continuity.

They play an essential role in everything from ensuring the integrity of diplomatic communications to ensuring national security and democratic processes and facilitating the continuity of public services and international cooperation. Cyber threats, including cyber warfare and espionage, have grown in sophistication and scale, representing a new frontier of international conflict. As a result, nations must be watchful and proactive, implementing comprehensive security measures and cultivating a cybersecurity culture. Moreover, the global nature of these threats involves new levels of international collaboration, from exchanging threat intelligence and best practices to coordinating responses to large-scale cyberattacks.

However, cybersecurity challenges extend beyond the reactive and into the proactive, involving the establishment of international norms and regulations to govern behavior in cyberspace. Balancing the need for security with privacy, freedom of expression, and economic growth is a difficult task that requires careful diplomacy and negotiation.

As we progress, the intersection of cybersecurity and international politics will continue to shape our global landscape, demanding innovative solutions, effective policies, and a shared commitment to a secure and stable digital future. How nations navigate this complex and ever-changing nexus will undoubtedly play a significant role in defining the geopolitical realities of the twenty-first century.

References

Alrajeh, N. A., & Lloret, J. (2013). Intrusion detection systems based on artificial intelligence techniques in wireless sensor networks. *International Journal of Distributed Sensor Networks, 9*(10), 351047.

Backman, S. (2023). Risk vs. threat-based cybersecurity: The case of the EU. *European Security, 32*(1), 85–103.

Bauböck, R., & Permoser, J. M. (2023). Sanctuary, firewalls, regularisation: Three inclusive responses to the presence of irregular migrants. *Journal of Ethnic and Migration Studies*, 1–18.

Bellovin, S. M., & Cheswick, W. R. (1994). Network firewalls. *IEEE Communications Magazine, 32*(9), 50–57.

Bhanot, R., & Hans, R. (2015). A review and comparative analysis of various encryption algorithms. *International Journal of Security and Its Applications, 9*(4), 289–306.

Bhatt, S., Manadhata, P. K., & Zomlot, L. (2014). The operational role of security information and event management systems. *IEEE Security & Privacy, 12*(5), 35–41.

Davis, R. (1978). The data encryption standard in perspective. *IEEE Communications Society Magazine, 16*(6), 5–9.

Egloff, F. J., & Shires, J. (2023). The better angels of our digital nature? Offensive cyber capabilities and state violence. *European Journal of International Security, 8*(1), 130–149.

Enck, W., Octeau, D., McDaniel, P. D., & Chaudhuri, S. (2011). A study of android application security. In *USENIX Security Symposium* (Vol. 2, No. 2).

Eriksson, J., & Giacomello, G. (2006). The information revolution, security, and international relations: (IR) relevant theory? *International Political Science Review, 27*(3), 221–244.

Fontaine, C., & Galand, F. (2007). A survey of homomorphic encryption for nonspecialists. *EURASIP Journal on Information Security*, 1–10.

Forbacha, S. C., & Agwu, M. J. A. (2023). Design and Implementation of a Secure Virtual Private Network Over an Open Network (Internet). *American Journal of Technology, 2*(1), 1–36.

Jiang, Y., Ritchie, B. W., & Verreynne, M. L. (2023). Building dynamic capabilities in tourism organizations for disaster management: Enablers and barriers. *Journal of Sustainable Tourism, 31*(4), 971–996.

Kalra, K., & Tanwar, B. (2023). Cyber security policy in India: Examining the issues, challenges, and framework. In *Cybersecurity issues, challenges, and solutions in the business world* (pp. 120–137). IGI Global.

Khan, S. U., Eusufzai, F., Azharuddin Redwan, M., Ahmed, M., & Sabuj, S. R. (2022). Artificial intelligence for cyber security: Performance analysis of network intrusion detection. *Explainable artificial intelligence for cyber security: Next generation artificial intelligence* (pp. 113–139). Springer International Publishing.

Kuthadi, V. M., Selvaraj, R., & Marwala, T. (2016). An enhanced security pattern for wireless sensor network. In *Proceedings of the Second International Conference on Computer and Communication Technologies: IC3T 2015, Volume 2* (pp. 61–71). Springer India.

Kuthadi, V. M., Selvaraj, R., & Marwala, T. (2018). Energy efficient secure data Transmission in wireless sensor network. In *Proceedings of the First International Conference on SCI 2016, Smart Computing and Informatics, Volume 1* (pp. 275–287). Springer Singapore.

Li, Y., & Liu, Q. (2021). A comprehensive review study of cyber-attacks and cyber security; Emerging trends and recent developments. *Energy Reports, 7*, 8176–8186.

Liang, H., Li, X., Xiao, D., Liu, J., Zhou, Y., Wang, A., & Li, J. (2023). Generative pre-trained transformer-based reinforcement learning for testing web application firewalls. *IEEE Transactions on Dependable and Secure Computing.*

Lipp, B., Blanchet, B., & Bhargavan, K. (2019). A mechanized cryptographic proof of the WireGuard virtual private network protocol. In *2019 IEEE European Symposium on Security and Privacy (EuroS&P)* (pp. 231–246)

Ma, X., & Wang, C. (2023). Hyper-chaotic image encryption system based on N+ 2 ring Joseph algorithm and reversible cellular automata. *Multimedia Tools and Applications*, 1–26.

Marais, E., & Marwala, T. (2004). Predicting global Internet instability caused by worms using neural networks. In *Fifteenth Annual Symposium of the Pattern Recognition Association of South Africa* (p. 81).

Marais, E., & Marwala, T. (2007). *Predicting the presence of internet worms using novelty detection.* arXiv preprint arXiv:0705.1288.

Massaro, A., Gargaro, M., Dipierro, G., Galiano, A. M., & Buonopane, S. (2020). Prototype cross platform oriented on cybersecurity, virtual connectivity, big data and artificial intelligence control. *IEEE Access, 8*, 197939–197954.

Muhammad, A. R., Sukarno, P., & Wardana, A. A. (2023). Integrated Security Information and Event Management (SIEM) with Intrusion Detection System (IDS) for live analysis based on machine learning. *Procedia Computer Science, 217*, 1406–1415.

Naas, M., & Fesl, J. (2023). A novel dataset for encrypted virtual private network traffic analysis. *Data in Brief, 47*, 108945.

Nekovee, M., Sharma, S., Uniyal, N., Nag, A., Nejabati, R., & Simeonidou, D. (2020). Towards AI-enabled microservice architecture for network function virtualization. In *2020 IEEE Eighth International Conference on Communications and Networking (ComNet)* (pp. 1–8)

Neto, E. P. D. A. R. J. (2023). *Paying for privacy in a digital age: willingness to pay for attributes in a VPN (Virtual Private Network) service, and its relation to privacy literacy* (Instituto Universitário de Lisboa Master's thesis).

Novikova, E., & Kotenko, I. (2013). Analytical visualization techniques for security information and event management. In *2013 21st Euromicro International Conference on Parallel, Distributed, and Network-Based Processing* (pp. 519–525)

Paul, B., & Rao, M. (2023). Zero-trust model for smart manufacturing industry. *Applied Sciences, 13*(1), 221.

Radoglou-Grammatikis, P., Sarigiannidis, P., Iturbe, E., Rios, E., Martinez, S., Sarigiannidis, A., Eftathopoulos, G., Spyridis, Y., Sesis, A., Vakakis, N., & Tzovaras, D. (2021). Spear SIEM: A security information and event management system for the smart grid. *Computer Networks, 193*, 108008.

Rajkumar, B., & Arunakranthi, G. (2023). Evolution for a secured path using NexGen firewalls. In *2022 OPJU International Technology Conference on Emerging Technologies for Sustainable Development (OTCON)* (pp. 1–6)

Ranjan, A., Selvaraj, R., Kuthadi, V. M., & Marwala, T. (2018). Stealthy attacks in MANET to detect and counter measure by ant colony optimization. In *Advances in Electronics, Communication and Computing: ETAEERE-2016* (pp. 591–603). Springer Singapore.

Saputra, T. A., Khairil, K., & Rohmawan, E. P. (2023). Design and implementation of network security system using Network Management System (NMS) and Firewall on SMA N 1 Bengkulu City. *Journal Media Computer Science, 2*(1), 15–22.

Selvaraj, R., Kuthadi, V. M., & Marwala, T. (2014). Enhancing intrusion detection system performance using firecol protection services based honeypot system. *International Journal of Computer Applications, 975*, 8887.

Selvaraj, R., Kuthadi, V. M., & Marwala, T. (2015a). An effective ODAIDS-HPs approach for preventing, detecting and responding to DDoS attacks. *British Journal of Applied Science & Technology, 5*(5), 500–509.

Selvaraj, R., Marwala, T., & Kuthadi, V. M. (2015b). An efficient web services framework for secure data collection wireless sensor network. *British Journal of Political Science, 12*(1), 18–31.

Selvaraj, R., Kuthadi, M., & Marwala, T. (2016a). Ant-based distributed denial of service detection technique using roaming virtual honeypots. *IET Communications, 10*(8), 929–935.

Selvaraj, R., Kuthadi, V. M., & Marwala, T. (2016b). Honey pot: A major technique for intrusion detection. In *Proceedings of the Second International Conference on Computer and Communication Technologies: IC3T 2015, Volume 2* (pp. 73–82). Springer India.

Selvaraj, R., Kuthadi, V. M., & Marwala, T. (2016c). EIDPS: An efficient approach to protect the network and intrusion prevention. In *Information Systems Design and Intelligent Applications: Proceedings of Third International Conference INDIA 2016c, Volume 2* (pp. 35–47). Springer India.

Setiawan, H. (2023). *SIEM (Security Information Event Management) Model for Malware Attack Detection Using Suricata and Evebox* (Universitas Kristen Satya Wacana Doctoral dissertation).

Singh, M., & Singh, A. K. (2023). A comprehensive survey on encryption techniques for digital images. *Multimedia Tools and Applications*, *82*(8), 11155–11187.

Sharikov, P. (2023). Contemporary cybersecurity challenges. In *The implications of emerging technologies in the Euro-Atlantic Space: Views from the Younger Generation Leaders Network* (pp. 143–157). Springer International Publishing.

Sharma, A., Singh, S. K., Kumar, S., Chhabra, A., & Gupta, S. (2023, February). Security of android banking mobile apps: Challenges and opportunities. In *International Conference on Cyber Security, Privacy and Networking (ICSPN 2022)* (pp. 406–416). Springer International Publishing.

Shneyderman, A., & Casati, A. (2003). *Mobile VPN: Delivering advanced services in next generation wireless systems*. Wiley.

Stevens, T. (2016). *Cyber security and the politics of time*. Cambridge University Press.

Titus, A. J., Hamilton, K. E., & Holko, M. (2023). Cyber and information security in the bioeconomy. In *Cyberbiosecurity* (pp. 17–36). Springer.

Tonge, A. M., Kasture, S. S., & Chaudhari, S. R. (2013). Cyber security: Challenges for society-literature review. *IOSR Journal of Computer Engineering*, *2*(12), 67–75.

Tseruashvili, M. (2023). Cyberterrorism and its reflection on international security. In *Global perspectives on the psychology of terrorism* (pp. 253–266). IGI Global.

Vanichchinchai, A. (2023). Links between components of business continuity management: an implementation perspective. *Business Process Management Journal*, (ahead-of-print).

Vilakazi, C. B., & Marwala, T. (2006, October). Application of feature selection and fuzzy ARTMAP to intrusion detection. In *2006 IEEE International Conference on Systems, Man and Cybernetics* (Vol. 6, pp. 4880–4885)

Viveka, S. (2023). Lessons learnt from COVID-19 for business continuity management in banking sector. In *Building resilient organizations* (pp. 241–251). Routledge.

Whyte, C., & Mazanec, B. M. (2023). *Understanding cyber-warfare: Politics, policy and strategy*. Taylor & Francis.

Wu, A. Y., Hanus, B., Xue, B., & Mahto, R. V. (2023). Information security ignorance: An exploration of the concept and its antecedents. *Information & Management*, 103753.

Yip, A., Wang, X., Zeldovich, N., & Kaashoek, M. F. (2009, October). Improving application security with data flow assertions. In *Proceedings of the ACM SIGOPS 22nd Symposium on Operating Systems Principles* (pp. 291–304).

Young-Geun, K., & Minjung, J. (2023). Disaster management and COVID-19 financial support for SMEs in Korea. In *Changing law and contractual relations under COVID-19: Reallocation of social risks in Asian SME sectors* (pp. 27–41). Springer Nature Singapore.

CHAPTER 10

Social Media in Politics

10.1 What Is Social Media?

Social media has become indispensable to modern life, significantly transforming our reality. It has evolved beyond simple communication to become a business, politics, education, and entertainment platform. Because of its pervasiveness, it is a powerful force with enormous promise, but it raises significant issues about privacy, mental health, and societal peace (McCay-Peet & Quan-Haase, 2017).

Social media has drastically changed how we communicate and exchange information, from platforms like Facebook, Twitter, and Instagram to newer entrants like TikTok. It has democratized content creation by transforming consumers into creators and dismantling conventional barriers to mass communication. As a result, information, views, and ideas circulate at an unprecedented rate and breadth. This widespread democratization of knowledge has had far-reaching consequences for industries, governments, and society.

On the one hand, social media can empower and connect people. It enables us to retain contacts across long distances, form communities based on common interests, and raise awareness about social, political, and environmental issues. It has given voice to those silenced, shed light on previously unnoticed situations, and sparked societal change. #MeToo, #RhodesMustFall, #BlackLivesMatter, #FeesMustFall, and the

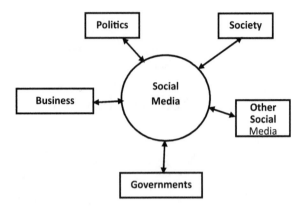

Fig. 10.1   The ecosystem of social network

Arab Spring have all demonstrated the potential of social media as a weapon for societal transformation. Figure 10.1 illustrates this.

Furthermore, social media has become critical for businesses in marketing, customer service, and public relations. It has opened up new opportunities for enterprise and creativity, from Instagram boutiques to TikTok viral marketing campaigns.

10.2   Social Media and Politics

Social media platforms have dramatically altered how individuals communicate and share information, impacting many cultural issues, including politics. Moreover, these digital platforms have expanded to affect public opinion and impact political discourse (Chekol et al., 2023; Karlsen & Aalberg, 2023; Kayode Mustapha et al., 2023; Matthes et al., 2023; Zhai & Luo, 2023). This section delves into the link between social media and international politics, including its effects, the challenges, and the implications for the future of international diplomacy and political activity.

Social media platforms have evolved into virtual spaces for political discourse, allowing for rapid, worldwide conversations about global issues. These platforms are used by politicians, diplomats, and political groups to engage directly with citizens, convey information, and shape narratives. These digital spaces, however, pose concerns, such as the propagation of misinformation and propaganda, which can alter public opinion and aggravate conflicts.

From the Arab Spring to the Black Lives Matter movement, social media has been critical in mobilizing activism and social movements worldwide.[1] These platforms empower activists to organize, communicate, and magnify their views on a worldwide scale. Governments, on the other hand, can employ them to monitor activists and stifle opposition.

The use of social media in diplomacy, often known as "Twiplomacy" or "Facebook Diplomacy," has changed the face of diplomatic communication. Diplomats utilize social media to communicate with international audiences, handle crises, and strengthen soft power. However, informal and public aspects of social media can lead to diplomatic errors and confrontations.

Politicians have used social media platforms to campaign and engage people, tremendously impacting political politics. Concerns have been expressed, however, about foreign meddling, "fake news," and the influence of social media algorithms in generating echo chambers and influencing election outcomes.

Social media platforms can help international collaboration by allowing direct communication between nations and encouraging cultural interchange. They can, however, escalate international disputes. State-sponsored disinformation operations, cyber warfare, and digital surveillance are major global problems.

Social media has undoubtedly transformed international politics, affecting political debate, activism, diplomacy, and elections. However, although this technology provides unparalleled potential for communication and involvement, it also poses enormous problems, ranging from disinformation propagation to the risk of cyber warfare. Understanding the delicate interplay between social media and international politics is critical in establishing a global digital landscape that supports transparency, cooperation, and peace as we traverse this digital era.

10.3   Social Media as a Political Discourse Platform

Social media has developed as a major venue for political discourse in the digital era, transforming how individuals, governments, and organizations engage in political debate (Gambetti & Biraghi, 2023; Hagemann &

---

[1] https://indianstrategicknowledgeonline.com/web/mayfield_strat_for_soc_media.pdf.

Abramova, 2023; Kim, 2023; Madhu et al., 2023; Noor & Turetken, 2023). This change has democratized political communication, breaking conventional barriers and enabling real-time, worldwide discussions about essential problems. This section looks into the complex dynamics of social media as a political discourse platform, highlighting its benefits and limitations.

One of social media's most disruptive consequences is democratizing political speech. Individuals can now express their views, participate in debates, and influence political narratives on a previously unfathomable scale. This broadens political debate participation, producing a more diverse and inclusive conversation.

Politicians now rely on social media to engage with their voters, present their policies, and shape their public image. It enables direct connection by avoiding established media venues and their associated biases. On the other hand, politicians' use of social media raises concerns about populist rhetoric, misinformation, and internet manipulation.

Social media have changed political campaigns. Candidates use various venues to rally supporters, raise funds, and spread campaign themes. However, disinformation has become a big issue during political campaigns, with false narratives and "fake news" potentially influencing voters and damaging democratic processes.

While social media allows for unprecedented political participation, it poses considerable problems. The propagation of misinformation and the construction of echo chambers, in which people are only exposed to material that confirms their existing beliefs, are serious concerns. These elements have the potential to polarize nations, escalate conflicts, and impede informed political debate.

In response to these difficulties, calls for social media platforms to be regulated have gotten louder. These talks center on responsibility, transparency, and control over content moderation. However, balancing the need to address these issues with the need to protect free speech and the open character of these platforms is a difficult task that will influence the future of political dialogue on social media.

Social media has radically modified political discourse, which has democratized political communication and transformed political campaigning. However, its concerns, ranging from misinformation to polarization, are significant and must be addressed carefully. How we handle social media as a venue for political debate as we navigate this new digital world will have enormous ramifications for the health of our democracies, the quality of political dialogue, and the future of political engagement. Balancing the benefits and drawbacks of social media in political debate is a crucial task for the digital era, requiring careful regulation and active citizen participation.

10.4   ACTIVISM AND SOCIAL MEDIA

The advent of social media platforms has had a significant impact on activism and social movements all over the world, giving new means for communication, organization, and global reach (Almazyad et al., 2023; Bitman, 2023; Cammaerts, 2015; Guedes & Carvalho, 2023; Velasquez & LaRose, 2015). In recent years, several initiatives have used social media to mobilize support, create awareness, and impact change. This section investigates the use of social media in activism and social movements, looking at how social media technology has empowered and linked activists while recognizing the obstacles and potential pitfalls of its use.

Social media is an effective tool for connecting and motivating campaigners across borders. Individuals can use platforms like Twitter, Facebook, and Instagram to share information, arrange events, and build networks of like-minded supporters. This worldwide connectivity and collaboration have given rise to new transnational social movements.

One of the most essential characteristics of social media activism is its ability to magnify disadvantaged perspectives. As a result, social media enables a more diverse and inclusive debate about social issues by offering a voice for individuals who have previously been underrepresented or silent, encouraging better empathy and understanding.

Social media platforms have increased public knowledge of various social issues and affected public opinion. Activists can draw attention to topics that traditional media might otherwise neglect by using hashtags, viral content, and online campaigns. This increased awareness can result in concrete actions and policy changes.

The influence of social media on activism is not limited to the digital realm. Social media has stimulated practical, real-world change by rallying support, creating awareness, and altering public opinion. From the #RhodesMustFall movement to the #BlackLivesMatter movement, social movements have used the power of social media to win important victories and long-term change.[2]

While social media has enormous potential for activists and social movements, it also comes with many problems and possible dangers. These include spreading misinformation, the risk of digital spying by governments or other actors, and the possibility of movements being split or co-opted. Furthermore, social media algorithms might contribute to echo chambers, limiting the diversity of viewpoints and reinforcing pre-existing convictions.

Social media has transformed activism and social movements by amplifying voices, connecting activists, and promoting global change. Individuals can now engage in political activity, and challenge established power structures thanks to the digital era. However, to fully realize social media's potential for positive change, it is critical to acknowledge and solve its difficulties, ranging from misinformation to spying. As activists continue to harness the power of social media, the future of social movements and the quest for justice will be significant.

10.5   Digital Diplomacy

Diplomacy in the twenty-first century has expanded to include digital technologies, with social media platforms playing a prominent role. This new type of diplomacy, known as digital diplomacy or e-diplomacy, has altered how governments communicate and negotiate with one another (Bjola, 2016; Khan et al., 2021; Manor, 2016; Rashica, 2018; Strauß et al., 2015). This section investigates the use of social media in digital diplomacy, exploring its effects, benefits, problems, and international relations consequences.

Twitter and Facebook have become indispensable tools for diplomats and foreign service personnel. They are used to express policy, interact with international audiences, and manage crises. These tools enable real-time communication while providing an informal diplomacy arena that goes beyond established diplomatic conventions.

Diplomats can communicate directly with the foreign public via social media, a practice known as public diplomacy. Diplomats can use social media to shape their country's image, promote its principles, and build

---

[2] https://blacklivesmatter.com/.

goodwill. This can boost soft power based on seduction rather than compulsion.

Social media has also evolved into a critical crisis communication and management instrument. During a crisis, ambassadors can immediately communicate information, provide updates, and clear up misconceptions via social media. This real-time communication can aid in the more effective management and mitigation of emergencies.

While social media provides numerous opportunities for diplomacy, it also poses innumerable obstacles. For example, disinformation or "fake news" can also aggravate tensions and confusion. Furthermore, digital diplomacy requires new skills and capabilities, necessitating comprehensive training and education for diplomats.

As social media rises in popularity, its function in diplomacy will become even more critical. Future advancements could include the growing use of artificial intelligence in diplomatic communication, the emergence of new social media platforms, and the need to resolve digital disparities between states. These changes will necessitate adaptation, technological literacy, and a commitment to digital ethics.

Social media has altered the diplomatic environment by providing new instruments for communication, public diplomacy, and crisis management. While the digital revolution gives several benefits, it also introduces new obstacles that must be handled. States' ability to adapt to this new diplomatic climate will be critical in defining international relations. Understanding and utilizing the potential of social media for digital diplomacy will be essential to the success of international relations in the digital era.

10.6 Elections and Social Media

The introduction of social media and AI has profoundly altered the political environment, particularly in the context of elections (Aral & Eckles, 2019; Fujiwara et al., 2021; Metaxas & Mustafaraj, 2012; Intyaswati & Fairuzza, 2023; Sarıtaş & Aydın, 2015). These technologies have reshaped how electoral processes are done and experienced, from voter mobilization to campaign strategies. This section delves into the relationship between elections, AI, and social media, emphasizing this digital growth's possibilities and substantial obstacles.

Social media platforms have evolved into indispensable instruments in modern election campaigns. They provide politicians and political parties with an unfiltered line of communication with citizens, allowing for real-time involvement and criticism. Campaigns may instantly share policy proposals, promote events, and respond to emerging challenges. Furthermore, social media serves as a grassroots organizing and mobilization platform, allowing regular citizens to participate in the voting process.

AI augments these advancements by providing sophisticated data analysis skills. Political campaigns, for example, employ AI to analyze massive amounts of data from social media and other sources better to understand voter behavior, attitude, and preferences. This information helps to inform campaign plans, allowing for more targeted messages and cost allocation. In addition, AI can automate campaign activities such as sending targeted messages to voters and finding major social media debate topics.

However, incorporating AI and social media into elections is fraught with difficulties. For example, AI-enabled micro-targeting might create echo chambers in which voters are exposed solely to information that supports their beliefs, thereby increasing polarization.

Furthermore, the strength of AI and social media has generated concerns about misinformation and manipulation. Deepfakes or artificial intelligence-generated bogus material that appears real can be used to create false narratives, while social media platforms can be used to disseminate misinformation quickly. Both scenarios have the potential to influence voters' views and judgments greatly.

Another significant issue is data privacy. AI-driven campaigning's vast data collection and analysis raises concerns about voter privacy and data security. Addressing these issues would necessitate a diverse strategy. Transparency in AI algorithms, data gathering procedures, and strict data privacy legislation are critical. Furthermore, digital literacy efforts can help voters evaluate online information and identify falsehoods.

Furthermore, social media sites must be held accountable for content control. Finally, an international collaborative effort is required to develop rules and legislation around using AI and social media in elections.

Artificial intelligence and social media have dramatically altered electoral processes, providing extraordinary involvement opportunities and considerable obstacles. As these technologies change, so must our approaches to maximizing their promise and mitigating hazards. Navigating this complex situation will be critical to guaranteeing electoral integrity and fairness in the digital era.

10.7   ONLINE ECHO CHAMBERS

The internet and social media platforms have transformed how people connect, engage, and access information. Politics, too, has been affected by this seismic shift. The formation of "online echo chambers" is an intriguing and concerning phenomenon in the digital sphere. These echo chambers are virtual spaces where people are exposed primarily to information and opinions that align with their own, reinforcing their pre-existing beliefs and potentially leading to polarization (Bastos et al., 2018; Brugnoli et al., 2019; Robson, 2023; Wolfowicz et al., 2023). This section delves into the idea of creating online echo chambers, its impact on political debate, and proposed remedies to reduce its harmful implications.

A variety of elements combine to form online echo chambers. These include algorithmic filtering on social media platforms, which favors content that corresponds with user preferences and behavior, and people's natural desire to seek out and connect with content that confirms their pre-existing opinions. This generates a feedback loop in which individuals are primarily exposed to similar viewpoints, restricting their worldview.

The insular character of online echo chambers has far-reaching consequences for political discourse. Firstly, it can lead to increased polarization of political beliefs because people are less likely to encounter or evaluate opposing viewpoints. This polarization can stifle healthy political conversation by instilling an "us vs. them" mentality and diminishing the possibility of compromise or consensus.

Second, echo chambers can contribute to the propagation of misinformation or 'fake news.' When information is constantly echoed within a closed group, whether factual or not, it obtains perceived credibility, which can dramatically influence public opinion and political results.

Finally, echo chambers can aid in political radicalization. Extremist views can look more popular and acceptable when repeatedly reinforced without contradiction, perhaps leading to increased radical thought and behavior.

A diversified approach is required to address the influence of online echo chambers. Digital literacy campaigns can enlighten the public about the presence of echo chambers and the significance of getting information from various sources. Social media sites must also accept responsibility for increasing openness about their algorithms and giving users more control over their content feeds.

It is also critical to promote cross-cutting political debate online. This could be enabled through platforms built for respectful discussion between people with opposing viewpoints or by features on platforms that encourage exposure to varied ideas.

While internet echo chambers pose enormous difficulties to democratic discourse and processes, they are not insurmountable. The detrimental impact of these echo chambers can be minimized through collaborative initiatives that include digital literacy, algorithmic transparency, and encouraging open dialogue. As the digital world evolves, so must our policies to ensure that it supports rather than undermines a dynamic and inclusive democratic process.

10.8   Social Media, Conflict and Politics

Social media has quickly developed as a significant force in modern society, with far-reaching repercussions for many parts of life, including war and international politics. Social media platforms such as Facebook, Twitter, and Instagram have transformed interpersonal communication and significantly impacted political discourse, conflict dynamics, and international diplomatic relations. This section investigates the interaction between social media, conflict, and international politics, highlighting its dual role as a trigger and a conflict mitigator (Gray & Gordo, 2014; O'Callaghan et al., 2014; Wolfsfeld et al., 2013; Woolley & Howard, 2016; Zeitzoff, 2017).

Social media has played a significant influence in initiating and exacerbating disputes. The democratization of information has enabled the mass transmission of diverse points of view, which, while encouraging conversation and understanding in certain circumstances, may also lead to polarization, misinformation, and incitement to violence in others. Notably, social media has been used to spread hate speech, radicalize individuals, and mobilize violent movements in many conflict situations worldwide.

However, social media can help resolve conflicts. It can serve as a platform for peace advocacy, encourages conversation among opposing parties, and is a real-time monitoring system during crises. Furthermore, it can raise international awareness and solidarity in crisis, influencing global reactions.

The reach of social media extends into international politics. In diplomacy, social media platforms are utilized for public diplomacy, crisis communication, and negotiation. Social media has also aided in the transition from traditional government-to-government diplomacy to public diplomacy, which involves direct interaction between governments and foreign communities.

A multi-pronged approach is required to address the issues provided by social media in conflict and international politics. First, disinformation and hate speech can be reduced by educating users about the possible misuse of social media and fostering digital literacy. Transparency and accountability in social media algorithms can also be important in avoiding spreading harmful content.

International rules and regulations governing cyber warfare, data privacy, and misinformation must be developed and implemented. These solutions necessitate international cooperation and a commitment to maintaining the integrity of digital spaces.

Social media has a wide-ranging and significant impact on war and international politics. Understanding its dynamics is critical for conflict resolution, diplomatic ties, and overall global security. As we struggle with the changing digital landscape, promoting responsible social media use and adequate regulation must remain a top focus.

10.9   Social Media, AI, and Mechanism Design in International Politics

With social media, artificial intelligence, and mechanism design, a new trio of influential tools in international politics has emerged. These digital tools are reshaping the landscape of international relations by transforming diplomacy, conflict, and collaboration. This section investigates the role of social media, artificial intelligence, and mechanism design in international politics, exploring its consequences and future implications (Kawasaki et al., 2021; Li et al., 2017; Paul et al., 2020).

Social media platforms are valuable tools for diplomatic communication, public diplomacy, and cyber warfare in international politics. These platforms enable real-time communication and the exchange of information and ideas. However, although this has democratized information access and facilitated global dialogue, it has also posed essential challenges, such as the spread of disinformation and the potential of foreign involvement in domestic politics.

Artificial intelligence is employed in international politics, with applications ranging from data analysis and predictive modelling to self-driving weapons systems. AI improves decision-making, increases efficiency, and delivers new civilian and military capabilities. However, it creates serious ethical, security, and governance issues, such as questions about responsibility, privacy, and the possibility of an AI weapons race.

Mechanism design, a branch of economics that entails creating systems or "mechanisms" to achieve desired results, is increasingly becoming important in international politics. Mechanism design can be used for international agreements, voting systems, and the management of global public assets. By carefully developing these channels, nations can foster cooperation, alleviate conflicts, and produce mutually beneficial outcomes. However, enforcing these systems can be difficult, especially in a diverse and complicated global landscape.

Social media, AI, and mechanism design interaction can significantly impact international politics. For example, artificial intelligence can examine social media data to forecast political trends or identify disinformation efforts. Similarly, mechanism design can aid in addressing the difficulties provided by social media and AI, such as developing legislation to prohibit the misuse of AI or social media in politics. On the other hand, the interactions between these technologies are complicated and can have unanticipated implications, needing careful investigation and oversight.

As social media, artificial intelligence, and mechanism design advance, international politics will fundamentally alter. Nations must respond to these developments by adopting new digital strategies, norms, and institutions. This requires dedication to technological knowledge, ethical concerns, and international cooperation.

Social media, artificial intelligence, and mechanism design alter diplomacy, conflict, and cooperation in international politics. One of the defining difficulties of international politics in the twenty-first century is navigating this digital terrain. Nations may improve their decision-making, foster cooperation, and negotiate the complexity of the digital age by using these tools effectively and responsibly. This will, however, necessitate careful oversight, creative thinking, and a commitment to international collaboration and ethical governance.

10.10   Policy and Regulation

Social media has provided numerous opportunities and difficulties. As a digital public square where billions of people interact and share content, it is becoming increasingly important to tackle regulatory and policy issues.

However, the digital public square character is compromised because social media is controlled by companies, governments, or even individuals. This section discusses the social media regulatory and policy landscape, outlining important difficulties and potential solutions.

Social media networks traverse national borders, posing considerable regulatory challenges. Traditional media sources are usually regulated at the national level, but the global character of social media calls this approach into question (Alkiviadou, 2019; Flew et al., 2019; Rochefort, 2020). As a result, policymakers must deal with challenges, including content moderation, data privacy, misinformation, and antitrust concerns in an ever-changing digital world.

Content moderation is one of the most pressing issues. On the one hand, damaging content such as hate speech, harassment, and false information must be limited. However, there is a risk of infringing on free speech and expression. Finding the correct balance requires a thorough understanding of cultural, social, and legal settings.

Another critical regulatory worry is data privacy. Business strategies that collect and commercialize user data are common on social media sites. Regulatory policies must guarantee that these activities are explicit, that users have control over their data, and that proper security measures to prevent breaches are in place.

Another significant issue is the dissemination of misinformation on social media, particularly concerning electoral integrity. Policies should prevent the spread of incorrect information while protecting free speech values. This could include measures like labelling or fact-checking content and holding platforms accountable for failing to control harmful content.

Finally, in the face of a few major social media networks, antitrust problems are becoming increasingly important. As a result, authorities must ensure a competitive digital market by discouraging monopolistic practices and fostering innovation.

A multi-stakeholder strategy is required to address these issues. Policymakers, platforms, users, and civil society must collaborate to create effective, fair, and adaptive policies. Platform self-regulation methods, such as community standards and internal review processes, are part of the answer. External oversight, however, is required to assure accountability.

Because of the worldwide character of social media, international cooperation is also required. As a result, policymakers must collaborate to create coherent and coordinated regulatory frameworks that respect national and regional diversity.

Regulating social media is a complex and ever-changing undertaking. Therefore, we must constantly examine and change our regulatory measures as we traverse this new digital terrain. We can, however, strive toward a regulatory framework that harnesses the benefits of social media while limiting its risks by encouraging collaboration among different stakeholders and promoting values of transparency, accountability, and respect for human rights.

10.11   Conclusion

The impact of social media on politics is growing. This game-changing media is ushering a real-time, interactive platform for state and non-state actors to engage, negotiate, and even clash. Furthermore, by broadening the reach of political discourse and diplomacy, social media has democratized engagement in politics by increasing transparency and encouraging public participation.

However, it is critical to recognize the dual-edged nature of social media in this context. It has aided democratic processes and public diplomacy but has also increased the possibility of disinformation, polarization, and foreign influence. The rapid dissemination of misinformation and the construction of echo chambers harm democratic ideals, while cyber warfare and digital espionage represent new threats to national and international security.

The international community must work together to navigate the potential and difficulties social media poses in politics. Policymakers, diplomats, engineers, and members of civil society must work together to set and enforce ethical standards, put in place solid cybersecurity measures, and encourage digital literacy. As the digital age progresses, striking a balance between exploiting the power of social media and controlling its potential disadvantages will be critical in sustaining a stable, egalitarian, and secure worldwide political scene.

References

Alkiviadou, N. (2019). Hate speech on social media networks: Towards a regulatory framework? *Information & Communications Technology Law, 28*(1), 19–35.

Almazyad, F., Shah, P., & Loiacono, E. T. (2023). Social media activism for resurrecting deleted brands: the role of consumers' psychological reactance. *Journal of Brand Management, 30*(4), 367–380.

Aral, S., & Eckles, D. (2019). Protecting elections from social media manipulation. *Science, 365*(6456), 858–861.

Bastos, M., Mercea, D., & Baronchelli, A. (2018). The geographic embedding of online echo chambers: Evidence from the Brexit campaign. *PLoS ONE, 13*(11), e0206841.

Bitman, N. (2023). 'Which part of my group do I represent?': Disability activism and social media users with concealable communicative disabilities. *Information, Communication & Society, 26*(3), 619–636.

Bjola, C. (2016). Digital diplomacy—The state of the art. *Global Affairs, 2*(3), 297–299.

Brugnoli, E., Cinelli, M., Quattrociocchi, W., & Scala, A. (2019). Recursive patterns in online echo chambers. *Scientific Reports, 9*(1), 20118.

Cammaerts, B. (2015). Social media and activism. In R. Mansell & P. Hwa (Eds.), *The international encyclopedia of digital communication and society* (pp. 1027–1034). Wiley-Blackwell.

Chekol, M. A., Moges, M. A., & Nigatu, B. A. (2023). Social media hate speech in the walk of Ethiopian political reform: Analysis of hate speech prevalence, severity, and natures. *Information, Communication & Society, 26*(1), 218–237.

Flew, T., Martin, F., & Suzor, N. (2019). Internet regulation as media policy: Rethinking the question of digital communication platform governance. *Journal of Digital Media & Policy, 10*(1), 33–50.

Fujiwara, T., Müller, K., & Schwarz, C. (2021). *The effect of social media on elections: Evidence from the United States* (No. w28849). National Bureau of Economic Research.

Gambetti, R. C., & Biraghi, S. (2023). Branded activism: Navigating the tension between culture and market in social media. *Futures, 145*, 103080.

Gray, C. H., & Gordo, Á. J. (2014). Social media in conflict: Comparing military and social-movement technocultures. *Cultural Politics, 10*(3), 251–261.

Guedes, H. F. A., & Carvalho, J. V. (2023). Portuguese sports fans reaction to professional athlete's activism on social media: A systematic literature review. In *Perspectives and Trends in Education and Technology: Selected Papers from ICITED 2022* (pp. 609–623). Springer Nature.

Hagemann, L., & Abramova, O. (2023). Sentiment, we-talk and engagement on social media: Insights from Twitter data mining on the US presidential elections 2020. *Internet Research* (ahead-of-print).

Intyaswati, D., & Fairuzza, M. T. (2023). The influence of social media on online political participation among college students: Mediation of political talks. *Southern Communication Journal, 88*(3), 257–265.

Karlsen, R., & Aalberg, T. (2023). Social media and trust in news: An experimental study of the effect of Facebook on news story credibility. *Digital Journalism, 11*(1), 144–160.

Kawasaki, T., Wada, R., Todo, T., & Yokoo, M. (2021). Mechanism design for housing markets over social networks. In *Proceedings of the 20th international conference on autonomous agents and multiagent systems* (pp. 692–700).

Kayode Mustapha, L., Hameed Olufadi, O., Lukuman Azeez, A., Udende, P., & Lasisi Mustapha, M. (2023). Social media and changing political behaviors among the youth in Kwara state of Nigeria. *Democratic Communiqué, 31*(2), 3.

Khan, M. L., Ittefaq, M., Pantoja, Y. I. M., Raziq, M. M., & Malik, A. (2021). Public engagement model to analyze digital diplomacy on twitter: A social media analytics framework. *International Journal of Communication, 15*, 29.

Kim, S. J. (2023). The role of social media news usage and platforms in civic and political engagement: Focusing on types of usage and platforms. *Computers in Human Behavior, 138*, 107475.

Li, B., Hao, D., Zhao, D., & Zhou, T. (2017). Mechanism design in social networks. *Proceedings of the AAAI Conference on Artificial Intelligence, 31*(1).

Noor, H. M., & Turetken, O. (2023). What drives sentiments on social media? An exploratory study on the 2021 Canadian federal election. In *Proceedings of the HICSS.*

Madhu, H., Satapara, S., Modha, S., Mandl, T., & Majumder, P. (2023). Detecting offensive speech in conversational code-mixed dialogue on social media: A contextual dataset and benchmark experiments. *Expert Systems with Applications, 215*, 119342.

Manor, I. (2016). Are we there yet: Have MFAs realized the potential of digital diplomacy?: Results from a cross-national comparison. *Brill Research Perspectives in Diplomacy and Foreign Policy, 1*(2), 1–110.

Matthes, J., Heiss, R., & van Scharrel, H. (2023). The distraction effect: Political and entertainment-oriented content on social media, political participation, interest, and knowledge. *Computers in Human Behavior, 142*, 107644.

McCay-Peet, L., & Quan-Haase, A. (2017). What is social media and what questions can social media research help us answer. In *The SAGE handbook of social media research methods* (pp. 13–26). Sage.

Metaxas, P. T., & Mustafaraj, E. (2012). Social media and the elections. *Science, 338*(6106), 472–473.

O'Callaghan, D., Prucha, N., Greene, D., Conway, M., Carthy, J., & Cunningham, P. (2014). Online social media in the Syria conflict: Encompassing the extremes and the in-betweens. In *2014 IEEE/ACM international conference on advances in social networks analysis and mining (ASONAM 2014)* (pp. 409–416).

Paul, A., Suppakitpaisarn, V., & Rangan, C.P. (2020). Smart contract-driven mechanism design to mitigate information diffusion in social networks. In *Mathematical research for blockchain economy: 1st international conference MARBLE 2019, Santorini, Greece* (pp. 201–216). Springer International.

Rashica, V. (2018). The benefits and risks of digital diplomacy. *Seeu Review, 13*(1), 75–89.

Robson, G. J. (2023). Social media firms, echo chambers, and the good life. In *Technology ethics* (pp. 204–214). Routledge.

Rochefort, A. (2020). Regulating social media platforms: A comparative policy analysis. *Communication Law and Policy, 25*(2), 225–260.

Sarıtaş, A., & Aydın, E. E. (2015). Elections and social media: An overview. *International Journal of Social Ecology and Sustainable Development (IJSESD), 6*(1), 59–72.

Strauß, N., Kruikemeier, S., van der Meulen, H., & van Noort, G. (2015). Digital diplomacy in GCC countries: Strategic communication of Western embassies on Twitter. *Government Information Quarterly, 32*(4), 369–379.

Velasquez, A., & LaRose, R. (2015). Youth collective activism through social media: The role of collective efficacy. *New Media & Society, 17*(6), 899–918.

Wolfsfeld, G., Segev, E., & Sheafer, T. (2013). Social media and the Arab Spring: Politics comes first. *The International Journal of Press/Politics, 18*(2), 115–137.

Wolfowicz, M., Weisburd, D., & Hasisi, B. (2023). Examining the interactive effects of the filter bubble and the echo chamber on radicalization. *Journal of Experimental Criminology, 19*(1), 119–141.

Woolley, S. C., & Howard, P. N. (2016). Social media, revolution, and the rise of the political bot. In *Routledge handbook of media, conflict and security* (pp. 302–312). Routledge.

Zeitzoff, T. (2017). How social media is changing conflict. *Journal of Conflict Resolution, 61*(9), 1970–1991.

Zhai, X., & Luo, Q. (2023). Rational or emotional? A study on Chinese tourism boycotts on social media during international crisis situations. *Tourism Management Perspectives, 45*, 101069.

CHAPTER 11

Robotics in Politics

11.1 WHAT IS ROBOTICS?

Robotics is an interdisciplinary field that blends elements from various branches of science and engineering, including computer science, electrical engineering, and mechanical engineering. At its core, robotics is the design, construction, and operation of machines (robots) that can automate tasks that humans previously performed. This section looks at the fundamentals of robotics and its applications, problems, and future directions (Birk, 2011; Koditschek, 2021; Tarassoli, 2019; Xing & Marwala, 2018). Its working is illustrated in Fig. 11.1.

Robots are programmable machines that interact with their surroundings. They are typically designed to perform tasks autonomously or semi-autonomously, frequently in hazardous or unpleasant environments. The capabilities of a robot can range from simple, predefined movements, such as those of an assembly line robot, to complex, adaptable actions, such as those of a self-driving car or a humanoid robot.

In robotics, there are three major components: mechanics, electronics, and programming. Mechanics comprises the physical design and structure of the robot, ensuring it can accomplish essential duties. Electronics involves the sensors and actuators that allow the robot to interact with its environment. Furthermore, programming entails developing algorithms and control systems to guide the robot's behavior.

© The Author(s), under exclusive license to Springer Nature Singapore Pte Ltd. 2023
T. Marwala, *Artificial Intelligence, Game Theory and Mechanism Design in Politics*, https://doi.org/10.1007/978-981-99-5103-1_11

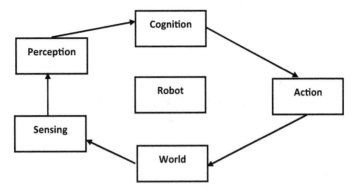

Fig. 11.1   An illustration of the report interacting with the world

Robotics has wide-ranging applications across numerous fields. In manufacturing, for example, robots do repetitive jobs swiftly and precisely, enhancing efficiency and production. Robots assist in complex surgeries in medicine, enabling higher precision and less invasive procedures. Robots such as the Mars Exploration Rovers study extraterrestrial environments in space exploration.[1] In the consumer market, robots do things like vacuum floors and act as personal assistants.

Despite its advancements, the area of robotics confronts several hurdles. Technical issues include increasing robot autonomy, adaptability, and energy efficiency. Furthermore, as robots become more integrated into society, legal considerations such as liability for robot actions are becoming increasingly important.

The future of robotics is promising, with several exciting developments. These include developments in AI that could lead to more intelligent and autonomous robots, improvements in materials science that could result in more durable and flexible robots, and ongoing miniaturization that could lead to nanorobots for application in medical and environmental monitoring.

Robotics is a dynamic and fast-expanding discipline that has the potential to impact society substantially. As we continue to develop and integrate robotics into our lives, it is critical that we carefully navigate the associated challenges and ethical considerations. By doing so, we

[1] https://mars.nasa.gov/mer/.

can leverage the full potential of robotics to increase human capabilities, improve quality of life, and tackle some of the world's most critical concerns.

11.2   ROBOTICS AND POLITICS

Robotics technology has added a new dimension to international relations, reshaping diplomacy, conflict resolution, and global governance. As a result, the dynamics of international relations are changing as nations grapple with the opportunities and challenges posed by robotics. This section investigates the effects of robotics on diplomacy, conflict, economic relations, and global norms (Borges, 2017; Carpenter, 2016; Kiggins, 2018a, 2018b; Michalec et al., 2021;).

Using robotics in diplomacy marks a fundamental change in international communication and negotiation. Telepresence robots, for example, improve diplomatic processes by allowing real-time communication and interaction regardless of geographical constraints. This, however, brings new challenges, such as ensuring secure and private communication channels in the face of potential cyber threats.

In conflict, deploying robotic technology, particularly autonomous weapons systems or drones, has profound implications. Such technology can potentially transform military strategy and reduce human casualties in conflict zones. However, it creates complex ethical and legal challenges, such as accountability concerns, the risk of escalation, and the possibility of an arms race in autonomous weapons.

The expanding use of robotics has far-reaching consequences for global economic relations. As robotics technology improves productivity and changes labor dynamics, it has the potential to reshape global supply chains and trade relationships. At the same time, disparities in access to robotics technology can exacerbate national economic inequalities, posing challenges to global economic governance.

Robotics' emergence needs the creation of global norms and rules to control its use and address associated concerns. International cooperation will be critical in establishing ethical robotics standards, mitigating risks associated with autonomous weapons, and addressing the economic implications of robotics technology. However, due to differing national interests and levels of technological advancement, reaching an agreement on these issues may be difficult.

Robotics technology is ushering in a new era in international relations, reshaping diplomacy, conflict, and economic ties. As nations navigate this new landscape, they must grapple with complex ethical, legal, and governance challenges. The ability to harness the benefits of robotics while effectively managing its risks will determine the future of international relations in the age of robotics. This will necessitate creative thinking, strong international cooperation, and a dedication to ethical and equitable technology use. Decisions made today will shape the dynamics of international relations for decades to come as we stand on the verge of a technological revolution.

11.3   Robotics in Diplomacy

Introducing robotics has resulted in significant changes in various fields, including diplomacy. Incorporating robotics into diplomatic affairs heralds a new era of international relations marked by efficiency, immediacy, and novel challenges. This section investigates the role and influence of robotics in diplomacy, analyzing the opportunities and challenges given by this technology (Carpenter, 2016; Luo et al., 2022; Puaschunder, 2019; Takayama et al., 2008.).

One of the primary benefits of robotics in diplomacy is facilitating communication and interaction. Telepresence robots, for example, enable diplomats to simultaneously be 'present' in multiple locations, engaging in real-time communication without regard for geographical boundaries. This can potentially speed up diplomatic negotiations, improve cultural exchange, and foster a greater sense of global interconnectedness.

Robotics can also improve diplomatic safety and accessibility. For example, in conflict zones or areas affected by natural disasters, robots can be deployed to carry out diplomatic missions that may be too dangerous for human diplomats. Similarly, robots can reach remote or difficult-to-reach areas, allowing diplomatic efforts to reach all corners of the globe.

With the rise of social media and digital communication, public diplomacy—the participation of foreign publics in diplomatic efforts—has grown in importance. Robotics, especially with AI, can help diplomats manage and analyze massive amounts of data, allowing them to understand public sentiment, tailor communication strategies better, and engage effectively with foreign audiences.

While robotics offers many benefits, it also presents significant challenges. The use of robots in diplomacy involves complex ethical and legal problems. For example, how can privacy and confidentiality be ensured when telepresence robots are used? Who is accountable if a robot malfunctions or is involved in an incident? Addressing these issues necessitates clear guidelines and stringent regulation.

As robotics technology advances, its role in diplomacy is expected to grow. For example, robots could automate administrative tasks, allowing diplomats to focus on strategic decisions. Advanced AI robots could even participate in negotiations, armed with vast amounts of data and sophisticated algorithms. However, this future also demands vigilant control to prevent misuse and guarantee that diplomacy's human aspect is not lost.

Robots transform diplomacy, providing new tools to improve communication, increase safety and accessibility, and shape public diplomacy. However, incorporating robotics into diplomacy poses significant issues requiring careful regulation and ethical thought. As we enter a new era of diplomatic relations, we must capitalize on robotics' benefits while effectively managing its risks. The future of diplomacy will depend on technological advancements and our ability to navigate the ethical and legal landscape these advancements create.

11.4 Robotics in Conflict

As technological breakthroughs continue to influence our society, the role of robotics in warfare is becoming apparent. Robotics transforms warfare and peacekeeping operations from autonomous drones to unmanned ground vehicles. While these improvements can bring critical strategic advantages, they also present complicated ethical and legal problems. This section explores the complex role of robotics in conflict, examining its impacts, challenges, and implications for the future of international relations (Barrett, 2023; Modliński et al., 2023; Morioka et al., 2023; Russell, 2023; Scollick, 2023).

Robotics has transformed the way fights are waged in the military. Unmanned aerial vehicles (UAVs), also known as drones, have been extensively used for surveillance, reconnaissance, and targeted strikes. These robotic technologies can potentially reduce risk to human soldiers, improve precision, and provide strategic advantages. However, using autonomous weapon systems raises concerns about accountability, the potential for escalation, and the risk of civilian casualties.

Robotics can help preserve safety and mission success in peacekeeping operations. Robots can be deployed to defuse explosive devices, monitor cease-fire agreements, and offer logistical support, lowering the risk to peacekeepers and increasing operating efficiency. However, implementing these technologies in high-risk conflict zones requires careful assessment of their possible impact on local populations and conflict dynamics.

The use of robotics in conflict raises significant ethical and legal challenges. For example, who is accountable if an autonomous weapon system does unintended harm? Furthermore, in the age of autonomous combat, how can proportionality and discrimination, two fundamental principles of the laws of war, be ensured? These problems underline the necessity for extensive rules and international agreements governing the use of robotics in conflict.

Future developments in robots and artificial intelligence will undoubtedly modify the nature of conflict. As more countries access these technologies, the possibility of a robotic arms race grows. At the same time, technological improvements may result in new forms of conflict, such as cyber warfare and wars for technological domination.

The rise of robotics in conflict is reshaping the landscape of warfare and peacekeeping. At the same time, these technologies provide tremendous benefits while also posing serious ethical and legal concerns. Navigating this new landscape will require a commitment to international cooperation, strict laws, and careful consideration of the ethical implications of robotic warfare. As we stand on the precipice of a new era of conflict, the decisions we make today will shape the nature of warfare and peacekeeping for decades to come.

11.5   Autonomous Weapons

Autonomous weapons, commonly called "killer robots," are a new class of military equipment that can choose and engage targets without human interaction. Driven by developments in AI and robotics, these technologies promise to change warfare and create profound ethical, legal, and security challenges. This section analyzes autonomous weapons' nature, problems, and necessity for regulation (Bode et al., 2023; Christie et al., 2023; de Vries, 2023; Kwik, 2023; Misselhorn, 2023).

Autonomous weapons systems are distinct from traditional weaponry due to their capacity to function without human control. Instead, they use artificial intelligence to process information from their surroundings, make judgments, and carry out activities. Examples are autonomous drones that can identify and strike targets, robotic tanks that can navigate battlefield terrain, and unmanned naval vessels that can perform various operations.

The rise of autonomous weaponry raises a slew of ethical and legal issues. One of the most fundamental ethical issues concerns accountability. In the event of an error or violation of international humanitarian law, determining who is to blame—the operator, the manufacturer, the programmer, or the military authority—becomes difficult.

There are issues regarding whether these systems can comply with the norms of distinction and proportionality—core aspects of international humanitarian law. The concept of distinction requires that fighters be differentiated from civilians. At the same time, the principle of proportionality necessitates that the harm caused by an attack must not be disproportionate in relation to the military advantage obtained. Whether an AI can make such nuanced judgments remains questionable.

From a security standpoint, autonomous weapons have the potential to aggravate hostilities or spark accidental confrontations. An autonomous system, for example, may misinterpret a situation and launch an attack, resulting in retaliation and escalation. Furthermore, an arms race in autonomous weapons is risky because nations may feel compelled to develop and deploy these weapons to maintain strategic balance.

Given these ethical, legal, and security concerns, it is crucial to develop robust international regulations governing the use of autonomous weapons. In addition, these regulations should address issues of accountability, adherence to international law, and measures to prevent misuse.

Developing such regulations is difficult because of the rapidly evolving nature of technology and the need for broad international consensus. Furthermore, policymakers must weigh the potential military benefits of autonomous weapons against their associated risks.

To summarize, autonomous weapons represent a significant shift in warfare, offering potential benefits and posing significant risks. As a result, the development and application of these weapons must be guided by careful ethical and legal considerations. Establishing international standards as we navigate this new terrain will ensure that this technology is used properly and ethically while maintaining peace and security.

11.6   ROBOTICS AND ECONOMIC RELATIONS

Robotics and automation technologies are rapidly transforming global economic landscapes. Its impact extends to labor markets, manufacturing methods, and global trade, fundamentally altering international economic relations. However, although it offers higher productivity and efficiency, it also brings substantial concerns, such as job displacement and widening economic inequities. This section explores the impacts of robotics on international economic relations, delving into both the opportunities and challenges it presents (Abdel-Keream, 2023; Barrett, 2023; Gil et al., 2023; Li & Tian, 2023; Seyitoğlu & Ivanov, 2023).

Robotics has the potential to significantly increase productivity and efficiency across a wide range of industries. Advanced robots can perform tasks faster, more correctly, and for more extended periods than humans, resulting in more productivity and cheaper production costs. This can boost a country's global competitiveness by opening up new trade opportunities and alliances.

The rise of robotics is also transforming labor markets. While it may result in employment displacement in industries where robots may replace human labor, it may also create new jobs in robotics-related industries. This transformation, however, necessitates a comparable evolution in workforce capabilities, necessitating substantial investment in education and training.

Global supply chains and trade patterns are being reshaped by robotics. Automation allows businesses to bring manufacturing closer to home, potentially reversing the trend of offshoring and impacting trade relations. Furthermore, countries that lead in robotics technology can significantly influence international trade, potentially influencing power relations.

While robotics offers numerous benefits, it can also exacerbate economic disparities. Countries with access to advanced robotics technology can leapfrog those without. This digital divide can potentially exacerbate the divide between developed and developing countries, posing challenges to international economic relations and global governance.

Appropriate regulation and policy are required to navigate the economic implications of robotics. Countries must balance supporting innovation and reducing the harmful consequences of automation on jobs. Furthermore, international cooperation will be critical in managing the effects on global trade and mitigating the risk of growing economic disparities.

In conclusion, the rise of robotics ushers in a new era of economic relations characterized by greater productivity and efficiency, labor market reforms, shifts in global trade, and expanding economic inequities. Effective policy, rigorous regulation, and international cooperation will be vital as we navigate this quickly shifting terrain. The challenge is to capitalize on robotics' benefits while mitigating potential drawbacks, ensuring a fair and inclusive global economy.

11.7 ROBOT TAX

The concept of a "robot tax" has emerged as an essential topic in political debates over the influence of automation on the labor force. As robotics and AI systems advance, their potential to replace human labor becomes clearer. This section delves into the concept of a robot tax, its political ramifications, and the broader socio-economic issues it raises (Gasteiger & Prettner, 2022; Guerreiro et al., 2022; Marwala, 2018; Vishnevsky & Chekina, 2018; Zhang, 2019).

Some policymakers and thinkers have proposed levying a tax on companies that use robots or AI systems to replace human workers. The tax income might be used to pay social security measures or retraining programs for displaced workers, minimizing the impact of automation on employment.

The robot tax has become a political problem. Proponents argue that widespread automation is required to address income inequality and social instability. Furthermore, it is considered a strategy to decrease the automation rate and give society time to adapt to the changing work landscape.

According to critics, a robot tax would stifle innovation and economic growth. They contend that automation, like other technological advancements, creates new jobs by spurring economic development and creating demand for new skills. Taxing robots, in this opinion, could impede this process and reduce companies' global competitiveness.

Aside from the political implications, the robot tax proposal poses broader socio-economic concerns. It emphasizes the importance of rethinking our employment, income distribution, and social security concepts in an increasingly computerized society.

It also emphasizes the significance of education and skill development in preparing the workforce for the future. Workers must have the necessary skills to fill these roles if automation is to create new jobs. As a result, some argue that the proceeds from a robot tax should be used to fund education and retraining programs.

The concept of a robot tax reflects broader societal challenges in adapting to technological change. Whether or whether such a tax is enacted, the debate highlights the necessity for proactive measures to address the impact of automation on the labor. As we navigate this complex issue, our goal should be to maximize the benefits of robotics and AI while ensuring a fair and inclusive transition to an automated economy.

11.8   Robotic Norms and Regulations

The fast development and integration of robotics across various industries have substantially altered the worldwide landscape. The impact of robotics is far-reaching, ranging from transforming industries to influencing international politics. As these technologies advance, developing global standards and legislation to address the ethical, legal, and security issues they raise is critical. This section investigates the significance of developing global robotics norms, examining key areas that require international cooperation as well as potential barriers to reaching an agreement (Chatterjee, 2019; Leenes & Lucivero, 2014; Leenes et al., 2017; Nagenborg et al., 2008; Wallach & Marchant, 2019).

The rise of robotics presents several ethical and legal challenges that demand global regulations. To enable responsible development and deployment, issues such as privacy, responsibility, and the ethical use of robotics in conflict must be addressed collectively. International treaties and frameworks, such as the United Nations Convention on Certain Conventional Weapons (CCW), can be a foundation for creating global rules in this arena.[2]

Concerns about cyber threats and the possibility of an arms race in autonomous weapons are growing as robotics becomes more integrated into the defense and security sectors. Therefore, it is critical to

---

[2] https://www.unmas.org/en/resources/convention-certain-conventional-weapons-ccw#:~:text=It%20is%20also%20known%20as,or%20to%20affect%20civilians%20indiscriminately.

adopt universal standards governing the use of robotics in military applications to avoid destabilizing consequences on international security. Furthermore, confidence-building measures, information-sharing agreements, and joint research endeavors can enhance international trust and cooperation.

The economic impact of robotics technology, particularly regarding job displacement and wealth disparities, emphasizes the importance of international cooperation on labor policies and economic governance. Establishing global norms that promote inclusive growth, reskilling workers, and bridging the digital divide can all contribute to a more equitable economic landscape.

Robotic technology has environmental and sustainability issues. Developing global norms that encourage responsible robotics use and disposal, as well as promoting research into environmentally friendly materials and energy sources, can help reduce the environmental impact of this technology.

Due to differing national interests, levels of technological development, and cultural perspectives, reaching a consensus on global robotics norms is difficult. Balancing the benefits of innovation with the need for regulation necessitates a nuanced approach that considers diverse points of view and promotes international collaboration.

Developing global robotics rules is critical to guarantee a sustainable, secure, and fair future. International cooperation, open conversation, and a commitment to common goals are required to address ethical, legal, security, economic, and environmental challenges. While reaching an agreement on these issues may be complex, responsible robotics technology's stakes and potential benefits are enormous. As we negotiate the quickly changing robotics landscape, collaboration and establishing global norms will be critical to crafting a better world for future generations.

11.9   AI, Game Theory, Mechanism Design, and Robotics

Artificial intelligence, game theory, mechanism design, and robotics are increasingly important in international relations. These interconnected fields provide tools for comprehending, predicting, and influencing global events, from diplomatic negotiations to conflict resolution. They do, however, create new obstacles that must navigate carefully. This section looks at how these four areas intersect in the context of international relations, shedding light on their potential and the issues they raise (Cui et al., 2013; Iwase et al., 2020; Jaleel & Shamma, 2020; Murphy, 2019; Zhang et al., 2021).

AI and robotics are rapidly transforming various industries, from defense to diplomacy. AI-powered autonomous systems can perform complex tasks quickly and precisely, potentially reducing risks and increasing efficiency. In diplomacy, AI can help process vast amounts of data for decision-making, while robotics can facilitate real-time communication in international negotiations. These technologies, however, raise ethical, legal, and security concerns, necessitating stringent regulatory frameworks.

Game theory, the study of strategic interactions, has long been utilized in international relations to describe and predict state behavior. It can help understand power dynamics, predict conflicts, and inform negotiation strategies. In an increasingly AI-driven society, game theory can be utilized to analyze the strategic implications of AI-driven decision-making, revealing potential scenarios of cooperation or conflict.

Mechanism design, frequently dubbed 'reverse game theory,' involves building systems to produce specified outcomes. For example, in international relations, mechanism design could establish diplomatic conventions, economic agreements, or peace treaties that promote collaboration and discourage violence. Mechanism design takes on new dimensions with AI and robotics, as these technologies may be used in the designed systems.

The intersection of AI, game theory, mechanism design, and robotics can offer new approaches to addressing global challenges. AI and robotics, for example, could be used to implement mechanisms designed to promote cooperation in international politics. Game theory can aid in predicting these mechanisms' outcomes, informing their design. However, careful consideration and oversight are required due to the complexity of these systems and the possibility of unintended consequences.

In summary, artificial intelligence, game theory, mechanism design, and robots alter international relations by providing new instruments for understanding, predicting, and influencing global events. These technologies present significant opportunities while posing considerable obstacles, such as ethical, legal, and security considerations. Fostering international cooperation, developing robust regulatory frameworks, and ensuring these powerful tools are used responsibly and for all benefits are critical as we navigate this new terrain. Furthermore, the future of international relations will become increasingly entwined with these fields, necessitating a proactive and deliberate approach to their integration.

11.10 Conclusion

The intersection of robotics and international politics is becoming increasingly important, influencing diplomacy, conflict, economic relations, and global norms. With the potential to transform human activity across a broad spectrum, robotics technology is a change agent with enormous potential and significant challenges.

Its involvement in diplomacy has opened up new communication channels, improving efficiency and security. However, it also involves a reconsideration of conventional diplomatic conventions as well as the development of new abilities within the diplomatic corps. In conflict, robotics has ushered in a paradigm shift in warfare and peacekeeping operations, enhancing precision, and lowering human risk while presenting fundamental ethical and legal concerns.

Economic interactions are also changing as robotics and automation disrupt labor markets, redefine productivity, and restructure global supply networks. While this provides chances for growth and development, it also highlights the importance of addressing rising economic gaps and the need for a competent workforce.

Furthermore, the rapid growth of robotics emphasizes the importance of establishing worldwide norms and rules. International cooperation is pivotal as we grapple with robotics' ethical, legal, security, economic, and environmental implications. Despite the obstacles in reaching an agreement, adopting agreed norms will guide ethical robotics innovation and use.

Finally, the future of international politics in the age of robotics will be determined by our collective ability to maximize the benefits of this technology while effectively managing its drawbacks. It advocates for proactive policymaking, robust regulatory frameworks, and adherence to ethical principles. As we enter this new era, fostering dialogue among policymakers, technologists, and society is critical to ensure that robotics serves humanity's best interests.

REFERENCES

Abdel-Keream, M. (2023). Ethical challenges of assistive robotics in the elderly care: Review and reflection. In *Robots in care and everyday life* (pp. 121–130). Springer International.

Barrett, G. D. (2023). Technological catastrophe and the robots of Nam June Paik. *Cultural Critique, 118*(1), 56–82.

Birk, A. (2011). What is robotics? An interdisciplinary field is getting even more diverse. *IEEE Robotics & Automation Magazine, 18*(4), 94–95.

Bode, I., Huelss, H., Nadibaidze, A., Qiao-Franco, G., & Watts, T. F. (2023). Prospects for the global governance of autonomous weapons: Comparing Chinese, Russian, and US practices. *Ethics and Information Technology, 25*(1), 5.

Borges, J. V. (2017). Robots and the military: A strategic view. In *A world with robots: International conference on robot ethics: ICRE 2015* (pp. 199–205). Springer International.

Carpenter, C. (2016). Rethinking the political/-science-/fiction nexus: Global policy making and the campaign to stop killer robots. *Perspectives on Politics, 14*(1), 53–69.

Chatterjee, S. (2019). Impact of AI regulation on intention to use robots: From citizens and government perspective. *International Journal of Intelligent Unmanned Systems, 8*(2), 97–114.

Christie, E. H., Ertan, A., Adomaitis, L., & Klaus, M. (2023). Regulating lethal autonomous weapon systems: exploring the challenges of explainability and traceability. *AI and Ethics*, 1–17.

Cui, R., Guo, J., & Gao, B. (2013). Game theory-based negotiation for multiple robots task allocation. *Robotica, 31*(6), 923–934.

de Vries, B. (2023). *Individual criminal responsibility for autonomous weapons systems in international criminal law* (Vol. 65). BRILL.

Gasteiger, E., & Prettner, K. (2022). Automation, stagnation, and the implications of a robot tax. *Macroeconomic Dynamics, 26*(1), 218–249.

Gil, G., Casagrande, D., Cortés, L. P., & Verschae, R. (2023). Why the low adoption of robotics in the farms? Challenges for the establishment of commercial agricultural robots. *Smart Agricultural Technology, 3*, 100069.

Guerreiro, J., Rebelo, S., & Teles, P. (2022). Should robots be taxed? *The Review of Economic Studies, 89*(1), 279–311.

Iwase, T., Beynier, A., Bredeche, N., & Maudet, N. (2020). A game theoretical approach to self-assembly in swarm robotics. In *2020 IEEE/WIC/ACM international joint conference on web intelligence and intelligent agent technology (WI-IAT)* (pp. 90–97).

Jaleel, H., & Shamma, J. S. (2020). Distributed optimization for robot networks: From real-time convex optimization to game-theoretic self-organization. *Proceedings of the IEEE, 108*(11), 1953–1967.

Kiggins, R. D. (2018a). *Political economy of robots*. Palgrave Macmillan.

Kiggins, R. (2018b). Robots and political economy. In *The political economy of robots: Prospects for prosperity and peace in the automated 21st century* (pp. 1–16). Springer International.

Koditschek, D. E. (2021). What is robotics? Why do we need it and how can we get it? *Annual Review of Control, Robotics, and Autonomous Systems, 4*, 1–33.

Kwik, J. (2023). Mitigating the risk of autonomous-weapon misuse by insurgent groups. *Laws, 12*(1), 5.

Leenes, R., & Lucivero, F. (2014). Laws on robots, laws by robots, laws in robots: Regulating robot behaviour by design. *Law, Innovation and Technology, 6*(2), 193–220.

Leenes, R., Palmerini, E., Koops, B. J., Bertolini, A., Salvini, P., & Lucivero, F. (2017). Regulatory challenges of robotics: Some guidelines for addressing legal and ethical issues. *Law, Innovation and Technology, 9*(1), 1–44.

Li, X., & Tian, Q. (2023). How does usage of robot affect corporate carbon emissions?—Evidence from China's manufacturing sector. *Sustainability, 15*(2), 1198.

Luo, L., Ogawa, K., Peebles, G., & Ishiguro, H. (2022). Towards a personality AI for robots: Potential colony capacity of a goal-shaped generative personality model when used for expressing personalities via non-verbal behaviour of humanoid robots. *Frontiers in Robotics and AI, 9*, 103.

Marwala, T. (2018). *On robot revolution and taxation*. arXiv preprint. arXiv: 1808.01666

Michalec, O., O'Donovan, C., & Sobhani, M. (2021). What is robotics made of? The interdisciplinary politics of robotics research. *Humanities and Social Sciences Communications, 8*(1), Article 65.

Misselhorn, C. (2023). Three ethical arguments against Killer Robots. In *Social robots in social institutions* (pp. 24–31). IOS Press.

Modliński, A., Fortuna, P., & Rożnowski, B. (2023). Human–machine trans roles conflict in the organization: How sensitive are customers to intelligent robots replacing the human workforce? *International Journal of Consumer Studies, 47*(1), 100–117.

Morioka, M., Inaba, S. I., Kureha, M., Zárdai, I. Z., Kukita, M., Okamoto, S., Murakami, Y., & Muireartaigh, R. Ó. (2023). Artificial intelligence, robots, and philosophy. *Journal of Philosophy of Life, 2023*, 1–146.

Murphy, R. R. (2019). *Introduction to AI robotics*. MIT Press.

Nagenborg, M., Capurro, R., Weber, J., & Pingel, C. (2008). Ethical regulations on robotics in Europe. *Ai & Society, 22*, 349–366.

Puaschunder, J. M. (2019). Artificial diplomacy: A guide for public officials to conduct artificial intelligence. *Journal of Applied Research in the Digital Economy, 1*, 39–54.

Russell, S. (2023). AI weapons: Russia's war in Ukraine shows why the world must enact a ban. *Nature, 614*(7949), 620–623.

Seyitoğlu, F., & Ivanov, S. (2023). Service robots and perceived discrimination in tourism and hospitality. *Tourism Management, 96*, 104710.

Scollick, A. (2023). The Irish Defence Forces in the drone age. In E. U. The (Ed.), *Irish Defence Forces and contemporary security* (pp. 295–314). Springer International.

Takayama, L., Ju, W., & Nass, C. (2008). Beyond dirty, dangerous and dull: What everyday people think robots should do. In *Proceedings of the 3rd ACM/ IEEE international conference on human robot interaction* (pp. 25–32).

Tarassoli, S. P. (2019). Artificial intelligence, regenerative surgery, robotics? What is realistic for the future of surgery? *Annals of Medicine and Surgery, 41*, 53–55.

Vishnevsky, V. P., & Chekina, V. D.(2018). Robot vs. tax inspector or how the fourth industrial revolution will change the tax system: A review of problems and solutions. *Journal of Tax Reform, 4*(1), 6–26.

Wallach, W., & Marchant, G. (2019). Toward the agile and comprehensive international governance of AI and robotics. *Proceedings of the IEEE, 107*(3), 505–508.

Xing, B., & Marwala, T. (2018). *Smart maintenance for human–robot interaction.* Springer.

Zhang, P. (2019). Automation, wage inequality and implications of a robot tax. *International Review of Economics & Finance, 59*, 500–509.

Zhang, L., Zhu, T., Xiong, P., Zhou, W., & Yu, P. S. (2021). More than privacy: Adopting differential privacy in game-theoretic mechanism design. *ACM Computing Surveys (CSUR), 54*(7), 1–37.

CHAPTER 12

AI-Powered Blockchain in Politics

12.1 Artificial Intelligence-Powered Blockchain in Politics

As artificial intelligence (AI) and blockchain technology evolve, their convergence creates new opportunities for innovation and application across various industries. AI-powered blockchain systems have the potential to significantly transform diplomacy, security, and economic relations in international politics, providing unprecedented opportunities for cooperation and transparency (Kumar et al., 2022; Marwala & Xing, 2018; Raja et al., 2020; Sivarethinamohan et al., 2022). However, these developments bring new issues that must be navigated carefully to ensure responsible development and deployment. This chapter investigates the role of artificial intelligence-powered blockchain in international politics and its consequences on essential facets of global relations.

The combination of AI and blockchain technology has the potential to establish new diplomatic communication platforms, improving the efficiency and security of information transmission. Encrypted, decentralized networks can provide safe, tamper-proof communication routes, promoting international trust. Furthermore, AI-powered diplomatic data analysis can provide insights into possible areas of collaboration or conflict, informing diplomatic strategy and discussions.

T. Marwala, *Artificial Intelligence, Game Theory and Mechanism Design in Politics*, https://doi.org/10.1007/978-981-99-5103-1_12

AI-powered blockchain systems can improve cybersecurity and defense capabilities. The decentralized structure of blockchain can increase resistance to cyberattacks, while AI-driven threat analysis and response systems can help detect and counter threats more efficiently. This combination can potentially significantly improve national security and international cooperation in cyberspace.

Incorporating artificial intelligence and blockchain into international trade and commercial interactions offers enhanced efficiency, transparency, and accountability. AI-driven blockchain platforms can streamline and automate trade procedures, lowering transaction costs and promoting easier cross-border trade. Furthermore, these technologies can create trust by enabling greater transparency in transactions and supply chains, promoting fair and ethical trading practices.

As artificial intelligence and blockchain technologies become more integrated into international politics, global standards and rules are needed to ensure their ethical usage. Establishing international agreements on the ethical use of AI, data privacy, and blockchain network security can help to build a stable and secure environment for these technologies to thrive.

While AI-powered blockchain systems can potentially benefit international politics, they pose obstacles and threats. Privacy, accountability, and the digital divide between nations with uneven access to new technologies are among them. Furthermore, the intricacy of these systems may present new vulnerabilities and the possibility for misappropriation, requiring robust regulatory frameworks and international cooperation to address these problems.

AI-powered blockchain technologies can reshape international politics by revolutionizing diplomacy, security, and commercial interactions. These technologies can potentially change how nations communicate and collaborate by building trust, increasing efficiency, and promoting transparency. On the other hand, addressing the problems and risks connected with their use is critical to assuring their responsible development and deployment. Fostering international cooperation and building global rules and regulations will be essential as we traverse this quickly changing terrain to realize AI-powered blockchain's potential in international politics.

12.2   Blockchain Technology

Blockchain technology is based on a decentralized, transparent, and tamper-resistant framework that fundamentally challenges existing data storage, transaction processing, and trust management approaches (Belotti et al., 2019; Pilkington, 2016; Wang & Su, 2020; Yaga et al., 2019; Yli-Huumo et al., 2016). This section goes into the fundamentals of blockchain technology, its various uses, and the difficulties and opportunities it brings in our increasingly digital world.

Blockchain is a distributed ledger technology that uses a network of computers, or nodes, to validate and store transactions in blocks jointly. Cryptography connects these blocks, creating a chain of safe, verifiable, and unchangeable records. Decentralization, transparency, security, and trustlessness are vital properties of blockchain technology, enabling a system without a central authority for validation or control, illustrated in Fig. 12.1.

While blockchain technology is connected with cryptocurrencies, its potential applications are not limited to digital money. Finance is one industry that can benefit from blockchain technology by streamlining cross-border transactions, reducing fraud, and enabling safe asset management. In addition, it improves global supply chains' transparency, traceability, and efficiency. Blockchain technology is also utilized in healthcare to safeguard medical information, enable data collaboration, and enhance patient privacy. Finally, blockchain is used to secure intellectual property, such as copyrights, patents, and other forms of intellectual property.

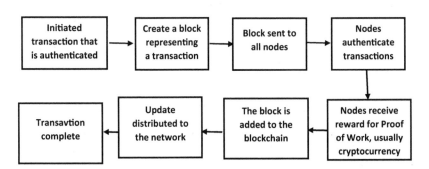

Fig. 12.1 An example of a blockchain process

Despite its potential benefits, blockchain technology also has some drawbacks. For example, many blockchain networks suffer from limited transaction processing capacity, resulting in slower and more expensive transactions as the network grows. Furthermore, the consensus process used by some blockchains, such as Proof of Work, can necessitate significant computational power, resulting in high energy consumption and environmental issues. Furthermore, it presents regulatory problems as governments wrestle with decentralized technology's consequences because they lack a central authority in blockchain networks. Finally, integrating blockchain technology into current systems and procedures can be expensive and time-consuming, limiting its general adoption.

Despite these obstacles, blockchain technology provides numerous opportunities for innovation and growth. Interoperability is an emerging trend and development in the area, where the creation of solutions enables seamless communication between different blockchain networks, enabling increased collaboration and efficiency. Furthermore, it provides opportunities for sustainability by investigating more energy-efficient consensus processes, such as Proof of Stake, which decreases the environmental impact of blockchain networks. Finally, new opportunities across multiple sectors can be unlocked by merging blockchain with complementary technologies such as artificial intelligence, the Internet of Things (IoT), and big data.

Blockchain technology represents a paradigm change in trust and decentralization, with numerous applications in various industries. While scalability, energy consumption, and regulatory obstacles remain challenges, the potential benefits of blockchain are enormous. Therefore, as we continue to investigate and develop this novel technology, we must handle its limits while capitalizing on its opportunities. By doing so, we may realize blockchain technology's full promise and harness its ability to revolutionize our increasingly digital world.

12.3   Diplomacy and Communication

AI and blockchain technologies are developing as potent instruments that can alter diplomacy and communication in the rapidly changing landscape of international politics (Bârgăoanu & Cheregi, 2021; Georgescu, 2022; Miegbam & Bariledum, 2022; Patnaik & Biswal, 2023). By providing secure, transparent, and fast information sharing and analysis platforms, these technologies can improve confidence and cooperation between states while solving inherent problems in traditional diplomatic processes. This section investigates the role of artificial intelligence and blockchain in diplomacy and communication and their potential to transform important facets of international relations.

One of the most significant advantages of using AI and blockchain technology in diplomatic communication is the greater security and trust these systems provide. The decentralized and tamper-proof blockchain structure ensures that sensitive information may be securely transmitted between nations, lowering the danger of data breaches and strengthening communication trust. Furthermore, AI-driven encryption and security measures can protect diplomatic communications from cyber threats.

AI and blockchain technology can help to streamline information flow in diplomatic contexts, resulting in more efficient communication and decision-making. AI systems can mine enormous amounts of data for significant insights that can be used to inform diplomatic strategy and negotiations. Similarly, blockchain technologies can enable faster and more transparent information transfers, improving the overall efficiency of the diplomatic process.

AI and blockchain technology can also help international diplomacy by allowing states to work more effectively together on complicated global concerns. By offering a secure and transparent data-sharing platform, these technologies can help develop trust and cooperation among many parties, leading to more productive talks and collaborative problem-solving.

While incorporating AI and blockchain technology into diplomacy and communication has tremendous advantages, several obstacles must be addressed. One of these is data privacy, sovereignty concerns, and the digital divide between nations with uneven access to new technologies. Furthermore, the rate of technology change may outpace diplomatic institutions' ability to adapt, demanding constant efforts to guarantee that new technologies are used responsibly and ethically.

As AI and blockchain technology progress, so will their potential applications in diplomacy and communication. Future advances could include using AI-powered virtual diplomats in discussions, developing blockchain-based global voting systems, and creating tools for monitoring and forecasting geopolitical trends. In addition, these technologies can potentially improve diplomatic processes' efficiency, security, and transparency, creating greater confidence and collaboration among states.

To summarize, AI and blockchain technologies can potentially change diplomacy and communication in international relations, providing significant security, efficiency, and transparency benefits. However, as we continue to investigate and develop these technologies, we must address the difficulties they raise and ensure their responsible and ethical application. By doing so, we can fully utilize the capabilities of AI and blockchain in diplomacy and communication, ultimately promoting more trust and collaboration among states in an increasingly interconnected world.

12.4   SECURITY AND CYBERDEFENSE

AI and blockchain technologies have emerged as critical instruments for boosting security and cyberdefense in a period of rapid technological breakthroughs and increased interconnection (Ameen et al., 2023; Muhati et al., 2022; Muheidat & Tawalbeh, 2021; Qiu et al., 2020; Singh et al., 2022). Moreover, these cutting-edge technologies have distinct capabilities to address cybersecurity's complex concerns while protecting sensitive data from unscrupulous actors. This section investigates the role of artificial intelligence and blockchain in security and cyberdefense, analyzing their potential to change digital security and boost global cybersecurity activities.

AI has shown considerable promise in cyberdefense because of its ability to scan massive amounts of data and detect patterns and abnormalities that may indicate a potential cyber threat. AI-driven security systems can adapt and respond to evolving threats by applying machine learning algorithms, making them more successful in identifying and mitigating possible attacks. Furthermore, AI can assist with automated incident response, lowering the time necessary to contain and remediate threats and, as a result, lessening the effect of cyberattacks.

Blockchain technology, with its decentralized, transparent, and tamper-proof nature, has the potential to improve cybersecurity significantly. Blockchain decreases the risk of single-point vulnerabilities that hackers can exploit by eliminating the requirement for centralized data storage. Furthermore, the immutable ledger of blockchain ensures that any attempts to edit or tamper with data are immediately detectable, deterring potential attackers and boosting overall system security.

The integration of AI and blockchain technology has the potential to provide novel cyberdefense capabilities. AI-powered security systems, for example, can be connected with blockchain platforms, allowing for the secure and transparent sharing of threat intelligence data between enterprises and governments. This collaboration has the potential to result in more efficient and coordinated responses to cyber threats, thereby improving global cybersecurity measures.

Despite the potential benefits of AI and blockchain in security and cyberdefense, several obstacles and issues must be addressed. Concerns about data privacy and sovereignty and the ethical use of AI in cybersecurity applications are among them. Furthermore, the rapid rate of technical progress may result in a digital arms race between hackers and security professionals, needing continual efforts to keep up with developing threats and vulnerabilities. Another issue is that general users do not fully understand how blockchains work. For example, thousands of people have had cryptocurrency investments stolen by failing to manage their private keys.

As AI and blockchain technology advance, so will their potential uses in security and cyberdefense. For example, future advances could include using AI-powered autonomous systems for threat hunting, developing blockchain-based identity management solutions, and creating decentralized cybersecurity infrastructure. In addition, it is possible to construct more robust and secure digital systems by harnessing the specific capabilities of these technologies, eventually strengthening global cybersecurity efforts.

Finally, artificial intelligence and blockchain technologies have the potential to transform security and cyberdefense by providing new capabilities that can meet the complex difficulties of digital protection. By incorporating these technologies into cybersecurity programs, defenses against increasingly sophisticated cyber threats can be strengthened. As we continue to investigate and develop new technologies, we must address the underlying challenges and ensure they are used responsibly and ethically. By doing so, we will be able to fully realize the potential of AI and blockchain in security and cyberdefense, resulting in a safer and more secure digital world.

12.5   Economic Relations and Trade

AI and blockchain technologies are reshaping the future of economic relations and trade by enabling more significant innovation, efficiency, and transparency (Akter et al., 2022; An et al., 2021; Charles et al., 2023; Di Prisco, 2019; Jekov et al., 2018). In addition, these technologies can improve trade processes, reduce transaction costs, and increase confidence among trading partners, resulting in greater economic cooperation and prosperity. This section looks at the role of AI and blockchain in economic relations and trade and their potential to alter global business and facilitate international cooperation.

AI-powered solutions transform different facets of economic interactions and commerce, providing valuable insights and efficiency to public and private stakeholders. Artificial intelligence, for example, can improve supply chain management by anticipating demand, identifying bottlenecks, and promoting more effective resource allocation. Furthermore, by analyzing massive volumes of economic data, AI-powered analytics can inform trade negotiations and policymaking, allowing governments and corporations to make more educated decisions.

Blockchain technology has emerged as a potent tool for improving the security and transparency of commercial transactions. Blockchain can prevent fraud and protect the integrity of supply chains by offering a decentralized, tamper-proof ledger for recording and verifying transactions. Furthermore, smart contracts on blockchain systems can automate numerous trading operations, lowering transaction costs and increasing overall efficiency.

The combination of AI and blockchain technologies can facilitate cross-border trade by expediting customs procedures, decreasing bureaucratic inefficiencies, and increasing confidence between trading partners. AI, for example, can be used to predict and avoid impending trade disputes. Simultaneously, blockchain can enable safe information sharing between customs administrations, resulting in faster and more accurate trade document processing.

AI and blockchain technology can aid international commerce cooperation by providing a safe and transparent data-sharing and collaboration platform. These technologies can boost international trust and collaboration by providing real-time access to trade data and simplifying collective decision-making, ultimately fostering more equitable and sustainable global economic growth.

Despite the potential benefits of artificial intelligence and blockchain in economic ties and commerce, various challenges and considerations must be addressed. Concerns about data privacy, the necessity for harmonized legal frameworks, and the possible impact of automation on employment are among them. Furthermore, the digital divide between nations with varying access to new technology has the potential to worsen existing economic inequities, necessitating deliberate measures to guarantee that the advantages of these technologies are shared equally.

To summarize, AI and blockchain technologies can transform commercial relations and commerce by providing new opportunities for efficiency, security, and cooperation. As a result, it is feasible to create more significant economic growth and international collaboration by incorporating these technologies into global trade operations. However, as we continue to investigate and develop new technologies, we must address the underlying challenges and ensure they are used responsibly and ethically. By doing so, we will be able to fully realize the promise of AI and blockchain in commercial relations and commerce, resulting in a more affluent and integrated global economy.

12.6   Governance and Regulation

Artificial intelligence and blockchain technologies have the potential to profoundly alter global governance and regulation by providing creative solutions to improve transparency, efficiency, and international cooperation. As a result, these technologies have the potential to simplify regulatory processes, improve international collaboration, and promote more effective and equitable global governance. This section investigates the role of AI and blockchain in global governance and regulation, analyzing their potential to revolutionize how governments manage complex challenges and collaborate to promote international stability and prosperity.

By providing superior analytics and decision-making capabilities, AI-driven systems offer promising opportunities for strengthening global governance. AI can analyze massive amounts of data to detect trends and patterns, allowing politicians and international organizations to make better decisions and devise more effective methods to handle global concerns. Furthermore, AI can assist in optimizing resource allocation, prioritizing actions, and tracking progress toward global goals, ultimately improving the effectiveness of governance operations.

Blockchain technology can improve transparency and security in global governance by providing a decentralized and tamper-proof platform for recording and validating transactions and data exchanges. Increased transparency can help nations develop trust and ensure the integrity of regulatory systems. Furthermore, the potential of blockchain to permit safe information sharing might encourage international cooperation and improve the overall efficiency of governance initiatives.

AI and blockchain technology can enhance international collaboration in global governance by enabling secure, transparent, and efficient platforms for data exchange and collective decision-making. In addition, these technologies can improve trust and cooperation among states by allowing real-time access to information and supporting coordinated solutions to global crises, ultimately encouraging more effective and equitable global government.

AI and blockchain technology can aid in automating regulatory processes, decreasing administrative burdens and increasing compliance with international standards. AI-powered regulatory systems, for example, can automate the analysis of compliance data. Simultaneously, blockchain provides secure and transparent reporting and verification platforms, improving the overall efficiency of global regulatory activities.

Despite the potential benefits of artificial intelligence and blockchain in global governance and regulation, we must address various issues. Concerns about data privacy and sovereignty, the necessity for unified legal frameworks, and the ethical usage of AI in governance applications are among them. Furthermore, the digital divide between nations with varying access to new technology may worsen existing disparities and obstruct equitable sharing of these technologies' benefits.

Finally, AI and blockchain technologies can transform global governance and regulation, providing transparency, efficiency, and international cooperation prospects. It is feasible to encourage more effective and equitable international collaboration and handle complex global concerns by incorporating these technologies into governance procedures. As we continue to investigate and develop new technologies, we must address the underlying challenges and ensure they are used responsibly and ethically. As a result, we will be able to fully utilize the potential of AI and blockchain in global governance and regulation, ultimately creating a more stable and affluent world.

12.7   BLOCKCHAIN AND ENERGY CONSUMPTION

Blockchain technology has emerged as a transformative force in a variety of industries, enabling secure, transparent, and decentralized data management solutions (Abed et al., 2023; Devi et al., 2023; Kohli et al., 2023; Luo et al., 2023; Oudani et al., 2023). However, besides its various advantages, the energy consumption connected with blockchain has prompted environmental concerns. This section investigates blockchain technology's energy footprint, explains the variables that contribute to its energy usage, and assesses potential solutions to this problem.

To validate and add transactions to the distributed ledger, blockchain technology, particularly in the context of cryptocurrency mining, necessitates substantial computing power. This approach, known as Proof of Work (PoW), requires enormous energy to answer complex mathematical problems, resulting in significant energy consumption. The Bitcoin network, for example, is believed to require more energy than certain small countries.

The PoW consensus method, the growing complexity of mining algorithms, and the competitive nature of cryptocurrency mining all contribute to the energy consumption of blockchain technology. Furthermore, as mining grows more complex and resource-intensive, miners are encouraged to invest in more durable and energy-consuming technology to retain profitability, compounding the energy consumption issue.

Blockchain technology's high energy usage has substantial environmental ramifications, particularly regarding greenhouse gas emissions. Because a significant amount of the electricity required in blockchain operations is derived from non-renewable sources such as fossil fuels, the technology's energy footprint contributes to climate change and other environmental challenges.

In blockchain technology, several potential solutions address the issue of energy consumption. The first is to replace PoW with more energy-efficient consensus methods like Proof of Stake or Delegated Proof of Stake, which can drastically cut energy usage by eliminating resource-intensive mining procedures. Second, increasing the use of renewable energy sources for blockchain operations, such as solar or wind power, can assist in reducing the environmental impact of its energy usage. Third, implementing scalability improvements can help reduce the energy consumption of blockchain networks by lowering the demand for computational power and resource-intensive processes and developing and promoting energy-efficient hardware for blockchain operations, which can contribute to reducing the technology's overall energy footprint.

While blockchain technology has numerous applications, its energy consumption is a significant concern with serious environmental repercussions. It is possible to reduce the energy footprint of blockchain technology by investigating alternate consensus techniques, encouraging the use of renewable energy sources, and investing in energy-efficient hardware and scalability enhancements. As blockchain use grows, industry, governments, and researchers must collaborate to address this challenge and ensure this new technology's sustainable and responsible growth.

12.8   CHALLENGES AND RISKS OF AI AND BLOCKCHAIN IN POLITICS

AI and blockchain technologies have the potential to alter international politics by improving efficiency, security, and international collaboration. However, these technologies bring several obstacles and concerns that must be addressed to ensure responsible and ethical usage. This section examines the key challenges and risks associated with artificial intelligence and blockchain in politics, emphasizing the importance of careful consideration and strategic planning in navigating the complex ethical and geopolitical landscape (Al-Saqaf & Seidler, 2017; Batubara et al., 2018; Chang et al., 2020; Shava & Mhlanga, 2023).

Using artificial intelligence and blockchain technology in international politics presents various ethical considerations. These include the potential misuse of artificial intelligence in surveillance, the development of autonomous weapons systems, and the risk of aggravating existing inequities due to the digital divide. Furthermore, using AI and blockchain for political reasons may violate individual privacy rights and data sovereignty, demanding the development of ethical principles and legal frameworks to control their usage.

Rapid development and use of AI and blockchain technologies may worsen geopolitical conflicts and generate new power dynamics. Nations with advanced artificial intelligence and blockchain capabilities may gain a competitive advantage, sparking an arms race in developing and deploying these technologies. Furthermore, state-sponsored cyberattacks and misinformation campaigns employing AI and blockchain technology potentially threaten international security and stability.

The growing use of AI and blockchain technology in international politics raises worries about data privacy and security. Safeguarding sensitive data and avoiding unwanted access are significant issues that must be addressed. To reduce these dangers, robust cybersecurity measures and the implementation of worldwide standards for data protection and exchange are required.

As nations rely more on AI and blockchain technology in international politics, they may become more exposed to system disruptions or failures. To solve this difficulty, the development of resilient and redundant systems, as well as international cooperation on disaster response and recovery, is critical.

AI and blockchain technology growth exceed existing legal and regulatory frameworks, creating uncertainty and potential conflicts in international politics. As a result, clear rules and standards and international cooperation in drafting harmonized regulations are required to ensure that these technologies are used responsibly and ethically. The primary challenge for using blockchain in international politics is control. The appeal of blockchain is decentralization, but it is hard to imagine nation-states approaching high-stakes diplomacy problems and voluntarily ceding control to a decentralized network.

AI and blockchain technologies have the potential to alter international politics significantly, but they also provide several obstacles and concerns that must be carefully addressed. Nations may reduce these risks and fully utilize the promise of AI and blockchain technology in international politics by adopting ethical principles, regulatory frameworks, and collaboration procedures. Policymakers, technologists, and other stakeholders must collaborate to negotiate the complicated ethical and geopolitical terrain, supporting responsible innovation and fostering global peace and prosperity.

12.9 Conclusion

AI and blockchain technologies have the potential to significantly alter the face of international politics, providing new prospects for efficiency, security, and international collaboration. It is feasible to encourage more cooperation and understanding in the international arena by incorporating these technologies into diplomacy, trade, global governance, and security activities. As we continue to investigate and develop new technologies, addressing the problems and risks connected with them is critical to ensure their responsible and ethical usage. By doing so, we may fully realize the potential of AI and blockchain in international politics, fostering a more stable, wealthy, and linked global community in the long run.

REFERENCES

Abed, S. E., Jaffal, R., & Mohd, B. J. (2023). A review on blockchain and IoT integration from energy, security and hardware perspectives. *Wireless Personal Communications, 129*(3), 2079–2122.

Akter, S., Michael, K., Uddin, M. R., McCarthy, G., & Rahman, M. (2022). Transforming business using digital innovations: The application of AI, Blockchain, cloud and data analytics. *Annals of Operations Research, 308*, 7–39.

Al-Saqaf, W., & Seidler, N. (2017). Blockchain technology for social impact: Opportunities and challenges ahead. *Journal of Cyber Policy, 2*(3), 338–354.

Ameen, A. H., Mohammed, M. A., & Rashid, A. N. (2023). Dimensions of artificial intelligence techniques, Blockchain, and cyber security in the Internet of medical things: Opportunities, challenges, and future directions. *Journal of Intelligent Systems, 32*(1), 20220267.

An, Y. J., Choi, P. M. S., & Huang, S. H. (2021). Blockchain, cryptocurrency, and artificial intelligence in finance. In *Fintech with artificial intelligence, big data, and blockchain* (pp. 1–34). Springer Singapore.

Bârgăoanu, A., & Cheregi, B. F. (2021). Artificial intelligence: The new tool for cyber diplomacy: The case of the European Union. In *Artificial intelligence and digital diplomacy: Challenges and opportunities* (pp.115–130). Springer International.

Batubara, F. R., Ubacht, J., & Janssen, M. (2018, May). Challenges of blockchain technology adoption for e-government: A systematic literature review. In *Proceedings of the 19th annual international conference on digital government research: Governance in the data age* (pp. 1–9). Association for Computing Machinery.

Belotti, M., Božić, N., Pujolle, G., & Secci, S. (2019). A vademecum on blockchain technologies: When, which, and how. *IEEE Communications Surveys & Tutorials, 21*(4), 3796–3838.

Chang, Y., Iakovou, E., & Shi, W. (2020). Blockchain in global supply chains and cross border trade: A critical synthesis of the state-of-the-art, challenges and opportunities. *International Journal of Production Research, 58*(7), 2082–2099.

Charles, V., Emrouznejad, A., & Gherman, T. (2023). A critical analysis of the integration of blockchain and artificial intelligence for supply chain. Annals of *Operations Research, 327*(1), 7–47.

Devi, K. M., Sai, D. S., Rao, N. T., Swathi, K., & Voddi, S. (2023). Blockchain and its idiosyncratic effects on energy consumption and conservation. In *Smart technologies in data science and communication: Proceedings of SMART-DSC 2022* (pp. 263–269). Springer Nature Singapore.

Di Prisco, D. (2019). Blockchain and AI: The technological revolution's impact on corporate governance relationships. In *New Challenges in corporate governance: Theory and practice* (pp. 368–381). Virtus Interpress.

Georgescu, A. (2022). Cyber diplomacy in the governance of emerging AI technologies—A transatlantic example. *International Journal of Cyber Diplomacy, 3*, 13–22.

Jekov, B., Petkova, P., Parusheva, Y., & Shoikova, E. (2018). Disruptive technologies-artificial intelligence and blockchain in education. In *ICERI2018 Proceedings* (pp. 6784–6793). IATED.

Kohli, V., Chakravarty, S., Chamola, V., Sangwan, K. S., & Zeadally, S. (2023). An analysis of energy consumption and carbon footprints of cryptocurrencies and possible solutions. *Digital Communications and Networks, 9*(1), 79–89.

Kumar, R., Singh, D., Srinivasan, K., & Hu, Y. C. (2022). December. AI-powered blockchain technology for public health: A contemporary review, open challenges, and future research directions. *Healthcare, 11*(1), 81.

Luo, H., Liu, S., Xu, S., & Luo, J. (2023). LECast: A low-energy-consumption broadcast protocol for UAV blockchain networks. *Drones, 7*(2), 76.

Marwala, T., & Xing, B. (2018). *Blockchain and artificial intelligence.* arXiv preprint. arXiv:1802.04451

Miegbam, A. T., & Bariledum, K. (2022). Artificial intelligence and diplomacy in the 21st Century: The African perspective. *Central Asian Journal of Theoretical and Applied Science, 3*(10), 49–65.

Muhati, E., Rawat, D. B., & Sadler, B. M. (2022). A new cyber-alliance of artificial intelligence, internet of things, blockchain, and edge computing. *IEEE Internet of Things Magazine, 5*(1), 104–107.

Muheidat, F., & Tawalbeh, L. A. (2021). Artificial intelligence and blockchain for cybersecurity applications. *Artificial intelligence and blockchain for future cybersecurity applications* (pp. 3–29). Springer International.

Oudani, M., Sebbar, A., Zkik, K., El Harraki, I., & Belhadi, A. (2023). Green blockchain based IoT for secured supply chain of hazardous materials. *Computers & Industrial Engineering, 175*, 108814.

Patnaik, S., & Biswal, S. K. (2023). Use of artificial intelligence and blockchain technologies in detecting and curbing fake news in journalism. *AI-Based Metaheuristics for Information Security and Digital Media, 14*, 1.

Pilkington, M. (2016). Blockchain technology: Principles and applications. In *Research handbook on digital transformations* (pp. 225–253). Edward Elgar.

Qiu, M., Liu, X., Qi, Y., Zhao, H., & Liu, M. (2020, October). AI enhanced blockchain (II). In *2020 3rd international conference on smart blockchain (SmartBlock)* (pp. 147–152). IEEE.

Raja, G., Manaswini, Y., Vivekanandan, G. D., Sampath, H., Dev, K., & Bashir, A. K. (2020, July). AI-powered blockchain—A decentralized secure multiparty computation protocol for IoV. In *IEEE INFOCOM 2020-IEEE conference on computer communications workshops (INFOCOM WKSHPS)* (pp. 865–870). IEEE.

Shava, E., & Mhlanga, D. (2023). Mitigating bureaucratic inefficiencies through blockchain technology in Africa. *Frontiers in Blockchain, 6,* 1.

Singh, P., Elmi, Z., Lau, Y. Y., Borowska-Stefańska, M., Wiśniewski, S., & Dulebenets, M. A. (2022). Blockchain and AI technology convergence: Applications in transportation systems. *Vehicular Communications, 38,* 100521.

Sivarethinamohan, R., Jovin, P., & Sujatha, S. (2022). Unlocking the potential of (AI-powered) blockchain technology in environment sustainability and social good. In *Applied Edge AI* (pp. 193–213). Auerbach Publications.

Wang, Q., & Su, M. (2020). Integrating blockchain technology into the energy sector—From theory of blockchain to research and application of energy blockchain. *Computer Science Review, 37,* 100275.

Yaga, D., Mell, P., Roby, N., & Scarfone, K. (2019). *Blockchain technology overview.* arXiv preprint. arXiv:1906.11078

Yli-Huumo, J., Ko, D., Choi, S., Park, S., & Smolander, K. (2016). Where is current research on blockchain technology?—A systematic review. *PLoS ONE, 11*(10), e0163477.

CHAPTER 13

Conclusion

13.1 INTRODUCTION

Merging artificial intelligence (AI), game theory, and mechanism design can fundamentally transform the political environment by providing new methods for analyzing and addressing complex global politics. In the interconnected world of the twenty-first century, the ability to model and analyze strategic interactions between varied actors and develop effective institutions and policies has become increasingly vital. AI, game theory, and mechanism design give valuable insights that can help decision-makers through the complexities of politics (McCarty & Meirowitz, 2007; Narahari, 2014; Schulze-Horn et al., 2020).

13.2 ARTIFICIAL INTELLIGENCE

AI technologies have helped us comprehend politics by analyzing massive volumes of data and generating predictions, simulations, and analysis. This has allowed researchers and policymakers to make more informed decisions and predict the results of diverse strategic interactions. Furthermore, AI has eased the incorporation of game theory and mechanism design into politics by providing more sophisticated and efficient computer approaches capable of dealing with the complexity and uncertainty inherent in global interactions.

© The Author(s), under exclusive license to Springer Nature 207
Singapore Pte Ltd. 2023
T. Marwala, *Artificial Intelligence, Game Theory and Mechanism Design in Politics*, https://doi.org/10.1007/978-981-99-5103-1_13

13.3   GAME THEORY

Game theory has substantially contributed to politics as a framework for analyzing strategic interactions. It has shed light on underlying motivations and limitations in various global contexts, including conflict and war, diplomacy and negotiations, international trade, and international institutions. Game theory has assisted scholars and policymakers in designing more effective policies and strategies by formalizing the analysis of strategic interactions, contributing to more stable and cooperative global solutions.

13.4   MECHANISM DESIGN

Mechanism design, an extension of game theory, is concerned with developing institutions and rules that control strategic behavior in pursuit of specified goals. Mechanism design can assist in creating international treaties, accords, and organizations that promote collaboration, dispute resolution, and global well-being. Furthermore, by comprehending the strategic motives of various actors, mechanism design can aid in developing more robust and effective mechanisms that promote cooperation and stability in the international arena.

13.5   ARTIFICIAL INTELLIGENCE, GAME THEORY, AND MECHANISM DESIGN

The convergence of AI, game theory, and mechanism design can address some of politics' most important issues. For example, developing AI-powered early warning systems can aid in detecting and preventing potential conflicts. Accordingly, game-theoretic models can reveal the most effective conflict resolution and crisis management solutions. Furthermore, mechanism design can help develop international norms and institutions that promote collaboration in climate change, global security, and trade.

Despite the apparent benefits, it is critical to recognize the limitations and constraints of using AI, game theory, and mechanism design in politics. Concerns include using rationality assumptions, the potential simplifying of complicated dynamics, and the difficulty in accurately modelling and forecasting real-world interactions. Furthermore, the growing use of AI in politics creates ethical and security concerns, such as the possible exploitation of AI technologies for surveillance, disinformation, or autonomous weapons systems.

To fully realize the potential of AI, game theory, and mechanism design in politics, scholars, and politicians must confront these constraints and problems. This could include improving existing models to account for emotions, biases, and inadequate data, or inventing new approaches to better represent the complexity and ambiguity of global interactions. It is also critical to develop ethical principles and norms for using AI in politics, ensuring that these technologies are used ethically and to benefit all parties involved.

13.6 Conclusion

Incorporating AI, game theory, and mechanism design into the study of politics offers a viable option for furthering our understanding of global dynamics and addressing the world's pressing concerns. Furthermore, scholars and policymakers may build a more cooperative, stable, and prosperous international environment by exploiting the potential of these creative instruments. Nonetheless, it is critical to remain aware of the limitations and constraints connected with their use and to strive for responsible and ethical employment of these technologies in politics.

References

McCarty, N., & Meirowitz, A. (2007). *Political game theory: An introduction*. Cambridge University Press.

Narahari, Y. (2014). *Game theory and mechanism design* (Vol. 4). World Scientific.

Schulze-Horn, I., Hueren, S., Scheffler, P., & Schiele, H. (2020). Artificial intelligence in purchasing: Facilitating mechanism design-based negotiations. *Applied Artificial Intelligence, 34*(8), 618–642.

INDEX